THE Mathematics Program Improvement Review

A COMPREHENSIVE EVALUATION PROCESS FOR K–12 SCHOOLS

Acknowledgments

THE MATHEMATICS PROGRAM IMPROVEMENT REVIEW COULD NOT HAVE BEEN developed without valuable assistance from several individuals. I would like to thank Stephen Henderson and Karen Kidwell, for their suggestions that got the process initiated, and Michael Howard, for help with some of the rubrics. I would also like to thank David Shepard for input that he provided as a review team member. Support also came from many different individuals who participated in training and served on review teams. There are too many to name individually (I am certain I will leave someone out), but their contributions helped lead to the final product. The published results would not be in as fine a shape as they are without the excellent suggestions made by Katie Martin. Finally, and most importantly, I would like to thank my wife, Marta, who was not only willing to put up with my extended trips away from home, but eventually joined me as a team member and provided valuable support.

What Is the Mathematics Program Improvement Review?

ACCOUNTABILITY IS A HUGE ISSUE IN EDUCATION. POLITICIANS MAKE it the centerpiece of their education policy. School board members say they want their school system run like a business, with each child seen as a profit to the community and no child seen as a loss. As all educators know, this emphasis on measurable success has inspired an increase in standardized testing. In the United States, nearly every state has instituted its own high-stakes testing in mathematics. The federal No Child Left Behind Act requires annual mathematics testing in grades 3 through 8 and sets serious consequences for those schools that do not make adequate yearly progress.

One consequence of this accountability focus is that school officials, parents, and politicians have come to view standardized test scores as perhaps the most important measure of a school's effectiveness. But what do all these test scores really tell us, and how useful are they for schools focused on program improvement? To develop and maintain high-quality academic programs, school personnel need specific information that clarifies what is working and what is not. The standardized test results they receive are reports that compare their students' scores with those of students at other schools or in other districts, other states, and even other nations. In addition, testing companies often provide results as percentile scores based on isolated skills and concepts that have little relationship to state or local objectives.

The data available to the public, such as the mathematics score information depicted in Figure 1.1, are often even more obscure about the strengths and weaknesses of schools and programs. For example, parents trying to decide whether Somerville Elementary or Wilkins Elementary will offer their children the best mathematics instruction would be hard-pressed to make a decision based on the data in these tables or on the accompanying reports' discussion of percentile ranks, scale scores, normal curve equivalents, and grade-level equivalents. What's more, if the principals at Somerville or Wilkins were asked to explain what their schools are going to do to move more students from "proficient" to "advanced," or to reverse the

FIGURE 1.1	SAMPLE STANDARDIZED TEST DATA

Somerville Elementary School: Mathematics Results

Grade Level	2	3	4	5	6
Reported Enrollment	71	66	68	98	100
Students Tested	70	65	67	97	100
% of Enrollment	99%	98%	99%	99%	100%
Mean Scaled Score	394.8	388.9	370.7	344.4	369.3
% Advanced	38%	40%	31%	14%	25%
% Proficient	36%	28%	33%	30%	30%
% Basic	17%	28%	22%	26%	30%
% Below Basic	7%	5%	12%	19%	14%
% Far Below Basic	1%	0%	1%	11%	0%

Wilkins Elementary School: Mathematics Results

Grade Level	2	3	4	5	6
Reported Enrollment	90	89	87	71	105
Students Tested	89	89	87	71	105
% of Enrollment	99%	100%	100%	100%	100%
Mean Scaled Score	404.3	400.2	376.6	399.6	383.8
% Advanced	46%	44%	33%	28%	27%
% Proficient	36%	35%	38%	49%	35%
% Basic	9%	11%	16%	11%	30%
% Below Basic	8%	8%	10%	6%	4%
% Far Below Basic	1%	1%	2%	6%	4%

Note: Figure reflects actual test data. Rounded percentages may not add to 100.

trend of scores declining from grade 2 to grade 5, they would have a difficult time finding the answers in the test data.

For school officials, the receipt of a packet of test result information is only the first step in a long and tedious process of test interpretation. It is not a question of spinning the data so that our programs are seen in the best possible light, but of trying to wring from the data the information that will help us to maintain effective programs and improve those that are faltering. Here is what we need to know:

■ Where do the students' specific areas of strength and weakness lie? For example, can we identify how well students have done with both the concepts and the skills related to specific objectives?

■ Do low scores reflect an overall deficiency in the program, or are they a result of students' problems with the concepts or skills in a single strand, such as geometry?

■ Do low scores reflect a lack of conceptual understanding or difficulty applying conceptual understanding? For example, when the same concept is tested with a multiple-choice question and an open-response question, are students able to answer one correctly but not the other?

■ Do low scores reflect a deficient curriculum or a mismatch between what the program teaches and what the test measures?

■ Do low scores reflect deficient instruction or a mismatch between an instructional approach (e.g., drill and practice versus manipulative-based instruction) and the test's methodology (e.g., critical thinking and problem solving versus no manipulatives allowed)?

■ Have factors beyond the mathematics curriculum and instruction influenced the scores? Examples might be teachers' content knowledge, classroom climate, and students' reading readiness (and by extension, the language arts curriculum and instruction).

The truth is, no matter how a district aggregates or disaggregates data from standardized tests, these data alone will not yield the detailed information necessary to improve a school's academic program.

An alternative to relying on standardized tests data is for administrators and teachers to decide on and engage in a method of program evaluation that *will* provide all the detail they need. Nancy Love (2002) describes schools that do this as "inquiry-based" and points out that in these schools, "teachers and administrators continually ask questions about how to improve student learning, experiment with new ideas, and rigorously use data to uncover problems and monitor results" (p. 7). Inquiry-based schools don't wait for the release of state test data. Their teachers and administrators develop professional learning communities that examine every facet of the school's instructional program and then focus on ways to produce improved learning. These schools avoid being reactive to test results and instead are proactive in seeking improvement.

I have used an inquiry-based model in developing the Mathematics Program Improvement Review (MPIR), a proven evaluation process focused on standards for high-quality mathematics programs in grades K–12 and the means to measure those standards. It can be used effectively by individual teachers, teachers and administrators within a school, and teachers and administrations within an entire district. With the MPIR, you can establish a baseline for the quality of your mathematics program, identify the elements that are most in need of change, and continuously monitor your program's improvement.

The MPIR process is based both on research into other effective evaluation processes (DuFour & Eaker, 1998; English, 1999; Frase, English, & Posten, 2000; Louis, Marks & Kruse, 1996; Love, 2002) and on my own experience working to improve opportunities for mathematics teachers to excel in their classrooms. This handbook is designed so that any school or district can use the tools and procedures of the review to bring about positive change in students' mathematics learning.

The Development of the Mathematics Program Improvement Review

The MPIR is not a theoretical answer to the general dilemma of accountability. It was born out of a real need I encountered while serving as a mathematics consultant for the Appalachian Rural Systemic Initiative (ARSI), a project funded by the National Science Foundation to help improve the math and science programs in a six-state area (Kentucky, West Virginia, Tennessee, Ohio, North Carolina, and Virginia).

My primary responsibility at ARSI was to work with the mathematics teachers and administrators of schools in 22 rural districts in Kentucky. I met individually with the supervisors and superintendents of all of these districts to find out what they needed. Their requests for help varied from school to school; however, they all asked me to critically evaluate their mathematics programs and provide suggestions for systemic improvement. This request coincided with ARSI's need for a tool to evaluate itself. In 1996, ARSI administrative staff determined that they could not judge the success of the project solely upon standardized test data. One reason for this ruling was that the schools studied used a multitude of standardized assessments. Most of them used norm-referenced tests (designed around national percentiles and normal curve equivalents), but some used criterion-referenced test (focused on specific grade-level objectives). This made it impossible to compare all the schools within the six-state area based on test scores.

A more significant reason to develop a new review process was ARSI's goal to make systemic changes to the region's mathematics and science programs. Project managers simply could not measure these changes (e.g., in curriculum design, development and use of authentic assessments, community involvement) with the kinds of tests that the states and districts were using. Consequently, I began to develop tools and procedures to evaluate the programs of all the schools that ARSI served.

The first step in devising an evaluation process was to ask the question that opens this book: what are the elements of a high-quality mathematics program? I conducted a literature study to identify standards and also drew from my own experience: a decade as a mathematics teacher and 20 years as a mathematics supervisor focused on observing, assisting, and modeling instruction.

The standards I settled on for the review address 10 key program components: curriculum, instruction, equity and diversity, school climate, usefulness, professional environment, community, organization and leadership, assessment and evaluation, and financial material resources. The curriculum standard, for example, is that the curriculum uses problem-centered content that develops students' conceptual understanding of mathematics, their ability to apply mathematics, their ability to communicate mathematically, and their knowledge and skills in mathematics algorithms.

After identifying standards for each of the program components, I developed indicators of whether each of the standards was being met. The first indicator of the curriculum standard, for example, is that the math curriculum is written and is used in planning the instructional program. Some indicators have multiple parts. For example, the indicator specifically addressing a K–8 program curriculum (Indicator 1.7) is that the curriculum develops students'

- Number and operation sense and computational skills.
- Mastery of estimation and mental computation.
- Understanding of patterns and sequences.
- Knowledge of measurement and geometry.
- Spatial sense and reasoning.
- Ability to collect, organize, represent, and interpret data.
- Facility using statistical methods and exploring chance probability models.
- Facility using algebraic skills and concepts.

A complete list of the MPIR's standards and indicators is presented in Appendix B as Figure B.1, beginning on page 147.

With standards and indicators in place, the next step was to work backward to determine what data were needed to rate them. After all, you cannot measure success without data. You cannot cite improvements unless you have a baseline measurement of where you began and take subsequent measures to judge success. I designed or modified a set of tools for gathering that data:

- Questionnaires to be filled out by school principals and teachers.
- Interview questions for teachers, students, parents, and principals.
- A guide for classroom observation.
- A list of supplemental materials (standardized test scores, mathematics program budgets, lesson plans, etc.) that would contribute relevant information.

Because each method of gathering data has its strengths and weaknesses, using data from at least three sources to determine a score for each standard indicator results in a more accurate rating.

I also created a scoring rubric that gives specific descriptors for how to rate each indicator—another way to ensure accuracy and consistency in using the review, especially if teams are used to evaluate different schools. The rubric helps ensure that rating scores mean the same thing in each of the different schools. The scoring rubric is included in Appendix B as Figure B.2, beginning on page 153.

Of course, the decision to rely heavily on interviews and classroom observation meant the process would include a site visit to schools under review. I trained examiners to use the various on-site data collection tools and then sent the examiners to evaluate ARSI's "catalyst" schools—those schools that the districts had chosen as the lead schools in the project. After the visits, the review teams, consisting of the trained examiners and usually at least one experienced "review veteran," compiled all the data to score each indicator and standard. Next, they generated a report identifying both strengths and areas for improvement within each standard. The reports went both to the schools reviewed and to the ARSI leadership for use as baseline data for the project as a whole.

Because the Appalachian Rural Systemic Initiative was conceived as a five-year project, trained review teams revisited the catalyst schools four to five years after the initial review to measure improvements. Over the course of the project, the MPIR process was conducted at each and every school within the participating districts. In annual evaluations of ARSI services, participating schools regularly identified it as one of the most important services provided.

How Schools Have Used MPIR Reports

To clarify how the MPIR process can improve mathematics programs, let's look at some sample recommendations taken from actual MPIR reports and then at some of the ways that the evaluated schools have responded.

The first school is Foster Elementary. As with many schools, Foster's mathematics curriculum was limited to the adopted textbook series (and its scope and sequence) and the curriculum guide provided by the state department of education. Within the school, there did not seem to be any consistency among teachers, even teachers at the same grade level, as to expectations for instruction and assessment and what objectives they should pursue. Some teachers reported that they taught the textbook from beginning to end, whereas others indicated they emphasized the skills or concepts included in the state document.

The MPIR report's recommendation for Foster was for the mathematics faculty to develop a curriculum document that included components that would assist teachers in planning: scope and sequence, level of expectation, available resources, instructional strategies, suggested time line, assessment suggestions, and so on. The leadership team at Foster reviewed the report and determined that development of a usable curriculum was their highest priority. Ultimately, they went on to use professional development funds to release teachers by grade level so that the teachers could create a new curriculum that included the following:

- Grade-level objectives and expectations for these objectives (such as introduce, reinforce, master, apply).
- Alignment to state documents and alignment to resources, including but not restricted to the adopted texts.
- Common authentic assessment items to be used for objectives.
- A pacing guide or curriculum map indicating when each unit of study will be taught, to help ensure that all instructional expectations are met.

The leadership team at Foster Elementary agreed that the curriculum would be a work in progress, continually revised as they incorporated new resources, assessments, and other materials.

Similarly, an MPIR conducted at Cramer Elementary reported the need for the development of a curriculum aligned to state and national standards. Based on the recommendation, Cramer's principal awarded full-time release to Ms. Davis, a 25-year veteran teacher with strong talents and interest in math, so that she could work with all grade levels within the school to revise the mathematics curriculum. Ms. Davis consulted with a mathematics specialist to draft curriculum objectives. One of her major tasks became assisting Cramer's teachers with the consistent use of this curriculum. With the guidance of Ms. Davis, the teachers completed an alignment between the curriculum objectives and the adopted texts, and found the text did not provide sufficient coverage to develop the understanding that was expected for several curriculum objectives. Ms. Davis then found additional resources to teach these objectives.

Cartwright Middle School used its MPIR findings to improve recognition of students' accomplishments in mathematics, an indicator for the standard in school climate. This school already provided honor rolls for its high-achieving students and published their names in the local newspaper. However, it had no other means of recognizing academic achievement. The MPIR report recommended developing additional means of celebrating success and providing tangible rewards for students who excel academically. Cartwright's leadership team decided that this could be done easily and with little investment of time or money. The review team's report to the rest of the faculty also recommended these changes:

- Recognize members of the school's academic team through activities such as placing a photo of team members in the local newspaper, having the team lunch with the school principal, and displaying the names and pictures of team members and information about upcoming competitions on the bulletin board in the front hall.
- Ask each teacher to select a mathematics student of the month, alternating the award criteria between highest academic performance and most improvement.
- Develop a "hall of fame"—a display in the school containing names of students who scored "distinguished" on the state assessment.
- Hold an honors assembly in which students who scored "distinguished" on the previous year's assessment would be recognized in front of the entire student body and would receive certificates.

Upon general approval of the proposal, the leadership team at Cartwright agreed that it would revisit this issue each year to develop additional means of recognizing students' accomplishments.

As these examples demonstrate, schools have used MPIR reports to identify areas needing improvement, but they also have used reports to identify areas of success for which the staff may not have received adequate recognition. Recognition is perhaps one of the most important components of the process. Too often, the outstanding work teachers do does not receive the recognition it deserves. In these schools, the MPIR process enabled positive recognition to take place in a professional manner. Schools have also generated news releases to parents about strengths of the mathematics program based on review results. Rather than reporting only state test results, these schools are sharing the effective practices that are improving their mathematics programs.

Word about the success of the MPIR process has spread. When schools that followed the review's recommendations began to show improvements in their mathematics programs, leaders of schools *not* served by ARSI took notice. They questioned the superintendents or principals involved with ARSI about factors that led to improving their mathematics programs. After hearing these administrators cite the MPIR process, hundreds of schools outside of ARSI have requested that I or other trained review teams conduct MPIRs within their schools.

Tools from the Mathematics Program Improvement Review have now been used in schools in multiple states and within rural, suburban, and urban environments. The Coastal Rural Systemic Initiative conducted MPIRs in schools it serves in North Carolina, South Carolina, and Virginia. West Virginia has used an adaptation of MPIR within many of its schools through two different federal grant-administered programs. The Kentucky Department of Education performs MPIR reviews (with minor modifications) in schools that have not shown satisfactory progress on annual state assessments. The MPIR process has been revised though the years and continues to provide valuable information to mathematics teachers and school administrators.

Using This Handbook

Your school or district can also benefit from the tools developed for the Mathematics Program Improvement Review, whether you use them to conduct a formal and complete evaluation or to assess your program more informally. In some schools, teachers and administrators have developed internal discussions centered on the standards and indicators without ever undergoing a complete program improvement review. These teachers used the MPIR scoring rubric as the basis for discussion and examined each indicator. They determined as a group what score they felt they would receive on the rubric and what steps they would need to make improvements.

Other schools have formed study groups based on the standards. For example, all schools need a high-quality mathematics curriculum. Indicators like 1.3 ("problem solving is an integral part of all mathematical activity") can form a basis for discussion.

The remaining chapters in this handbook will guide you through all the steps and tools used in conducting a Mathematics Program Improvement Review:

- Preparing for the review.
- Understanding the standards and indicators.
- Using the questionnaires.
- Conducting interviews.
- Making classroom observations.
- Analyzing other source material.
- Compiling data and writing a report.

Appendix A explains an effective training program for MPIR review team members and clarifies the benefits of training faculty and administrative staff in the process even if they are not going to conduct formal reviews. As noted, Appendix B contains all the materials needed for a review: the standards and indicators; the templates for questionnaires, interviews, and classroom observations; the rubrics for assigning ratings to indicators; and the forms for compiling these ratings.

Finally, each chapter's discussion includes examples derived from actual reviews conducted at real schools. I have distilled them into a small number of composite schools, with pseudonyms selected to protect confidentiality. Foster Elementary is a composite of schools found to have poor or poorly implemented mathematics programs. Its complement is Abbott Elementary, a composite of schools found to have high-quality mathematics programs in place. The three other schools I reference are Cramer Elementary, Cartwright Middle, and Collingwood High. They represent the most common reality: schools with mathematics programs that are neither clearly excellent nor obviously deficient. The purpose of the MPIR is to provide a structure for evaluation that will clarify what schools like these are doing right, where they are going wrong, and how they can do better. It's a process that can improve mathematics education at every school—yours included.

■   ■   ■

## 2

Planning for the Review

A VARIETY OF CIRCUMSTANCES MOTIVATE SCHOOL PRINCIPALS OR central office administrators to formally evaluate their mathematics programs. Most commonly it's because scores have declined or failed to improve in the mathematics portion of a state or national assessment. Administrators who begin analyzing mathematics scores with their faculties may quickly notice a pattern of "up one year, down the next." This pattern is typical in schools that focus improvement plans on mathematics one year and reading the next, constantly targeting the area with lower scores. Over the years, however, the gains may not match the declines. This was the case at Cramer Elementary School.

As you can see in Figure 2.1, Cramer's scores revealed a typical up–down pattern. After seeing the decline in reading scores in 2001, the staff decided to take action to focus on reading instruction. As a result, 2002 reading scores improved, although they did not attain the earlier levels. Meanwhile, mathematics scores declined and did not recover. This is symptomatic of alternating attention to content areas. The approach is not systemic and so does not lead to sustained improvement.

Another frequently cited reason for having a program review is a change in staff—either a large turnover in mathematics faculty or a change in administration. Many schools view these junctures as opportunities to determine the best direction for the mathematics program. That was the situation at Collingwood High School. Collingwood's student population and staffing formula had consistently shown the need for eight mathematics teachers. Over the two years leading up to the review, five of Collingwood's eight teachers left the school (four retired and one moved out of state). With five new teachers in the department, the principal and mathematics chair agreed it was a good time to reexamine the mathematics program. Scores had not been declining, but they weren't increasing to the degree that the administration had hoped either. During the previous year, the faculty had reviewed the program internally, using a process that incorporated surveys of parents and students. Although the teachers felt they had received valuable data from these surveys, they

FIGURE 2.1	CRAMER ELEMENTARY SCHOOL NATIONAL PERCENTILE (NP) SCORES			
Subject	2000	2001	2002	2003
Reading	64	59	63	61
Mathematics	64	66	59	52

knew they needed more data—and data that examined all the issues instead of just those that could be addressed through parent and student surveys.

Collingwood teachers agreed to have an outside team of evaluators conduct a Mathematics Program Improvement Review. After the review was complete and recommendations were made, the teachers felt they could focus attention on some of the areas identified as needing improvement and move forward in making the mathematics program more effective.

Ultimately, schools opt for a review because they want improvement. The MPIR process analyzes each and every component of the mathematics program, including

- The instructional delivery system.
- The methods of internal assessment used by the school staff.
- External assessment results, such as surveys by the Association for Effective Schools.
- Resources available to the mathematics teaching staff.
- Communication with, and involvement of, the parents and school community.

When a mathematics program is effective, all these components work together. Each might adhere closely to research-based best practices, but if they are out of balance or disjointed, the school staff will probably not obtain the results they desire in terms of student mathematic achievement and understanding. The review is also valuable because it provides data that describe the mathematics program in a non-judgmental way, meaning that the data can support discussion about the *program*— its strengths and weaknesses—rather than discussion about individuals.

If you are considering having a review done at your school, you may find it helpful to take the short survey in Figure 2.2. The survey provides a quick means of analyzing the current status of a mathematics program. If you answer "No" or "Don't Know" to most of the questions, your program would benefit from a review.

FIGURE 2.2	DOES YOUR SCHOOL NEED A MATHEMATICS PROGRAM IMPROVEMENT REVIEW?

Directions: Please respond "Yes" (Y), "No" (N), or "Don't Know" (DK) to the following questions. Tally the number of each response. A majority of "No" and "Don't Know" responses indicates that the school would benefit from a Mathematics Program Improvement Review.

_____ Does the school have clearly defined instructional and assessment goals for the whole mathematics program that are known to all school personnel and community members?

_____ Is the curriculum written, implemented consistently, and aligned with state standards?

_____ Is the curriculum monitored by the principal and utilized to make decisions regarding resources, budget, and personnel?

_____ Do student assessment data indicate that students are proficient in mathematics and achieving at the highest level possible?

_____ Do teachers use a variety of strategies (inquiry, modeling, demonstration, flexible grouping, etc.) consistently in the instructional program?

_____ Are day-to-day student assessment strategies consistent with the instructional strategies used, and do they assess students' use of higher-order thinking skills?

_____ Do teachers and administrators understand how to disaggregate assessment data for the purpose of modifying and improving the instructional program?

_____ Are student assessment data utilized by both administrators and teachers for program planning and improvement efforts?

_____ Are policies in place to ensure high-quality student learning opportunities in mathematics for all students, regardless of gender, race, ability, socioeconomic status, and learning style?

_____ Are sufficient resources available to support a high-quality instructional program?

_____ Are budget decisions based on program needs?

_____ Is there adequate communication to parents regarding mathematics program expectations and student achievement in mathematics?

_____ Do parents have opportunities to become involved in their child's learning of mathematics?

_____ Do all teachers have high expectations for all learners?

_____ Has the professional development program for mathematics teachers improved the program and, consequently, student achievement?

_____ Does the principal provide strong instructional leadership for mathematics program improvement efforts?

Totals: _____ **Yes**   _____ **No**   _____ **Don't Know**

Review Team Configurations

Although each of the components that are key to effective mathematics programs can be analyzed internally, within the school staff, it is often much more valuable to bring in a team of reviewers from outside the district. I have worked with three different configurations of review teams over the course of the past nine years: *internal*, *exchange*, and *external*. Each has strengths and weaknesses.

Internal Review

In an internal review, a school or school district assembles the review team from among its own staff. There is relatively little expense to the school or district—just release time for team members to conduct the review and write the report. Another benefit is that members of an internal review team usually know of one or more issues that may be preventing the mathematics program from reaching its full potential: a lack of vision from the principal or central office administrator, a failure of the central office or school administration to provide necessary financial support (particularly toward sustained professional development in mathematics), or the presence of a well-liked teacher at a key assessment grade who is fundamentally weak in mathematics content knowledge or pedagogy.

The downside of the internal review is that although the team members may be aware of these problems, they may also be politically or personally reluctant to identify them in a written report submitted to the school faculty. Consequently, there's a relatively high risk that the team's recommendations may be superficial and fail to seriously address the underlying reasons why the mathematics program is ailing.

An internal review team evaluating Foster Elementary School faced just this kind of difficulty. After Foster's 5th graders again achieved low scores in the annual state-required mathematics assessment, the principal decided that a review of the mathematics program might identify what they needed to do to reverse the years-long trend of disappointing results. He selected four teachers to conduct an internal review. Because the school is departmentalized in grade 5, he selected the 5th grade math teacher. He also selected the librarian, a strong 2nd grade math teacher, and a 4th grade teacher who was one of his most experienced faculty members.

The team began their interviews, and came away with . . . almost nothing. Other teachers in the school were reluctant to discuss what they saw as problem issues with the very teacher whom they saw as the primary problem: the 5th grade math teacher on the review team, an individual who believed strongly in lecture- and demonstration-based instruction and expected her students to use the same solution methods on state assessments that she used during her lessons, despite the state assessment's emphasis on problem solving. Teachers also felt that a lack of administrative support from the central office was hindering the mathematics program. Each teacher received only $300 each year for purchasing classroom materials and resources, and this was meant to cover supplies for all the subjects they taught. Yet not one teacher mentioned this in the interviews, because they were afraid that complaints would get back to the superintendent or others within the administration. In this district, other teachers had been reassigned to less desirable positions after making complaints.

The report that the internal team at Foster finally generated did not contain any recommendations that could have a major impact on the mathematic achievement results. For example, the recommendation for Standard 1, which addresses the curriculum, was for the faculty to consider the adoption of a new mathematics textbook series that contained more computational review. The report did not address the basis for this recommendation, such as whether or not more computational review would alleviate the overall mathematics concerns and how this would be accomplished. It did not address the perceived need for more instruction on nonroutine problem solving. In general, the Foster faculty felt that the entire review process was a waste of time. They knew many of the problems that existed, and they didn't see any of them mentioned in the report.

Exchange Review

The second type of review configuration I've observed is the exchange review: an exchange of staff-based review teams between neighboring districts. This approach can be a valuable professional development for the team members, as they have an opportunity to observe the teaching practices with a critical eye. However, there are both advantages and disadvantages to this approach with regard to school improvement.

The first and most obvious advantage is that the reviewers are from outside the district; personal loyalties, internal politics, and concerns about blame and reprisal do not factor in the recommendations as they tend to do in internal reviews. However, because the team is from a district close by, the members can usually understand the culture of the school and its community and can make recommendations that are politically sensitive and will have some likelihood of being followed through a subsequent improvement plan.

The second advantage is that an exchange review can be economically feasible because, as with an internal review, it involves just the funds for released time.

A disadvantage that I have observed in nearly every exchange review is that the two teams are composed of teachers only. Teachers do make excellent review team members, and every review team should primarily be made up of either current or retired classroom teachers. However, although teachers tend to be very knowledgeable about the courses or the grades they teach, they often lack the "big picture" understanding of a total mathematics curriculum and the mathematics program. For example, the daily demands of the classroom tend to limit the amount of time teachers have to follow the latest research being published in professional journals like the *Journal for Research in Mathematics Education*. Relatively few mathematics teachers have an opportunity to attend regional or national meetings of the National Council of Teachers of Mathematics (NCTM) or the School Science and Mathematics Association (SSMA). In one state, I conducted MPIRs in more than 50 schools; only one teacher among the hundreds who were interviewed had even heard of SSMA. Similarly, teachers seem familiar with only one or two of the various suppliers of mathematics resources (such as ETA, Delta, Creative Teaching Associates, and Dale Seymour Publications).

In short, teacher-only review teams tend to produce recommendations that are specific in terms of courses or grades, but fall short when it comes to addressing overall program needs. In my experience, this is most evident when it comes to professional development. The recommendations made by a teacher-only exchange team that reviewed Cartwright Middle School's mathematics program are typical of this problem.

The review team had had success in its own school using manipulatives and graphing calculators in algebra classes. When the team members did not observe any use of such resources at Cartwright, they recommended that Cartwright's algebra teachers do what they had done: receive training on the use of manipulatives (algebra tiles), graphing calculators, and computer-interfacing devices. With their own experience foremost in their minds, the exchange team members missed the more fundamental issue: Cartwright had not provided any mathematics-specific professional development that addressed the effective use of technology for *any* of its mathematics teachers, let alone its algebra teachers. Teachers had received generic training on presentation software and e-mail, but no training focused on technology's true instructional applications.

A second factor to consider before initiating an exchange review between neighboring districts is competition. Here in the United States, the media and most state departments of education put schools in a sort of competition with one another. Many newspapers publish best-to-worst rankings of schools or school districts based on student achievement results. No faculty wants to see their school ranked lower than another school. Generally, all feel that they are working as hard as they can to produce outstanding students, and nothing lowers a faculty's morale like seeing their school ranked below another school with which they are familiar, especially if they feel that they are working "harder and smarter."

If neighboring schools or districts that have been ranked in this way are involved in an exchange review, the teachers serving on the review teams may feel reluctant to provide helpful suggestions that will create an improved program. They may feel that any such suggestions will place the reviewed school higher than their own school in the rankings. Similarly, teachers may not totally trust the recommendations that they receive. Consequently, exchange reviews can lead to more superficial and less meaningful recommendations.

Some schools I have worked with have tried to alleviate the inherent problems often found within teacher-only internal or exchange teams by including a university or college mathematics educator on the team. In most instances, this has proved to be a successful solution. University mathematics educators typically remain well-informed about current research in mathematics education and can provide valuable assistance to the team as the report is written. Suggestions based upon recent research add credibility to the report and can move a mathematics program in a positive direction.

At the same time, classroom teachers can be reluctant to trust recommendations that seem based more on research than on their reality ("That may have worked with the kids in the study, but my situation is different"). Likewise, they may not readily accept that specific manipulatives or tools will really be instructional assets rather than "toys" that divert time and attention from their real objective of mastering computation.

The Best Review Team Configuration for MPIRs: The External Review

Based on my experience, the ideal review team for MPIRs is external, with all members coming from outside the district. The discussion of review procedures presented in the remainder of the book assumes an external team, although as noted, you will be able to adapt the information to the configuration best suited to your own situation. An external review team should consist of at least two members but may feature as many as five, depending on the size of the school to be reviewed. Here are the core team members:

- **A mathematics leader, such as a district mathematics supervisor or a university mathematics educator.** A supervisor or university educator brings knowledge of the research and resources as well as the "big picture" understanding of the mathematics program. This individual should be both aware and supportive of the national mathematics standards and the state reform efforts that apply to the school under review—even if he or she does not totally agree with those standards. Some of the professors of mathematics education who have served on my review teams have been highly critical of public school reform measures undertaken as a reaction to national standards, to No Child Left Behind, or to both, and have tried to used review reports as diatribes against the reforms rather than as instruments for school improvements.

This is never appropriate. If the MPIR is to be conducted in a state pursuing standards that are out of sync with or somewhat in opposition to national standards, all review team members still must be willing to support the school's efforts to meet these state standards. And from a purely practical standpoint, if the report is to be used, it must adhere to both local and state guidelines.

■ **A current or recently retired expert mathematics teacher.** The teacher brings experience related to the school's grade structure (elementary, middle, or high) and contributes an understanding of practicality within that grade range.

Additional members, who may be needed for reviews of larger schools, should be more of the same: mathematics supervisors or university educators or expert mathematics teachers.

As a general guideline, the number of team members must be sufficient to conduct interviews of staff and students and to complete classroom observations of mathematics lessons. In elementary schools, every teacher should be interviewed, even if, as in large schools, it's only feasible to observe a random selection of all the classroom teachers during math class. (Teacher interviews are key to the perceived legitimacy of the review; teachers must feel that they had input during the process and that their concerns were heard.) The size of the review team for a middle or high school should be determined by the number of mathematics faculty to be observed and interviewed and the school's schedule. For secondary schools on a traditional schedule, the general guideline is for the review team to have one member for every five mathematics faculty members. For schools on a block schedule, the team should generally have one member for every three faculty members.

Of course, there can be drawbacks to the external review as well. First among these is the cost. Members of external teams must be compensated for their time and travel. Depending on the travel expense and the number of team members required, external MPIR reviews can cost between $2,500 and $3,500.

Another potential problem is that external team members may not be aware of the culture of the school community they are visiting. I have always tried to ensure that at least half of the external team members came from cultures similar to the sites being visited.

A third complication is where to *find* these external reviewers. If you, as a principal (or a superintendent), decide that you would like to have an external team review your school's mathematics program, then you will need to find individuals who have already received training on the MPIR process or who would be willing to train themselves using this book as a guide.* You may want to begin by contacting a

---

*In addition to the use of this book for training purposes, you may find it beneficial to contact me. I continue to provide training in various locations, and you may find it helpful to send your selected team members to one of these sessions. However, if your team members carefully review the contents of this book, they will be able to succeed without attending specific training. They will become stronger reviewers as they gain more experience.

local university mathematics education program to determine the willingness of one or more of its faculty to serve on a team. It might also be helpful to contact a local or state mathematics association to identify recently retired mathematics educators who would be willing to develop an understanding of the MPIR process.

There is one final, major caution. When selecting external review team members, be wary of those who are ready to sell you the "magic bullet": the product or program that will be the perfect solution to your school's mathematics program. I have found that each school is unique in its culture, its faculty, its resources, its facilities, and its administration. Recommendations should be tailored to these unique characteristics, not to a canned solution that can be sold to the school by a consultant who served on the review team.

Review Team Training

Appendix A provides an overview of the procedures necessary to train review team members in the MPIR process. This training is absolutely essential for maximizing the potential benefits to schools under review.

First, review team members need to be very familiar with the process for the on-site visit. This includes understanding the standards and the questions that will be used in the interviews. Based on my experience conducting MPIRs, teachers responding to a question during an interview will invariably provide an answer or two that relates to a subsequent question. Rather than asking these questions later, I write their response in the appropriate location. This not only saves time during the interview but also helps to reassure the teacher that I know what I am doing and promote confidence in the review in general.

It's interesting to note that participating on a review team can be a very beneficial form of professional development for team members who are teachers or administrators. In fact, formal training in the MPIR process is a rich learning experience in itself and has routinely offered additional opportunities for those who complete the training. I have conducted MPIR process training for more than three years, and I often conclude the sessions that I lead by asking if participants would be interested in shadowing me or other experienced reviewers as we conduct a review. (Of course, we always request approval from the school to be reviewed before going forward with shadowing, and we are sure to inform those who shadow us that they are not to discuss observations with anyone else. We also collect any forms that they complete or notes that they take.) In every instance, the teachers and administrators who have participated in a shadowing experience have stated that it was one of the most valuable professional development opportunities they had ever had. One retired mathematics instructional supervisor who shadowed a one-day review commented at the conclusion that she felt she knew as much or more about the reviewed school's mathematics program than she did about those in the schools she had worked with for more than 10 years.

A number of the principals and supervisors who have shadowed reviews have subsequently had some of their mathematics teachers attend training sessions with the express intent of having them shadow on review visits. They were not interested in having the teachers trained to be team members, but they felt that the process of observing a review was an intense learning experience not to be missed.

Coordinating the On-Site Visit

Advance planning on the part of the review team and the school is the best way to ensure that an MPIR will be conducted in a professional manner and will yield accurate data that will support beneficial recommendations. Preparation responsibility falls to the school principal and the review team leader.

First, the review team leader must provide the principal with written notification of any advance work that needs to be done before the team's on-site visit (filling out questionnaires, gathering materials, arranging schedules, contacting parents, etc.). This communication should arrive at the school no later than one week before the team's scheduled visit. An example of a notification letter generated by an external review team appears in Figure 2.3. This information is critical, so it's advisable for the review team leader to contact the school principal to confirm its receipt. At this time, the review team leader should also answer any questions about the process and, if necessary, obtain directions to the school and the start time of the school day— information he or she must pass on to the other team members, along with a folder that contains all the forms to be used during the on-site evaluation.

Meanwhile, the school principal should announce to the entire school staff— not just to mathematics faculty—that there will be a review of the mathematics program. If the review will be conducted by an external team, it's important to explain that reviewers will be visiting the school to conduct the process. The principal is charged with making sure the staff has a full and clear explanation of the review's purpose, emphasizing that it will be a comprehensive evaluation of the mathematics program, not an evaluation of individual mathematics teachers, and that it will generate a final report with recommendations addressing these issues:

- The mathematics program's source of financial support.
- The use of classroom and schoolwide assessments to monitor program improvement.
- School and district administrative support for mathematics professional development.
- The availability and use of resources to support best-practices instruction in mathematics.

FIGURE 2.3	SAMPLE NOTIFICATION LETTER

Dear Principal:

We are pleased to have an opportunity to visit your school to conduct a Mathematics Program Improvement Review. The team will arrive approximately 30 minutes before the school day starts.

The purpose of the review is to collect as much data as possible concerning the mathematics instructional program. Following the site visit, the team will summarize the findings and issue a final report that includes recommendations for program improvement. You may also request that the report be presented orally to your teachers. The report will be confidential, for use at your discretion. Please note that although the team will spend time in classrooms observing mathematics instruction and conferring with individuals and groups, the findings will be presented in a generic fashion, and *no teacher or individual will be singled out or named in the report.*

Our site visit has several components. Please develop a schedule for the day that includes the following:

- A tour of the building.
- A 50- to 60-minute meeting with you, the principal. We would prefer to conduct this close to the end of our visit if this is possible.
- A 60-minute group meeting with all teachers who teach mathematics or, preferably, meetings with these teachers at their regular planning times during the day.
- A 30- to 45-minute meeting with 10 to 12 students representative of all academic levels in grades 3–5, unless you have mature and verbal 1st and 2nd grade students who can participate.
- A 60-minute meeting with 5 to 10 parents representative of your school's student body. This meeting is typically held after school.
- Observation time for teachers who teach mathematics. (*Note:* The group interview meetings should be spaced to allow maximum time for classroom visits.) We would like to observe *every* teacher of mathematics teaching a lesson if possible. If observing all teachers is not possible, please select a representative group including as a minimum the accountability grades. The schedule should allow for at least a 30-minute class visit for each teacher who is to be observed and, if time permits, we would like to stay for the entire class. The teachers should be encouraged to teach the math lesson they would regularly teach on the day of the visit and to utilize the same strategies and materials they would normally use. If possible, long videos and formal paper-and-pencil assessments should be avoided because it is important to observe teaching strategies.

In addition to interviewing and observing, the team will review various documents that the school uses in planning for or supporting the mathematics instructional programs. With the limited time for the site visit, we may need to take these items to use while writing the report. It would be helpful if the administrative staff could gather and make copies of the following materials (all that are available):

(continued)

FIGURE 2.3	SAMPLE NOTIFICATION LETTER *(continued)*

- Mathematics curriculum guide(s).

- Samples of lesson plans and assessments from each mathematics teacher (included in a separate folder for each teacher and including the teacher's completed class description questionnaire).

- Copies of the completed (anonymous) teacher self-perception questionnaires. (But see note below.)

- A copy of your completed principal's checklist and principal's self-perception questionnaire.

- Mathematics assessment data (national, state, and local if available), including trend data and disaggregated data.

- Parent information and communications pertinent to the mathematics program (newsletter articles, list of grade-level expectations, etc.) regarding the mathematics program.

- Memos (including e-mails) from you to teachers regarding mathematics instruction.

- Information related to professional staff development for improving mathematics instruction (number and type of sessions that have been presented and number of teachers who have attended).

- A copy of the school report card issued by the state department of education.

- A copy of your school improvement plan (particularly those pages that relate to mathematics).

- A copy of the school floor plan identifying teacher workstations, library, computer labs, and so on.

- A list of the school's computer software available for instructional use in mathematics. (Please indicate whether the software is stand-alone or on the school network.)

- An inventory of the school's math-related books, periodicals, and videos that are available to teachers or students and that are contained in the library or professional library.

- Any other materials you feel would help us understand the mathematics instructional program in your school, particularly the mathematics department budget and the school Web site (please provide the URL address).

Attached, you will find copies of the questionnaires mentioned above, along with a fourth questionnaire (the teacher's self-perception questionnaire, to be completed anonymously by staff who teach mathematics). Again, these questionnaires should be completed before the team arrives; if possible, we would like to arrange to pick up copies of the anonymous teacher self-perception questionnaires a few days before the site visit.

Please develop a tentative schedule for the visit based on this letter. If you have any questions, feel free to contact me at [phone number] or at [e-mail address]. We are looking forward to meeting with you and your staff and working with you toward the improvement of your mathematics instructional program.

Sincerely,
Review Team Leader

It should also be clear that although the review team will gather information from teachers through questionnaires, interviews, and classroom observation, *the review report will contain nothing that can be used to evaluate the performance of individual teachers*. Teachers should also know that the review team will give the final report only to the school principal.

In my experience, it is wise for the principal to address teachers' concerns about the MPIR before any review activities begin. Failing to explain the review process thoroughly can be quite detrimental to the review. This was certainly the case at a school whose faculty had no idea a program review was even scheduled until the team arrived. Needless to say, the teachers' anxiety level was very high throughout the day. Even though the team explained to interviewed teachers that they were not there to evaluate them individually, the teachers were highly stressed and suspicious of the process.

Tips for Review Team Members

Here are some general tips for review team members.

Dress appropriately. All team members should dress professionally for the on-site review, but not necessarily in suits, which teachers in some school cultures can perceive as threatening. Teachers being observed and interviewed need to feel as relaxed as possible. When conducting reviews, I try to dress at about the same level of formality as the school principal. Obviously this can only be done when I have been able to meet with the school principal prior to the site visit. If I have not had a prior planning meeting, I typically wear a dress shirt and tie. I never wear casual clothes like blue jeans or T-shirts, even if a review falls on the school's "casual Friday."

Plan to arrive early. Team members need to arrive at the school early and arrange the interview room or rooms in an appropriate way. Although the arrangement may vary from site to site, it is usually best to have a room with tables for interviewing parents and teachers. Most adults feel more comfortable when they can lean on (or hide behind) a table. Although it may seem adversarial, it is also best that the interviewer(s) sit across from those being interviewed. The interviewer will need to make notes throughout the interviews, and it is best if those being interviewed are not reading over the interviewer's shoulder.

The best place to interview teachers and the principal is within their own classroom or office. This is only possible if the schedule has been set up with time for individual interviews. In some instances, schools have found it necessary to schedule a group interview for large numbers of teachers. In such instances, it is best to have a room with tables.

Prepare some introductory remarks. One team members should be designated to introduce the review process to interview groups. The purpose of this introduction is to put those who will be interviewed at ease and make sure they understand that the team's purpose is to evaluate the mathematics program, not mathematics personnel. At this time, all the team members should introduce themselves to the members of their interview group, and the group members should introduce themselves.

Decide where and when to hold follow-up discussions. Before the on-site visit, the entire team should agree on a time and place to meet to discuss observations and decide on tentative ratings for each indicator. The place could be in the interview room in the school after all observations and interviews have been completed or even in a car on the way back to a meeting point.

Decide how to approach and present the report. After the on-site review, team members must decide whether to divide responsibility for drafting the report by standards or to have each member submit draft documentation of evidence to the team leader for writing the report. The team leader is responsible for collecting all drafts and compiling them into the report, editing as necessary after feedback from the team members, and printing and binding the reports to be sent to the school principal. It's also recommended that the team select highlights from the report and include them in a PowerPoint or overhead slide presentation if the school has made prior arrangements for the report to be presented orally to the entire faculty or to the mathematics department.

■   ■   ■

Now that you have a clear understanding of the advance work needed to initiate an MPIR and the options for how to conduct it, it is time to move on to the components underlying the evaluation: the standards of effective mathematics education.

## 3

The Standards

DuFour and Eaker's *Professional Learning Communities at Work* (1998) identifies key questions to be answered by school personnel in planning for continuous improvement. One of these questions revolves around the criteria schools use to assess their improvement efforts, and one method of establishing measurable criteria is the development of specific standards along with indicators of success. This is the approach I have taken with the MPIR.

Throughout my 20 years as a mathematics supervisor, my primary goal was to improve opportunities for teachers to excel in their classrooms. I visited classrooms nearly every day—observing, assisting, and modeling instruction. I used grant monies and federal funds to send teachers to regional and national mathematics conferences.

The investment paid off. The teachers in my district enhanced their knowledge of mathematics content and pedagogy and saw results in their classrooms. There were major improvements in the students' mathematics achievement scores, with the district average moving from percentile scores in the upper 40s to scores in the high 50s and low 60s. More important, gains were made in every school: the ones in affluent neighborhoods, the ones with high percentages of students receiving free and reduced-price lunch, and the ones with high minority-student percentages.

I identified a number of critical factors that contributed to our district's gains, and teachers and administrators worked with me to formally add these factors to our mathematics programs. Some of the elements we incorporated—such as a focus on problem solving—are now commonplace in schools, but at the time (the 1980s) they were a departure from the norm of a skills-based focus that was highly dependent on basal programs.

When developing the MPIR process for ARSI, I turned again to the elements I knew to be helpful in establishing high-quality mathematics programs. I also looked beyond my own experience, scouring the literature for research results that indicated best practices in mathematics programs. Some of the research I found confirmed the approach we'd taken within our district; other research presented elements that were new to me as practices a program should incorporate. I want to highlight some of the key external research underlying the MPIR's standards:

- Louis, Marks, and Kruse (1996) identify five elements that can lead to increased responsibility for student learning: shared norms and values, collective focus on student learning, collaboration, deprivatized practice, and reflective dialogue.

- Frase, English, and Posten (2000) identify five standards for quality control for curriculum management: control, direction, connectivity, feedback, and productivity.

- The National Review Panel selected by the U. S. Department of Education (2000; 2001) established a set of guidelines* to examine schools nominated for the prestigious Blue Ribbon Schools award. The Blue Ribbon Schools guidelines call for evaluating schools based on student focus and support; school organization and culture; challenging standards and curriculum; active teaching and learning; professional community; leadership and educational vitality; school, family, and community partnerships; and, indicators of success (assessment results).

The handbook you are now reading proposes 10 specific standards and supporting indicators for measuring the quality of a mathematics program:

1. Curriculum
2. Instruction
3. Equity and diversity
4. School climate
5. Usefulness
6. Professional environment
7. Community
8. Organization and leadership
9. Assessment and evaluation
10. Financial and materials resources

These represent the best of what I have winnowed from the literature and from my own experience. The standards are numbered, but this is a convenience for cross-referencing indicators and data, not an indication of priority. Each is critical to a successfully implemented mathematics program.

During the review, indicators are rated on a scale of 1 to 5, with 5 being the highest in terms of a high-quality, constructivist-based mathematics program. The final MPIR report submitted to the school should always include a copy of the rubric

---

*Note that The Blue Ribbon panels serve an entirely different purpose than what is proposed in this book. They don't set out to work to improve schools, but to identify schools that are already at or near the top of all schools in the country.

so that mathematics teachers and school administrators can determine for themselves how close they are to meeting the standards. The report extract that follows shows findings noted about a school that received a low rating for the diversity/equity standard. The specific statements of the evaluator were not included within the report provided to the school because a specific teacher could potentially be identified. However, the review team reported that, based on observations and other related information, an equity problem did seem to exist:

> . . . During one classroom observation, a reviewer noticed that the teacher virtually ignored an entire row of students throughout her lecture-style instruction. Although she interacted with the rest of the class, she never made eye contact with or directed questions to the students sitting in the row of desks lining the right side of the classroom. After class, and in response to the reviewer's inquiry, the teacher explained that this row consisted of special education students who had been placed in her classroom. She felt very strongly that she should not modify her lesson to accommodate these students; it was their responsibility to keep up. To change her instruction so that it was accessible to them, she said, would risk shortchanging the rest of the class, who would need the mathematics she was teaching. Other teachers at the school expressed similar feelings about mainstreamed special education students. Yet there was no perception of an equity problem; during the interviews, none of the teachers expressed a need for professional development on that topic.

The remainder of this chapter discusses the 10 quality standards and provides examples of actual MPIR findings related to each standard in the form of report extracts. As you review each of the standards, it may be helpful to refer to the standard rating form in Appendix B (Figure B.1, beginning on p. 147), which lists each standard's indicators. The rubric used to determine scores for each indicator is also included in Appendix B (see Figure B.2, beginning on p. 153).

Standard 1: Curriculum

The mathematics program uses problem-centered content that develops students' conceptual understanding of mathematics, ability to apply mathematics, ability to communicate mathematically, and knowledge and skills in using mathematics algorithms.

This standard calls for the presence and use of a locally developed curriculum that is aligned with the National Council of Teachers and Mathematics (NCTM) criteria or state standards or both. Local development and alignment creates teacher ownership;

teachers are more likely to use a curriculum they have worked on than an off-the-shelf curriculum from a publisher or other outside source.

A teacher-friendly curriculum is more than a textbook program. It includes an emphasis on both the teachers' understanding of the curriculum and the students' ability to demonstrate competencies in the curriculum objectives through problem solving, communication, multiple representations, reasoning, and connections. The MPIR curriculum standard also identifies specific concepts that should be taught within various grade spans.

In evaluating this standard, reviewers ask the following questions:

- Does the school have and do the teachers use a mathematics curriculum that has been developed and regularly revised by its own teachers of mathematics?

- Does the curriculum call for the students to be actively engaged in problem solving, or does it focus primarily on ensuring their proficiency with computational algorithms?

- Does the curriculum contain and do the teachers regularly exploit connections between the concepts being taught at one grade level or within one mathematical subject and concepts taught at other grade levels or within other mathematics subjects?

- Do all students have access to instructional resources that will support their exploration of the mathematics concepts contained within the curriculum?

The following MPIR report extracts reveal very different approaches to curriculum.

Cartwright Middle School

. . . Some important mathematics concepts are apparently being neglected. We saw little evidence of instruction on various estimation strategies (front-end with adjustment, compatible numbers, and clustering) and mental computation involving mathematics properties (e.g., using the commutative property to demonstrate that 16 percent of 25 is the same as 25 percent of 16 and thus is 4). Students do not have sufficient experience with manipulatives to develop spatial sense, including tessellations and transformations (translations, reflections, rotations, and dilations—no one reported teaching dilations).

Students also lack sufficient experience with hands-on measurement tools that help in developing measurement sense and measurement concepts (e.g., trundle wheels and platform scales). In fact, the responsibility for any hands-on instruction in measurement seems to have been left to the science department. Measurement instruction in the mathematics classrooms consists only of conversion of units.

Although vocabulary receives some emphasis (including Word Walls in some of the classrooms), it does not seem to be emphasized enough in view of the importance placed on vocabulary in state and national assessments.

Cartwright does not have one curriculum document that is used consistently by all teachers. Rather, teachers use a variety of sources for planning their instruction. Some use a district curriculum, some use the textbook scope and sequence, some use state guidelines, and some base their instruction on their years of experience teaching that grade level. Perhaps as a consequence, teachers' reports of content coverage revealed considerable inconsistencies. Teachers at the same grade level don't always teach the same concepts. For example, one teacher reported having students collect their own data, whereas another teaching the same grade level reported that data collection was not being done that year. Similarly, one teacher reported teaching interquartile range, whereas another teaching the same grade level did not.

Collingwood High School

. . . Two years ago, Collingwood's mathematics faculty began working on a curriculum document that was aligned to state objectives as well as to the resources they had access to within their program. The teachers have continued to monitor this curriculum's use and have revised it as they have conducted departmental assessments, purchased additional resources, and discovered new Web sites that support their curriculum.

Each of the teachers provided input into the original development of the curriculum, and it continues to be a primary pacing guide and reminder of resources that have been used successfully to teach each objective. Each content area teacher—the teachers for Algebra I, for Geometry, and so forth—knows what the expectations are for the course, what resources are available to teach the course, and how the students will be assessed. Interviews and test results seem to indicate that Collingwood's mathematics teachers have done a thorough job of teaching each of the objectives they have identified within their mathematics curriculum.

Standard 2: Instruction

The mathematics program engages students in a variety of learning experiences designed to develop mathematical discovery and reasoning.

The built-in assumption in assessing this standard is that classroom instruction will have a constructivist orientation, which includes the use of manipulatives and technology and the development of students' ability to communicate their mathematical understanding. The standard also assumes that teachers will use a variety of instructional strategies, such as changes in grouping patterns, mathematical discourse, and activities that extend instruction beyond the classroom.

Here are the questions reviewers must keep in mind while evaluating the quality of instruction:

- Does the instruction provide opportunities for student-initiated questions and discussion?
- Do the teachers' lessons reflect the use of written measurable objectives and multiple problem-solving strategies to develop understanding?
- Do teachers and the principal report that grouping patterns vary to suit the tasks to be accomplished, to address different learning styles, or to provide for differentiated instruction?
- Does daily instruction provide opportunities for students to reflect on the mathematics they are learning through writing or discussion?
- Do students regularly use manipulatives and technology and does their use include practicing/applying skills, developing concepts, problem solving, and verification?

The following extract addresses a school's implementation of instruction.

Cartwright Middle School
. . . Some lessons had a good balance of initial instruction, review, and homework, but there did not seem to be sufficient time for students to develop a full understanding of new concepts through either lecture or inquiry. All the interviewed students reported having regular mathematics homework, and all said they generally complete their homework in 20 minutes or less. However, the students reported that their homework is nearly always from textbooks or worksheets and is very rarely related to projects. Homework did not deal with appropriate grade-level applications (data collection, measurement, etc.).

Standard 3: Equity and Diversity

The mathematics program provides learning environments that meet students' diverse learning needs.

The equity standard addresses how well the mathematics program meets the needs of all students. An MPIR addresses a minimum of five different diversities: gender, race, socioeconomic status, learning style or multiple intelligence, and ability (gifted or special education). Depending on the school, other equity issues, such as culture, religion, and student assertiveness/bullying, might also need to be addressed. Evaluators ask questions like these:

- Do all students—regardless of ethnicity, culture, ability, race, learning styles, socioeconomic status, or gender—have access to the same quality of instruction and resources, including technology?
- Do teachers regroup students for different lessons to accommodate different learning styles and to ensure different working relationships?
- Do teachers vary their instructional strategies to accommodate students' varying abilities?
- Does the classroom setting depict the contributions of different cultures, races, and genders to the study of mathematics?

Sometimes schools have trouble recognizing inequities in the learning experience of their students. Consider the possible issues identified at Abbott Elementary.

Abbott Elementary School

. . . Parents reported no perceived inequities in teachers' dealings with students of different gender, race, and socioeconomic status, and we agree. In addition, teachers provided students with problems and activities aimed at different student interests. However, whereas the parents reported no perceived inequities in the teaching of students with different learning abilities, problems may exist in this area, specifically in a failure to adapt instruction to challenge the more capable students. Student interviews and classroom observations both suggest that the more capable students may not be challenged to the extent of their abilities.

The teachers did well grouping students to address different learning styles. Nevertheless, two of the teachers reported that they had not received much training on teaching to multiple learning styles, and an additional nine teachers felt they were only "somewhat prepared" to do this.

Standard 4: School Climate

The mathematics program creates positive attitudes toward and about mathematics and encourages and recognizes students' accomplishments in mathematics.

In evaluating this standard, reviewers ask the following questions:

- Does the mathematics program set high expectations for all students?
- Do both students and teachers receive appropriate recognition for their achievements?

■ Do the students perceive the classroom to be a risk-free environment? Do they feel comfortable asking questions of the teacher and of one another during discussion or dialogue?

■ Do persons in the school other than mathematics teachers actively promote the mathematics program?

The climate of the school and classroom has a definite impact on instruction, as illustrated by the contrasting climates described in the two extracts that follow.

Abbott Elementary School

. . . The teachers were welcoming, positive, and supportive. The parents and students both made positive comments about the teachers. They said teachers were "knowledgeable," "accessible," and "involved" and "cared that you learn." The school provides several methods of publicly recognizing academic achievements of students, such as honor rolls (including publication in the local newspaper and honor roll rallies). Some selected students participated in academic teams. Students are awarded certificates for completing computer lab units and receive medals for being "best in math." Each week, teachers nominate "most improved" students to have lunch with the principal.

Cramer Elementary School

. . . Cramer is a large, consolidated school composed of students from the town in which the school is located as well as students from the surrounding county. The parents of students from the county feel that their children are discriminated against within the school: denied opportunities to be placed in advanced-level classes and placed in classes with the lowest achieving students without regard to previous achievements. Although the school has access to state assessment results, placements are made based solely on teacher recommendations.

The only recognition program available to students is an honor roll each grading period. Teachers do not receive any public recognition for extraordinary efforts.

Standard 5: Usefulness

The mathematics program relates instruction and learning to students' interests, experiences, and future goals.

Here are the questions reviewers must keep in mind while considering usefulness:

- How well does the mathematics program relate learning to real-life applications?
- Are connections made between mathematics and other disciplines?
- Do teachers make efforts to involve student interests in their lessons and units?

In my experience, students' lack of motivation is a concern for both teachers and principals. Many teachers who successfully motivate their students do so by relating instruction to situations that would interest them. For example, a simple way that elementary school teachers can engage their class is to change the names used in mathematics problems to the names of their students. At some schools, teachers may be aware of the need to relate mathematics to their students' lives but unsure how to do that. The following extract from Collingwood High School's report describes a faculty that falls into this category.

Collingwood High School

. . . Many of the students interviewed indicated that their teachers *did* attempt to relate mathematics to individual interests. For example, the teachers asked students about their interests during a class early in the school year and then followed up with related problems or activities. However, 11 of the teachers indicated that they were only "somewhat prepared" through professional development or coursework to know how to encourage students' interest in mathematics. Greater student involvement could lead to both increased motivation and academic success.

Teachers were observed trying to connect mathematics to the real world in the opening portions of their lessons. However, at times both the observed examples and those examples teachers reported using in their classes were superficial. For instance, several teachers said they "included real-world connections in problem-solving discussions" without providing any specifics about how they did that. Teachers also indicated that they rarely tried to make connections between math and the real world by using speakers, films or videos, field trips, or software.

Standard 6: Professional Environment

The professional environment inspires collegiality and understanding among the faculty and the administrative staff to work together to implement an effective mathematics program.

This standard focuses on the professional learning community of the school. Data gathered from a review can answer important questions about that environment:

- Does the school or district provide appropriate professional development?
- Do teachers collaborate?
- Can teachers and other staff members articulate instructional goals for mathematics?
- Is the staff familiar with the school's improvement plan?
- Are teachers encouraged to pursue additional mathematics professional development—both within the school or district and at state or national professional association conferences?
- Is the principal involved in learning new ideas along with his or her teachers of mathematics?

Extracts from the Foster and Abbott MPIR reports illustrate different levels of success in developing a professional learning community.

Foster Elementary School

. . . The mathematics program lacks instructional goals and objectives and a mission statement. The school improvement plan addresses state assessment goals only, and only one mathematics teacher served on the committee that developed it. Another mathematics teacher served on the curriculum committee. Three of the teachers interviewed had seen a draft copy of the curriculum, but they didn't feel they would have input about possible revisions. Except for the committee member, none of the teachers was aware of what the school improvement plan contained related to mathematics.

It appears that professional development training sessions and attendance at conferences have not been evaluated to determine their impact on instruction, school culture, and other aspects of the program. Most of the teachers joined the staff after the adoption of the current textbooks, but none of these teachers has received training on the effective use of the textbook and its ancillary materials.

Abbott Elementary School

. . . The professional development committee routinely surveys all teachers about professional development needs. In response, the school annually sets aside at least two of the scheduled professional development days for subject-specific offerings, and all teachers are given opportunities to attend regional or national conferences at least once every three years. Every teacher of mathematics has been to a regional or national mathematics conference at least once in the past five years. Teachers regularly evaluate professional development offerings that they attend.

The school also has an early release day one Wednesday each month. This day is used for schoolwide initiatives. For example, in the current year, the school has used study groups to focus on reading in the content areas.

Standard 7: Community

The mathematics program involves the parents and the community in a collaborative effort to develop mathematical knowledge among students.

Schools that have shown the most improvement from their first MPIR to a subsequent review often have been those that involved their parents and community in the educational programs. Each review evaluates how successful a school faculty is at doing just that. The data collected should provide answers to questions like these:

- Are various means provided for communicating with parents and the community?
- How effective have these efforts been in involving parents and the community with the learning process?
- Do the parents know where and how they can get additional support for their children when they are having difficulties?

In answering these kinds of questions, reviewers at Cartwright Middle School discovered that the school had taken some steps toward parental and community involvement, but more were needed.

Cartwright Middle School

. . . The Parent–Teacher Organization and the principal at Cartwright are working hard to ensure that this group moves beyond the typical fundraising to greater engagement. However, at the time of the review, the overall parental involvement with the academic program appears minimal.

No proactive steps have been taken to increase two-way communication between the school staff and parents. Even though many of the interviewed parents are employees of the school, they have little awareness of the mathematics program. Parents said they have never been asked for specific suggestions about the mathematics program; however, they did think the school staff would be open to different approaches. They have received no reports about the overall mathematics program via newsletter, principal letters, or posting on the school Web site.

Standard 8: Organization and Leadership

The school faculty and school leadership enhance opportunities for effective and consistent mathematics instruction.

Review teams typically find this standard one of the most difficult to evaluate. Teachers are often reluctant to make statements about principals or administrators that might be perceived to be critical. They don't want to be the one who casts aspersions on their principal's character or leadership skills. At times, teachers have even plainly stated that they were not in a secure enough position to be able to make any statement—good or bad— that might get back to the principal. One of the first reports that I ever wrote and returned to a school was never seen by the school faculty because the principal thought the report was too critical of his administrative leadership.

That said, the leadership standard is one of the most critical. Principals are key to effective mathematics programs because they control so many factors that can lead to success. These may include the quality of the faculty, the budget, teaching loads, class size (teacher–student ratio), and assignment of classrooms with adequate space for conducting investigations. Here are some questions to consider in evaluating leadership:

- Is a structure in place to enhance opportunities for learning? Does it include support from the principal, adequate facilities, instructional time in the schedule, and so forth?
- Does the principal focus on instructional leadership?
- Does the principal effectively convey high expectations for students, faculty, and self?

Reviewers must be especially sensitive in reporting their evaluation of this standard. Unlike the other standards, which focus on the practices of a group, findings about leadership single out one person—and it happens to be the person who is most likely to decide whether to share the report recommendations and act on them. A review report that is too critical of a principal's decisions may never be seen and used by the faculty. I realize that softening results about principals is a delicate matter, but I have found it to be wise to curb some of the possible comments that could lead to the principal's perception that he or she is being criticized directly. This next report excerpt was tempered in light of the principal's personality and the overall school climate. As you read, think about how reviewers have indicated ways to improve while still being encouraging.

Collingwood High School

. . . The organization and leadership are present within Collingwood High School and its district to produce noteworthy gains in instruction and assessment. The principal is generally not perceived as a "people person," but appears to have the energy, knowledge, and leadership ability to enable the school to continue to make progress. Most of the classes lack adequate learning space (especially for large movement activities) and storage space, but all have appropriate furniture to conduct a variety of inquiry-type lessons in mathematics.

Standard 9: Assessment and Evaluation

The school continually assesses student achievement, evaluates program effectiveness, and uses the results to determine if there is a need for improvement.

With state and national tests, schools have access to a wealth of data on their students. They also have opportunities to collect data within their own classrooms using both standard and alternative assessments. Many schools use various surveys and questionnaires to collect data from parents and students. The review examines how effectively the school staff is using all of these data to improve its mathematics program and whether staff continuously monitor student learning. Reviewers also ask questions like these:

■ Does the school use a variety of data to assess the success of the mathematics program and to identify where improvements can be made?

■ Are the results of evaluations made available to parents and others in the community?

■ Is the mathematics program coordinated among the various schools in the district?

■ Do formal evaluations of teachers by the principal include an examination of effective teaching practices?

If teachers are not using alternative assessments in their classrooms, it may be because teachers simply don't know about them. Reviewers for Foster Elementary School made sure to list some alternative assessments in their report results, in case teachers and leadership were unaware of what else they could use besides traditional tests.

Foster Elementary School
. . . Most of Foster's teachers indicated that they seldom or never use any type of alternative assessment strategies for formative or summative evaluation. A primary purpose of student assessment is to help teachers better understand what students know and to help them make meaningful decisions about teaching and learning activities.

Most of the assessment samples provided were paper-and-pencil tests from the textbook series. Curriculum maps also indicated that assessments are primarily pencil-and-paper and include homework, which teachers grade and weigh equally with tests.

None of the teachers at Foster reported using any alternative assessments like math writing (journals, logs, exit slips, etc.), group projects, anecdotal records, self-assessments, individual hands-on investigations, performance events, and open-response questions. Even though the state assessment requires that students answer open-response questions, the current district policy (as given in the school improvement plan) only supports the inclusion of short-answer and extended-response questions.

Standard 10: Financial and Material Resources

The mathematics curriculum is supported by adequate financial and material resources.

This final standard is last in position but not in importance. Some schools may find that they need to make it their highest priority. Here are some guiding considerations in reviewing this standard:

- Do teachers have the financial support to maintain and enhance the development of the mathematics program?
- Do teachers have a say in the determination of the expenditures for the mathematics program?
- Does the school seek and use funds or resources from other agencies?

As illustrated in the following extract, a review team looking at resources at Cramer Elementary School found areas for improvement. Schools with funding issues, like Cramer, often use MPIR findings about resources to support requests for augmenting budgets.

Cramer Elementary School

. . . The funding of Cramer's mathematics program is a concern, as an allotment of $300 per teacher for all classroom expenditures, including replacement ink cartridges, seems to be inadequate to support a quality program. Although the school library has a good inventory of mathematics-related books and professional mathematics books and journals, the classrooms are inadequately equipped with technology (computers, software, and calculators), manipulatives, and mathematics tools.

■   ■   ■

You have seen the standards for a quality mathematics program and some sample findings for each standard, but these represent only the starting and ending points of the Mathematics Program Improvement Review. Most of the process happens in between and is related to data gathering.

4

The Questionnaires

The Mathematics Program Improvement Review depends on accurate data—and a lot of it.

Review teams use a number of different instruments to collect these data. Some of the tools are used in face-to-face interviews or discussions with school personnel. Other tools are used to gather data anonymously. Each instrument serves a specific purpose, but all are the means to gather data that can be triangulated to support the accuracy and consistency of the overall assessment. This chapter discusses the first of these data-gathering tools: questionnaires. Within the MPIR process, results are tabulated from four questionnaires: two completed by classroom teachers and two completed by the school principal.

The Strengths (and Limitations) of Questionnaires

As a data-gathering tool, questionnaires have some specific strengths that factor into their use within the MPIR process (see Figure 4.1). However, the advantages of all types of data-collection instruments are offset to some degree by their drawbacks, which is another reason the MPIR process relies on multiple approaches. I want to begin by looking at the strengths of the questionnaire approach and acknowledging some of its limitations.

Questionnaires are more efficient than face-to-face interviews. Especially in large schools with many teachers, they provide a fast, easy, and complete way to gather data. In group interview situations, it can be difficult to get every teacher's response to every question within the time allotted. With questionnaires, all teachers can respond to all the questions. *However:* The longer a questionnaire is, the greater risk that answers will be superficial, marked casually and without reflection. Given the number of questions included in two of the MPIR's questionnaires, this can be a concern.

FIGURE 4.1	STRENGTHS OF QUESTIONNAIRES

+ Fast and efficient

+ Easy to analyze

+ Minimize bias

+ Allow for anonymity and higher respondent comfort level

+ Convenient for respondents and reviewers

Questionnaires are relatively easy to analyze. Multiple-choice answers allow for fast tabulation, and computer software packages can make that tabulation even faster. *However:* The inclusion of open-response questions does slow the analysis process. Open-response questions are included in two of the MPIR questionnaires (one teacher questionnaire and one principal questionnaire). The two longer questionnaires are multiple choice.

Questionnaires have minimal bias. The format allows for careful crafting and prior review of questions to ensure they are not inadvertently biased. In contrast to an interview, where the interviewer may pose questions in slightly different ways at different times and may use verbal or nonverbal cues that influence interviewees' answers, questionnaires have a uniform question presentation and response format. *However:* The set format also means that if respondents find a question puzzling or unclear, they do not have the interviewee's option of asking for additional explanation.

Questionnaires are nonthreatening. Nearly everyone has had some experience completing questionnaires and, in contrast to face-to-face interviews, they generally do not make people apprehensive. *However:* The less threatening format of questionnaires does not guarantee a high response rate. Individuals asked to complete questionnaires might not wish to reveal the information, might think that they will not benefit from responding, and might even fear they will be penalized for giving their real opinion. The MPIR process tries to mediate such misgivings by asking teachers to complete the longer of their two questionnaires anonymously.

Questionnaires are relatively nonintrusive. The MPIR process calls for schools to receive, complete, and return their questionnaires in advance of the site visit. When teachers or principals receive a questionnaire in the mail or electronically, they are free to complete it on their own timetable, whenever it is most convenient. There is no need to rush through the information, as they might have to if there were time limits. *However:* Because questionnaires are completed in advance, there is a chance that some respondents may have difficulty relating the questions to the site visit that is to come, may forget important issues by the day of the visit, or may change their typical instruction to conform with what they think the review team may be looking for on the basis of the questionnaire content.

The inclusion of questionnaires in the review process serves a variety of purposes related to the discussed advantages. As noted, one of the more significant is that it functions as a valuable means of triangulating data with observations and other forms of data (test results, interviews, etc.). Because the questionnaires are given out, completed, and at least reviewed (and in some cases tabulated) *before* the review team makes the on-site school visit, they serve as early indicators of strengths and weaknesses in the program, providing the review team with an idea of areas that deserve particular focus. Reviewers are then able to validate or probe these issues in interviews and during observation. The response of teachers at Foster Elementary School to a question about use of manipulatives alerted a review team in this way.

One of the teacher questionnaires used in the MPIR process provides examples of manipulatives—such as geoboards, counters, algebra tiles, base-10 blocks—and asks teachers how often they are used in their classrooms: daily, weekly, monthly, rarely, or never. All the primary grade teachers at Foster responded that they used manipulatives daily; the intermediate grade teachers, however, marked that they used manipulatives rarely or never. Reviewers followed up on these responses during subsequent on-site interviews. They discovered that the intermediate grade teachers were reluctant to use manipulatives for three reasons: (1) "They take too much time away from teaching"; (2) "Students play with them instead of focusing on the task"; and (3) "The state assessment does not allow the use of manipulatives." The teachers also reported that they had never attended any professional development dealing with the use of mathematics manipulatives.

Predictably, such diverse philosophies between the primary grade and intermediate grade teachers had produced inconsistencies in students' achievement results on the state-mandated tests. The teachers within this school had never sat down as a faculty and established a unified philosophy of mathematics instruction. Although these issues may have come to light during the interview stage, the need to address them was first detected through analysis of the questionnaires before the review team arrived.

Within the MPIR process, the questionnaires can also be used to identify strengths of a program that may not be observable on the particular day of the visit. For example, one of the questionnaires asks teachers to mark if their students participate in mathematics field trips and, if so, how often. The mathematics teachers at Cartwright Middle School all marked that their students do participate in field trips. Follow-up interviews revealed that Cartwright faculty offer three interdisciplinary units each school year, and the culminating event for each unit is a related field trip.

Reviewers might have become aware of this very positive aspect of the mathematics program during the on-site visit, but the questionnaire ensured they would not miss it.

Sometimes, MPIR questionnaire responses from one group lead interviewers to pose follow-up questions to other groups. For example, a principal's response on a questionnaire could prompt follow-up questions for interviews with the principal, with teachers, or with parents. One principal gave this response to a question about the school's use of state funds: "We use state funds for after-school remediation. We also provide funds to fully support the academic team's competitions. Funds are available to support field trips as requested by teachers, but I don't recall any math teacher asking for field trips." Reviewers probed this issue during interviews. The parents interviewed indicated that they were not aware of their children ever going on a mathematics field trip. The mathematics teachers thought that budget constraints prevented them from taking any field trips. It appeared that a lack of communication may have kept students from a valuable learning opportunity.

Teacher Questionnaires

In schools with a large number of mathematics teachers, it can be difficult to observe or even interview each teacher during the site visit. The two questionnaires used in the MPIR process give all teachers the opportunity to describe the mathematics program according to their understanding; they ensure that every mathematics teacher has a voice in the review and give each teacher the option of making that voice an anonymous one. At one school, the teachers were uncomfortable being interviewed in their classrooms. They explained that it was because their principal had a habit of turning on classroom intercoms and listening in.

Teachers have used the MPIR questionnaires to express their opinions freely. One issue they tend to comment on in questionnaires rather than in interviews is insufficient support of the mathematics program. Often they mention a lack of financial or administrative support in relationship to other programs within the school. They perceive that mathematics is considered "less important" than reading, say, or athletics. In questionnaire responses, teachers also have identified a lack of professional development focused on mathematics. Similar opinions were not always expressed in personal interviews of these same teachers. This in itself may speak to the lack of a professional learning community within such schools.

Let's take a closer look at the two teacher questionnaires.

The Mathematics Teacher Self-Perception Questionnaire

This questionnaire, included in Appendix B as Figure B.3 (see p. 168), is given to all classroom teachers of mathematics at elementary schools under review and to all mathematics teachers at middle and high schools. It is designed to address Standard 6 (Professional Environment) primarily, but it does include questions related to every review standard except Standard 4. (Standard 4, dealing with school climate, is omitted because reviews have revealed that most teachers feel they create positive learning atmospheres in their classrooms.)

The teacher self-perception questionnaire covers the following topics:

- Professional background and affiliation.
- Instructional approaches (pedagogy).
- Concerns (e.g., budgetary support).
- Training (professional development).
- Preparation (professional development and coursework).
- Instruction (content).
- Technology use.
- Resources and equipment.
- Use of textbooks/commerical programs.

With the exception of the one question in the section on professional background, which asks teachers to indicate their total years of classroom experience by filling in a blank, this questionnaire is multiple choice. Each item—as with most of the MPIR data-collecting tools—is cross-referenced with the indicator and standard it supports. For example, the teachers are asked how often (daily, weekly, monthly, rarely, or never) students in their classrooms solve real-life problems. This question is cross-referenced with Indicator 5.4: "Teachers highlight applications of mathematics in the everyday life and culture of students and the community and its importance in students' future career choices." The review team member gathering the questionnaire data tabulates responses to this question as one piece of triangulated data (others will come from interviews and observations) for that indicator, which will help determine a rating for each indicator on the standard for usefulness.

The Class Description Questionnaire

The second teacher questionnaire, included in Appendix B as Figure B.4 (see p. 173), features a short list of open-response questions. It facilitates the review team's understanding of the environment during classroom observation by asking teachers to briefly describe the lesson plan they will teach on the day of the site visit and any materials they plan to use. It also asks for some detailed information about professional affiliations (readings, conferences, etc.) as a follow-up to the self-perception questionnaire. Please note that the class description questionnaire is not anonymous. Because its purpose is to help observers understand a particular class, it must contain the teacher's name.

Principal Questionnaires

The school principal controls many of the factors critical to teacher effectiveness. The *Interstate School Leaders Licensure Consortium: Standards for School Leaders* (ISLLC standards) developed by Council of Chief State School Officers (1996) sheds light on the important role principals play in the success of a mathematics program. For example, Standard 2 of the ISLLC standards is that principals should have knowledge and understanding of

- Student growth and development.
- Applied learning theories.
- Applied motivational theories.
- Curriculum design, implementation, evaluation, and refinement.
- The principles of effective instruction.
- Measurement, evaluation, and assessment strategies.
- Diversity and its meaning for educational programs.
- Adult learning and professional development models.
- The change process for systems, organizations, and individuals.
- The role of technology in promoting student learning and professional growth.
- School cultures.

There is an obvious close correlation between these standards and the standards and indicators used for the Mathematics Program Improvement Review. The MPIR process includes two questionnaires for principals. Both include specific questions developed to reveal the principal's support and understanding of the mathematics program within his or her school. All principals are asked to complete the two questionnaires, even if they have assigned specific responsibility for the oversight of the mathematics program to an assistant or associate principal.

The Principal's Self-Perception Questionnaire

This questionnaire, included in Appendix B as Figure B.5 (see p. 174), focuses directly on the principal's support of the mathematics program and uses open-response questions to gather data primarily about Standard 6 (the Professional Environment) and Standard 10 (Financial and Material Resources). Rather than examine each question, let's take a look at the "bigger questions"—the main issues that this questionnaire targets.

Does the school provide regular opportunities for mathematics teachers to attend mathematics-focused professional development relevant to their teaching? In many districts—especially smaller ones—professional development programs are restricted to general interest topics (diversity, awareness of blood-born pathogens, use of PowerPoint to develop presentations, etc.). I have been in districts where the mathematics teachers have never had an opportunity to attend mathematics-specific professional development. Teachers who are never exposed to current research and best practices in mathematics often "don't know what they don't know." They continue to teach what they were taught in the ways that they were taught and use the same types of resources (textbooks and a chalkboard or marker board) year after year. An NCTM task force (Campbell & Silver, 2000) cited research conducted by Haberman (1991) that schools of poverty have been found to have a "constant reiteration of core functions" that included

- Giving information.
- Asking questions.
- Giving directions.
- Making assignments.
- Monitoring seatwork.
- Reviewing assignments.
- Giving tests.
- Reviewing tests.
- Assigning homework.
- Reviewing homework.
- Settling disputes.
- Punishing noncompliance.
- Marking papers.
- Giving grades.

To determine what is being done to keep teachers and principals abreast of developments in mathematics education, the principal's self-perception questionnaire specifically asks principals what opportunities are provided for them and for the teachers to broaden and deepen their knowledge of subject matter, content-specific pedagogy, child pedagogy and adolescent development, new assessment strategies, learning differences and disabilities, teaching strategies, technology application within the curriculum, and parent collaboration.

What type of financial support does the mathematics program receive? Do teachers receive equal allocations or are the funds distributed based upon program needs? Principals filling out this questionnaire have sometimes responded that they provide equitable funding for their departments, even though they have not considered the varying needs of the programs. Is it really fair and equitable for all departments to receive an equal amount of dollars? To illustrate, one school's test scores in mathematics were consistently low. Under the equitable funding model, the teachers had sufficient funds to purchase mathematics manipulatives to use for demonstration, but not enough to begin purchasing classroom sets of manipulatives for student use.

A number of schools I have observed did not provide adequate financial support to newly employed teachers. Although never commented on in the report, this was often due to lack of oversight by the administrative staff. When a teacher retired, other teachers often scavenged through the classroom materials left behind, appropriating items for their own classrooms. Consequently, when a new teacher came into the classroom in the fall, that teacher found a room devoid of much of the necessary instructional materials. The problem was compounded when the principal allocated the same amount of money to all teachers. The new teacher did not have enough to bridge the gap.

The principal's self-perception questionnaire also asks principals to identify funds available to support extracurricular and cocurricular activities, such as remediation and enrichment programs, clubs, competitions, and field trips. I have found that it's common for principals to be unaware of all the sources of state and federal funds that the school might pursue for these uses. Oftentimes, funds are held at the district central office and doled out to the schools, but with priorities established at the central office level instead of by classroom teachers.

Do mathematics teachers have access to technology (such as computers, calculators, and data-collection devices) for student use? I have visited schools where mathematics classes do not have any time allocated for students to work in computer labs. These schools usually have had one or two computers in each mathematics classroom—numbers inadequate for student use. I have been in other schools where there were plenty of computers and other technology, but teachers were required to learn how to use these tools on their own time and did not receive any training from the school or district on how to use these tools within mathematics instruction.

Is there adequate instructional time for mathematics? I have seen elementary schools that allocate only 30 minutes for daily mathematics instruction and middle schools that allocate just 40 minutes (as compared with 80 to 90 minutes for language arts). While this may be sufficient to expose students to the required topics, few teachers can help their students achieve true mastery with so little time for instruction. The odds look even longer when you consider that the allocation of time in the mathematics classroom should include the following:

- Time for student investigations, reflection, and communication about the tasks at hand.
- Time for teachers to probe the depth of student understanding through planned developmental activities, observations, and conversations with individual students.
- Time for teachers to reteach high-priority concepts, skills, and applications until students demonstrate that they have learned them.

■ Time for students to connect the mathematics they are studying with applications of that mathematics in their daily lives and other topics in the curriculum (DuFour & Eaker, 1998).

Does the school provide mathematics teachers with personal reflective time and time for collaborative professional interaction? According to NCTM (2000), teachers need opportunities to deepen their understanding of mathematical content; to plan cooperatively with peers; to mentor new teachers; and to read, share, and discuss current research and educational literature.

The Principal's Checklist for the Mathematics Program

In contrast to the open-response format of the self-perception questionnaire, this checklist, included in Appendix B as Figure B.6 (see p. 176), has mostly multiple-choice questions that require a response of "Yes," "No," or "No Data." It addresses every MPIR standard and is divided into seven sections:

A. School Organization
B. Principal Leadership
C. Support for Teachers
D. Program Materials
E. Walk-Through Observations and Informal Discussions
F. Resources and Facilities
G. Summary

Despite the breadth of the checklist, its main thrust is to help determine how well the principal understands the mathematics program. Accordingly, curriculum and instruction standards receive the most attention. Again, let's look at the key issues that the checklist focuses on rather than examine each individual question.

Does the principal know and understand the constructivist philosophy? In a constructivist classroom

■ Student-initiated questions and discussion are accepted and encouraged.
■ The teacher asks open-ended questions and allows wait time for responses.
■ Higher-level thinking is encouraged.
■ Students are engaged in dialogue with the teacher and with each other.
■ Students are engaged in experiences that challenge assumptions and encourage discussion.
■ The class uses raw data, manipulatives, and interactive materials (Brooks & Brooks, 1993).

Does the principal know and understand the balance between skills, concepts, applications, and problem solving? For example, a student may be given the following problem from *Everybody Counts*:

> Design a dog house that can be made from a single 4-foot by 8-foot sheet of
> plywood. Make the dog house as large as possible and show how the pieces can
> be laid out on the plywood before cutting. (National Research Council Board on
> Mathematical Sciences & Mathematical Sciences Education Board, 1989, p. 32)

An observing principal should be able to recognize what skills, concepts, and applications are necessary to solve this problem. A 7th grade student would need skills in measurement and calculation of surface area and the concepts of surface area and nets. The teacher may further extend this problem into a real-life application by including cost of materials and other factors.

Does the principal know and support best practices in mathematics, such as the use of manipulatives, technology, and cooperative learning? For example, there are four major approaches to cooperative learning:

- The *structural* approach, which involves applying a variety of content-free ways of organizing social interaction in the classroom, each for particular purposes. Examples of these include Numbered Heads Together and Timed Pair Share. Some are quick activities to check knowledge; others are longer term to develop concepts, (Kagan, 1989).

- The *learning together* approach, which is built on the basic principles of cooperative learning. Teachers design structures appropriate to their classrooms (Johnson & Johnson, 1990).

- "*Student team*" *learning*, which provides a curriculum, activities, and ways to design student teams. Group rewards and individual accountability are integral parts of these programs, and they are usually fairly easy to add into current curriculum and school structures (Slavin, 1990).

- *Small-group discovery or inquiry*, in which the teacher acts as a facilitator. Students may pursue assigned, open-ended tasks or design their own tasks within given guidelines (Weissglass, 1990).

How familiar is the principal with each of these four approaches, and does he or she encourage their use?

The principal's checklist concludes with a summary portion that asks principals to total their responses and supply their perceptions of the strengths and weaknesses of the mathematics program. The principal is also asked to identify five high-priority actions for the next school year.

It is advisable for the review team to include most or all of the principal's high-priority actions in the final report back to the school, as this can help to ensure administrative support for the report recommendations. I've found that some principals, although aware of needs within their mathematics program, also need the outside confirmation of the review to move ahead. For example, one high school principal listed these high-priority actions for the following year:

1. Develop student interest in mathematics.
2. Identify and use real-world applications of the mathematics concepts.
3. Relate concepts to student interests.
4. Develop individual and group math-related projects.

All these actions related to the principal's perception that there was a problem of student apathy and resultant disruptive behavior. He saw that the teachers needed to increase students' involvement in their learning by focusing on student interests. However, he had not yet discussed the problem—or possible strategies to address it—with his faculty. Even though he managed the school through top-down administration, he didn't feel comfortable bringing up this issue until "outside experts" (the review team) expressed a similar concern.

In this instance, the MPIR report did make a recommendation related to the standard on usefulness (Standard 5) because there were numerous indications that the curriculum was not incorporating student concerns. However, it is interesting to note that the principal's top-down management style may have been the model for his teachers, who were making all of the instructional decisions in their classrooms without involving their students.

■　■　■

Although questionnaires are a very significant part of the data collection process, they are far from the only means. The next chapter introduces another process: interviews.

5

The Interviews

INTERVIEWS PROVIDE A SECOND SOURCE OF DATA THAT CAN BE TRIANGULATED to provide a fuller, more reliable picture of a school's mathematics program. They also allow those most concerned with the mathematics program to be involved in the improvement process. Review team members use sets of scripted interview questions that target each constituency of the mathematics program: teachers, students, parents, and the principal.

Although the question set for each group is different, all questions are keyed to specific standards and indicators, and many of the questions are parallel in construction to facilitate comparison. For example:

- Teachers are asked to rank the importance they place on the teaching of basic skills (computational algorithms), conceptual understanding, real-life applications, and problem solving.
- Students are asked which of these same four elements they believe is the most important for them to learn, and which they believe their teachers emphasize the most.
- Parents are asked which of the four they believe the school emphasizes the most.
- The school principal is asked which of these four he or she believes the teachers as a group are using most.

The responses to these parallel questions provide valuable data that can either support assertions made within the review process or, when contradictory, indicate a possible issue.

The interview question sets for teachers, students, and parents all have the same final two-part question: "What is the major strength of the mathematics program, and what most needs to be improved?" Reviewers often find similarities in the responses given by members of the same group (e.g., among teachers interviewed) and receive similar answers from all the constituent groups of the school. All the responses to this question are referenced in the review's summary report.

The Strengths (and Limitations) of Interviews

As mentioned in Chapter 4's discussion of questionnaires, every data-gathering tool has strengths and limitations that factor into their use within the process and raise certain cautions for review team members. Here is an overview of interviews, with strengths listed in Figure 5.1.

Interviews are interactive and open-ended. The format of interviews allows team members to focus on specific issues, such as those evident from questionnaire responses. If a response to a question doesn't seem complete or isn't clear, an interviewer can ask follow-up questions and probe for more information. *However:* This can be time-consuming, especially when the interviewer needs to interview many people, as is typically the case in MPIRs. Interviewers need to be conscious of schedule and judicious with follow-up questioning.

Interviews can yield very detailed information. In general, people give more detail when answering a question in an interview than when responding to a questionnaire. *However:* The degree of detail in the responses depends on the interviewees' understanding of the issues. The better the interviewer's grasp of the important issue underlying each question, the more detailed and valuable the responses are likely to be.

Interviews of a group reveal the general rules and procedures that group members follow. If two or more people are in the same interview session, common practices or even a shared philosophy may become evident to the interviewer. *However:* Group members—teachers, students, or parents—may conform in their responses to what they perceive as the majority answer. Given the group format used in the MPIR process, interviewers must be alert to assertive members who may obscure minority views.

Interviews create a feeling of involvement and satisfaction. Because they are a face-to-face experience requiring that someone ask questions and listen to and record the answers, interviews can be a very positive experience for those interviewed, leaving them with the feeling that their opinions are valued. *However:* For those who do not have the opportunity to be interviewed, the reverse is often true. Teachers who are not available during the site visit may feel excluded from the

FIGURE 5.1	STRENGTHS OF INTERVIEWS
+ Easily tailored to get at specific issues	
+ Yield detailed information	
+ Provide a "macro" view of attitudes and culture	
+ Satisfying for participants	

review process. The same holds true for parents and students who are not selected for interviews.

To recap, the MPIR incorporates four types of interviews: teacher, student, parent, and principal. Because of the number of questions in each set, we will focus on the most important issue each set addresses rather than discuss each question. We will also look at typical interview formats, possible concerns of those interviewed, ways to relax interviewees, and methods for circumventing a group dominator. At the end of the chapter, you will find a list of tips for successful interviewing.

Teacher Interviews

There are two teacher interview question sets: one for elementary and middle school teachers (available in Appendix B as Figure B.7, on p. 180) and one for high school teachers (available in Appendix B as Figure B.8, on p. 187). Each list has nearly 40 questions covering all 10 review standards.

Because of the number of questions and the time-consuming nature of the interview process, interviewers may not be able to ask every question of every teacher interviewed. However, some interview questions are foundational to the report and must be asked of all teachers; these questions are marked with an asterisk. (For example, one asterisked question on the elementary and middle school teacher form is, "Do you have an adequate number of resources to teach math? What do you feel you could use to improve your instruction?") These critical review questions provide an opportunity for teachers to identify their most pressing concerns. Accordingly, answers to these questions should always be included in the final review report, as inclusion there is a means of bringing these concerns to the administration's attention.

Due to time constraints, teacher interviews are conducted in groups, rather than one on one. I have found the most effective way to group teachers for interviews is by grade level (e.g., all 4th grade teachers) for elementary schools or by subject area (e.g., all algebra teachers) for secondary schools. These groupings allow teachers to focus on curriculum and professional development needs without feeling intimidated by the presence of colleagues from other grade levels. The drawback of interviewing this way is the amount of time it requires. Usually, it means at least one team member will need to focus on interviews throughout the entire site visit.

Before the site visit, review teams request through a notification letter (see Figure 2.3) that the principal schedule interview times for the day, noting the team's preference for interviewing teachers by grade level or subject area. Within elementary schools, teacher interviews typically take place during normal planning times: usually when the teachers' students are working in the library or in art, music, or physical education. Many schools do not and cannot, because of the shortage of elective teachers, provide common planning times for grade levels or subject areas.

Therefore, even though it is ideal to have only teachers of a single grade level for interviews, a mix of teachers of various grade levels is more typical. An advantage of the mixed group is that the teachers are able to examine the continuity of the curriculum as the questions are asked. A downside is that teachers may sometimes feel pressure to say they are doing more than they are in order to "save face" in front of their colleagues.

Another typical interview grouping is a gathering of the entire mathematics faculty after school. A concern with this format is the possibility that a vocal individual or small group of teachers will dominate the responses and thus hamper opportunities for other teachers to provide direct input. I've found that, in these larger groups, faculty are more likely to become defensive or worried that someone in the group will report what is said and who said it to the administration. Having the interview at the end of the day is also not ideal because the teachers may be anxious to leave, and thus may not be as thorough in their answers.

Whatever interview format the review team is presented with on the day of the site visit, it is best that the school has developed the interview schedule. If the principal schedules the interviews, each teacher can be notified in advance of the site visit. Contrast this with how anxious a teacher might become if, on the day of the visit, a reviewer suddenly asks for an interview during a planning time.

Making the interviews as nonthreatening as possible is important for gathering quality data. Reviewers can reduce anxiety by introducing themselves and setting the stage for the interview before beginning. Opening comments can make clear that the review process is voluntary and was initiated at the behest of the school and that no individual teacher will be identified in the review report. Yet even with ample notice and reassurance, some teachers have asked that their interviews (and observations) be scheduled first thing in the morning because they are so nervous—sometimes to the point of nausea. Most teachers, however, feel positive about the interview process and are appreciative that someone is listening to their comments and writing them down with the intention of acting on them.

Student Interviews

If nothing else, students are often brutally honest in their responses to questions about their school and the mathematics program. Although reviewers do not ask many questions of students (the interview generally lasts about 30 minutes), the responses can support findings that have been noted in teacher interviews or classroom observations. The full list of student interview questions appears in Appendix B as Figure B.9 (see p. 193).

Student interviews are also conducted in a group format. As noted, the interview begins with the interviewer soliciting the students' perceptions of what they feel is important in mathematics and what they feel their teachers believe is important. Other key questions relate to students' perception of connections. For example:

- Does instruction routinely make connections to previous learning (inside and outside of mathematics)?
- Does the teacher make connections to student interests (motivation)?

Anecdotal evidence from hundreds of school reviews seems to indicate that many teachers give lip service to relating instruction to student interests, but students don't feel that this is happening. In the many MPIR site visits that I have made, comparably few students have *ever* indicated that their teachers have made it a point to determine what interests (hobbies, sports, careers, etc.) they may have outside of the school environment. Even fewer of their teachers, they report, have tried to develop problems or activities around these interests. Studies (Blank, 1997; Brewster & Fager, 2000) have indicated that high motivation can lead to increased achievement, yet teachers seem reluctant to probe student interests.

The review team's notification letter asks the principal to select a random interview group of 10 to 12 students who are representative of varying abilities, the school's gender and racial makeup, and so forth. The students also need to be self-assured and verbal. For this reason, elementary school principals are asked to select only students who are in the 3rd grade and above.

Students, like teachers, are often nervous about the review process. The principal can provide reassurance by introducing the interviewer to the students and explaining that the questions they will be asked will help decide how to improve the school's mathematics program. Students should be encouraged to answer honestly and assured they will not be penalized in any way for what they say. The principal may make a statement like this:

> You are not here because you are in trouble. You have been selected to represent our school in this meeting. Mr. Jones is here to help us with improving our mathematics program. He will ask a series of questions. Please give him your honest answers. When you have completed answering all of the questions, Mr. Jones will dismiss you. At that time, return back to your classroom. I want to thank you for being here to help us improve our mathematics program.

It is important that the review team member conducting the interview ensure the participation of all students in the interview group. If a few individuals begin to dominate, then the interviewer should change the questioning procedure. For example, an alternative way of soliciting responses is to ask students to raise their hands to agree or disagree with statements derived from interview questions, like this:

> OK, here is our next statement: "My math teacher permits students to call out the answers to questions." Raise your hand if you agree with this statement.

The interviewer might also ask questions of each student in succession. This can be an effective way of getting information from the entire group, provided that the interviewer changes the order of the students questioned each time so that the same students' responses don't prejudice the responses of those who answer afterward. For example, the interviewer may ask the first question of 5th graders first, the second question of 4th graders first, and so forth.

Parent Interviews

The parent interviews gather data related to almost every standard, but are the prime medium for determining the degree of successful communication between the school and home. (For the full list of parent interview questions, see Appendix B, Figure B.10, on page 196.)

It is the principal's responsibility to randomly select a group of parents to be interviewed. The most beneficial course of action is to select parents who are representative of the student population. This means including parents of different "kinds" of students (gifted students, low-achieving students, special needs students, females, males) and parents with different cultural, economic, and racial backgrounds. It's fine to include some parents who are active in school activities, so long as others in the group are not active. I have interviewed "randomly selected" parent groups that were composed entirely of members of the site-based council, PTA or PTO officers, and others in school leadership positions, and I have interviewed groups that were all employees of the school district (e.g., bus drivers, instructional assistants, librarians, and teachers from other schools). Although one could argue that yes, these participants were parents of students in the school being reviewed, I have learned that their feedback is often not as helpful to the review process because they typically provide the same responses as the school's teachers and principal. In a sense, they are an extension of the faculty.

Principals who assemble "stacked" groups probably do so because they feel a random group of parents will be too negative about the school. Ironically, the random groups are typically more positive about the school than groups handpicked for their perceived support. The most negative group of parents I ever interviewed was made up of principal-selected "ringers." Interestingly, they had particularly negative things to say about the principal's leadership. This experience of mine is borne out in

Phi Delta Kappa's Gallup surveys, which indicate that parents randomly selected are usually very positive about their own school and especially positive about their children's teachers.

Now, let's look at timing. The parent interview is usually conducted at the end of the school day, when parents are more likely to be able to attend. Reviewers can take advantage of an end-of-the-day interview by targeting standards or indicators that may not have received sufficient attention in teacher interviews or observations. If the parent group cannot meet at any time during the day because of work requirements, reviewers may conduct phone interviews. Because of the time involved, and because there is not an opportunity for respondents to interact with each other, phone interviews are not ideal. And other problems can occur with phone interviews, as one MPIR interviewer discovered.

After spending the day on-site at a small, rural elementary school, a review team member returned to a local hotel for the night and began making parent interview calls. The principal had supplied the names and home phone numbers of the selected parents who were unable to participate in the daytime group. The interviewer called one number and learned that neither parent was at home, but a grandmother was available to take the call. The interviewer proceeded to explain to the grandmother that he wanted to ask questions related to a review of the mathematics program at her granddaughter's elementary school. On the other end of the line, the grandmother heard a stranger asking questions about her granddaughter and saw on her caller ID system that he was calling from a local hotel. She hung up and called the police. Fortunately, the police checked with the school principal before proceeding to the hotel for an arrest.

Parents' concerns about the interview usually are related to feeling that they have inadequate knowledge to answer the questions. The interviewer can respond by carefully explaining that many if not all the questions relate to the *perceptions* of the parents, so direct experience with the classroom or expertise in mathematics education is not necessary to answer them. The interviewer can also make clear that parent perceptions are important to the school because they can become the "realities" in the minds of many members of the community, and the school staff will be interested in taking countermeasures to correct any negative perceptions. Parents may also want to know that the school faculty is interested in what positive features of the mathematics program are noted.

For the parent interview, I recommend that interviewers create a simple matrix to gather information about the parents *before* asking questions. Interviewers need to understand the context of some of the parents' comments to draw the most complete data from them, and a matrix is an easy way to do that. Figure 5.2 provides an example. An interviewer asking about gender equity in the mathematics classroom can

FIGURE 5.2	SAMPLE PARENT INTERVIEW MATRIX									
Parent Data	**A**	**B**	**C**	**D**	**E**	**F**	**G**	**H**	**I**	**J**
Member of site-based council				X						
PTA/PTO officer	X		X							
Employee of the school or school district								X		X
Regular classroom volunteer		X		X	X					
Spouse of a school or district employee						X				
Number/gender of children in the school	1-F	1-M	1-F	2-F 1-M	1-M 1-F	1-F	1-F	1-F 1-M	1-M	1-F 2-M
Grade or math subject in which each child is enrolled	4	5	5	1, 3, 4	2, 5	1	3	1, 3	4	2, 4, 4

note that Parents A, C, and F were not aware of any gender differences, but that all had female children. On the other hand, Parents B and I—parents of males—felt that the teachers did *not* address the needs of their children. The remaining parents did not respond to the question or were uncertain if a problem existed. Such data, if supported elsewhere, may indicate that a gender problem does exist.

As when interviewing other school groups, interviewers should strive to ensure that all parent interviewees participate in the discussion. It is common for parents to lean on the responses of whomever they feel is the "expert" among the group. Thus, a teacher or site-based council member may dominate if allowed to do so. The interviewer needs to call on selected individuals if a pattern begins to emerge that everyone waits for a particular person to respond before giving their own answers.

The Principal Interview

The principal interview should always be a one-on-one conversation between the principal and a review team member. Typically, it lasts about 45 minutes, and ideally it is conducted at the end of day, after the review team has completed interviews with teachers, students, and parents, so as to allow follow-up questioning on issues raises by these constituent groups. However, scheduling is left to the principal, and any unnecessary disruption to his or her schedule should be avoided. In rare cases, this may mean that the interview takes place in multiple sittings, a few questions at a time. It is important, too, that the principal interview be conducted on the principal's home turf (e.g., his or her office). Just as many of the teachers feel some anxiety about the review process, many principals—even though they are generally the ones who requested the review—are anxious about how their school will look in the eyes of outsiders. After all, it is often the principal's management style and leadership that can produce exemplary efforts from teachers. To help put the principal at ease, at the beginning of the interview, the interviewer should reiterate that the MPIR focuses on the overall mathematics program. As such, the principal is singled out as the leader of the school, but the leader is only one of a multitude of factors that contribute to the success of the program.

When conducting principal interviews, I typically provide a very brief discussion about the 10 standards to underscore that a single factor does not make or break a program.

The principal interview complements the data-gathering done in advance with the principal's checklist and principal's self-perception questionnaire. The interviewer might, for example, follow up a questionnaire response by asking direct questions about the principal's knowledge of funds available to support the mathematics program (Title I funds to support professional development, local funds to purchase technology, etc.). The interview is also the means to seek answers to questions that have arisen during the site visit. Based on what the review team has seen during its classroom observations (see Chapter 6), the interviewer may ask the principal who is responsible for monitoring classroom instruction. Is it the principal or a designee? Are lesson plans reviewed by the principal? The answers to such questions provide insight into the principal's understanding of, and support for, the mathematics program. The full set of interview questions for the principal is given in Figure B.11 in Appendix B (see p. 199).

Taken together with the questionnaire responses, the interview responses from the principal are often critical to the acceptance and use of the final report. Whenever possible, suggestions or recommendations the principal makes should be included in the final report to help assure the principal's acceptance of the rest of the team's recommendations. After all, the principal is the building leader. Successes in implementing the recommendations within the report are contingent upon his or her willingness to act on them.

I learned this the hard way. One of the first program reviews I ever completed was at Collingwood High School. The written report was perceived by the principal as negative towards his leadership. Although the report was generally positive about the program, it noted that the school was failing to adhere to state safety regulations and lacked sufficient financial support to meet the needs of the department. Copies of the completed report were mailed to him but were then apparently destroyed. No one in the school or school district ever saw the report. I was not permitted back in the school even though his school was a member of a cooperative to which I was providing services to teachers. Interestingly enough, this principal subsequently became the district superintendent.

Principals like to use the interview time to get a feeling about how the process has gone so far. I usually provide some reassuring comments, such as, "Your teachers and students have been very cooperative and demonstrate a willingness to improve the mathematics program." However, I make it clear that I can't make any definitive statements until all of the data have been collected and reviewed by the team. At the conclusion of the interview, I give the principal an approximate date by which the report will be completed and ask how it should be delivered. Does the principal want to receive a copy of the report by mail, or should the report be hand-delivered? Should the review team leader plan to present highlights of the report in an after-school presentation before the mathematics faculty?

Tips for Interviewing

I have found that reviewers who are highly skilled at conducting interviews will collect the most useful data for the review. Because not everyone on a review team may have had the opportunity to develop these skills from long experience, I've assembled some tips for successful interviewing.

Use the questions as prompts. The questions do not have to be asked verbatim. They should serve only as prompts for the evaluator to address the pertinent issues and may be rephrased to suit the style of the interviewer or a particular school setting or school constituency.

Explain unfamiliar terms. Occasionally, a term used in a question may be unfamiliar to those interviewed. This happens most often when asking teachers content questions that may go beyond the scope of the grade level they teach. For example, an elementary grade teacher may not be aware of what a "line plot" or a "probability tree diagram" is, and the interviewer may want to define or give an example. Interviewers may also tell teachers at the start of the interview that some of the concept questions may not be relevant to the grade or subject of every teacher.

Know the questions. On nearly every MPIR visit that I have made, a teacher responding to a question during an interview provided an answer that related to a subsequent question on my list. Rather than asking that question later, I write their response to the "unasked" question in the appropriate location. Not only does this save time during the interview process, but it helps give the teachers confidence that the interviewer knows what he or she is doing and is not asking questions that have already been answered. But the interviewer has to know the questions well to be able to recognize an answer when it's given ahead of the question.

Skip questions that don't apply. For example, during interviews at one school, it became quickly apparent that the school had a "no homework" philosophy. All assigned work was to be completed in school, under the direction of the classroom teacher. Once the interviewer discovered this, she did not ask questions about homework in subsequent teacher interviews. Instead, she rephrased the homework-focused questions to ask about guided practice.

Ask follow-up questions. When a response seems incomplete or counter to what has been observed at the school or reported in questionnaires, an interviewer should probe further. For example, when asked about resources, one teacher responded that she had all she needed to teach mathematics; however, the interviewer had noted that important resources were not evident in the teacher's classroom. The interviewer then listed specific resources—unifix cubes, base-10 materials, geoboards, and several kinds of calculators—and asked the teacher to indicate which she had access to. The interviewer also listed some resource manufacturers and asked which the teacher was familiar with. These questions are not on the interview question form. The interviewer simply expanded on the resource question to gain more information. As this example shows, it is often advantageous to have a team member conduct the interviews of those teachers he or she has observed in the classroom so observations can be followed up with relevant interview questions.

Acknowledge responses without judging. The interviewer should acknowledge responses to questions by writing the response down and, possibly, by a neutral verbal response. The interviewer should not make statements such as, "That is great," or, "I can't believe that you don't _____." The interview is not the time to correct what the interviewer believes to be inappropriate teaching practices or teaching products. One interviewer used a portion of the interview to berate the teachers for the selection of what she felt was an inferior textbook because it relied heavily on basic skills computational practice. She felt the program was not consistent with the recommendations contained in the NCTM standards. However, the interview's purpose is to collect data, and the data may have revealed the text to have been consistent with the philosophy of the school's mathematics teachers.

Avoid conflicts of interest. Reviewers are often experts who could be helpful to the school in effecting changes. They may also be part of a program (like ARSI) that the school will have access to as a resource once the review is completed. The interview is an opportunity for these reviewers to introduce themselves to the principal and teachers and establish both the rapport and trust that may lead to a school asking the reviewer for help in implementing recommendations. However, it is not appropriate for interviewers to solicit work for themselves. One of the interviewers for an MPIR was a former mathematics teacher and principal who was a self-employed consultant. He used the interview time to suggest that the school employ him as a consultant once they received the report and read the recommendations that would be suggested. Such practices are not to be tolerated. The interview is for data collection and data collection only. There should not be any conflict of interest or even the perception of a conflict of interest with regard to the recommendations and subsequent efforts that the school may make to accomplish these recommendations.

Get the data. There is always the possibility of not collecting enough data during interviews to provide sufficient triangulation and support for a particular indicator. Scores of "N/O" (not observed) are given in such instances. The ideal is that "not observed" scores will not be necessary. The interview team needs as much quality data as can be obtained in order to write a quality report. Such a report will enable the receiving school faculty to move forward in improving the mathematics program.

■ ■ ■

Interview data go hand in hand with data collected from classroom observations. As noted, it is often advantageous for a review team member to interview a teacher he or she has observed. The next chapter provides additional clarity on the relationship between the interview and the observation.

## 6

The Classroom Observations

Observing individual teachers at work in their classrooms is the heart of the MPIR process. One of the review's main goals is to assess how effectively mathematics is being taught, and watching teachers teach is the most direct way to gather the data needed to make that assessment. The Classroom Observation Instrument (provided in Appendix B as Figure B.12, beginning on p. 201) is designed to guide review team members' data collecting as they observe lessons in progress. The results of the completed individual instruments are then summarized in the review report to present a global picture of instructional strengths and weaknesses.

The Classroom Observation Instrument is quite versatile and can also be used as a stand-alone tool to help improve instruction. For example, teacher peer groups may use the form to critique each other's performance as a means of self-improvement, and principals may use it for both formal and informal teacher observations.

As we have seen, each review tool has its positive and negative aspects. Let's take a look at the three chief advantages (see Figure 6.1) and related limitations of direct classroom observation.

Classroom observation allows for direct data gathering. Questionnaires and interviews rely on reports about activity; only observation allows data about activities to be collected directly. For the MPIR process, this means classroom observation is the only review element in which the reviewer truly looks at the quality of the mathematics instruction. Recommendations based on what teachers are actually doing can be enormously helpful in improving mathematics instruction. *However:* Each individual reviewer is doing the observing and data recording, and these individuals might introduce bias related to personal beliefs about teaching. Bias can be counteracted by having a number of reviewers observe each class, but usually time constraints and the number of team members preclude this. In addition, many teachers can perceive threat in being observed. Even though MPIR protocols stipulate that teachers must be told the review process does not reference individuals and that observations will not be used as evaluations, they may still view the observations as more of a "judging" experience than a data-gathering effort.

FIGURE 6.1	STRENGTHS OF CLASSROOM OBSERVATIONS

+ Yield "direct" data, not "reported" data

+ Provide opportunities for observed teachers to demonstrate their understanding of effective teaching (best practices)

+ Provide a comprehensive view of how various factors work together

Classroom observation provides an opportunity to view teachers' understanding of effective instructional practices. Every teacher wants to be considered a good teacher. Just as teachers carefully plan those lessons they know will be observed by their principal, they plan the lessons that will be observed by an MPIR team member. They almost always try to incorporate best practices, and the manner in which they do so sheds light on how well they understand these practices.

Classroom observation provides a comprehensive picture. For MPIR team members, the classroom observation is the best opportunity to view the relationship among various standards (curriculum, instruction, assessment, usefulness) as well as specific indicators, such as those related to technology, cooperative learning, and use of manipulatives.

Preparing Teachers for the Classroom Observations

The review notification letter (see Figure 2.3) asks the principal to ensure the faculty is briefed on the observation component of the MPIR. This must include assuring teachers they will not be singled out in the report or evaluated, and requesting that they teach the lesson they would normally teach on that day using resources they would normally use. Principals should ask faculty to avoid long videos or formal paper-and-pencil tests, as this will prevent the review team from truly seeing instruction in action.

As noted, it is not unusual for teachers to put on their best performance when they know that a review team will be visiting. This is not altogether bad; after all, if the faculty knows what best practices are, then they can—with encouragement—continue such practices and make them the norm. However, there have been instances when the teachers have not necessarily known how to incorporate best practices in their instruction. Reviewers found just this situation at Foster Elementary School.

All review team members came away from their first session of Foster classroom observations pleased to see the teachers using inquiry-based instruction to lead students in a mathematical investigation. The team's pleasure soon evaporated as they saw class after class following the exact same lesson plan. It became clear that the lessons did not fall into the sequence of the week's instruction, and what's more, the lesson was taught without any adaptation to the background knowledge or the grade-level objectives for each teacher's students, who ranged from grades 3 through 5. It turned out that, motivated by their desire to be well received, Foster's teachers had chosen a "best-practice lesson" that had been modeled for them just weeks before as part of a training session conducted by mathematics consultants from the state department of education.

Factors Leading to Successful Observation

The American Council on Education (1999) contends that the success of the student depends most of all on the quality of the teacher. But what factors should be used to determine the quality of the teacher? As noted, research into the current literature and my own experience informed the development of the MPIR's classroom observation tool. However, designing an instrument to examine various components of classroom practice was just a beginning.

I have conducted MPIRs in hundreds of schools for more than eight years, and in that time, I have modified the classroom observation instrument more than any other tool used in the review process. Research in instruction has led to continuous revision to incorporate additional factors that should be examined. But I have also added some factors based on evidence acquired while conducting reviews. For example, the current literature pays little attention to the classroom environment—elements such as the type and quality of mathematics posters and student work on display and the accessibility of mathematics manipulatives. Years of using the instrument have taught me that classroom environment is one of the factors that can be used reliably to measure teacher quality.

The Classroom Observation Instrument organizes these success factors into five sections:

1. Physical Setting/Classroom Environment
2. Lesson Effectiveness
3. Questioning Strategies
4. Classroom Climate
5. Development of Higher-Order Thinking Skills

In this chapter, we will look at each section and how to score and summarize observation findings. The multipage Figure 6.2 shows a completed classroom observation instrument for an Algebra I class on a 90-minute block schedule. It's included here to help demonstrate how to use the tool. You will see that the observer has not only marked factors to indicate strategies or activities the teacher used, but has also included notes and comments. At the end of the sample instrument, the observer has provided a rough script of the lesson. To complete the instrument form, an observer must mark all factors that he or she observes and supply pertinent comments, but also script what takes place during the lesson (e.g., questions asked, student responses), how it takes place, and when.

Physical Setting/Classroom Environment

The organization of visual displays, student work, materials, and so forth may not be essential to effective teaching, but most effective teachers seem to have well-organized and student-friendly classrooms. This section of the observation instrument is designed to help observers note all physical elements that may be influencing instruction.

The physical characteristics of mathematics classrooms vary extensively. I have seen high school mathematics classrooms that were entirely devoid of any type of display. Such classrooms appeared as sterile as hospital rooms, with absolutely nothing to motivate students to explore mathematics or to apply it in their daily lives. I have also seen elementary classrooms where the walls were completely covered with posters and mobiles of math vocabulary words were hanging from the ceiling. In one instance, the visual learner may have no support, and in the other, he or she may be overwhelmed with distractions.

The review has revealed a particular type of display as being especially helpful to boosting achievement: the work of the students themselves. Some teachers carefully select and display high-quality student work and then lead the students in a discussion of what makes this work particularly good. When teachers have posted such models, they have usually been able to see subsequent improvements in overall classroom achievement. Likewise, MPIR reviews have indicated that classrooms with few or no displays of mathematics work—either the students' or commercial—often produce students who score lower on achievement tests. Teachers in these classrooms have even said during the interview that they were uncomfortable with teaching their mathematics content. It is not uncommon to visit elementary school classrooms and see many posters related to reading and language arts. They may even include student work displaying haiku or other student writing. But these same classrooms exhibit little in the way of mathematics displays other than occasional commercial posters of multiplication tables, geometry terms, and so on. These do not require, or even invite, student discussion and interaction.

Observers should also look at what is stored in the classroom and how. I've seen rooms that have stacks of books, computer parts, and other collected memorabilia from years of teaching. The teachers for these rooms seemed to have just added to the clutter each year, with little or no effort at organization of resources.

FIGURE 6.2	CLASSROOM OBSERVATION INSTRUMENT AND SCRIPT—SAMPLE

TEACHER Trey Ditional   **LEVEL/CLASS** Algebra 1

LESSON TITLE Identify Absolute Value

1. Physical Setting/Classroom Environment   **Section Rating** 2
(Mark all that apply.)

A. Classroom Facility
☒ Classroom adequate size for student number
☐ Adequate storage for resources/materials/equipment
☐ Furnishings allow for activity-based instruction
☐ Student seating is flexible to allow for differing needs (projects, investigations, cooperative groups, etc.)
☒ Room size will accommodate activities (CBL, etc.)
☒ Flat-top surfaces are sufficient for investigations, projects, displays, etc.

B. Classroom Environment
☐ Math manipulatives/tools evident
☐ Math displays/posters promote learning
☐ Student textbooks evident
☒ Class set of calculators available
☒ Computers available, # 2
☒ Math student work displayed
☒ Adequate resources available for hands-on lessons (as appropriate)

Teacher has scientific calculators, but he's not using them this year. Materials are stacked on top of cabinets.

2. Lesson Effectiveness   **Section Rating** 2
(Mark all that apply.)

A. Major Instructional Resources Used

☒ Textbook	☐ Hands-on/manipulative materials	☐ Computer to learn or practice a
☐ Other print materials	☐ Calculators	skill or concept (software program)
☒ Overhead	☐ Overhead calculator	☐ The instructional resources were
☐ Videotape, audiotape	☐ Computer to access Internet	used appropriately
☐ DVD	☐ Computer to collect or	☐ The resources contributed to
☐ Math tools	analyze data	the quality of lesson

Textbook is Glencoe.

B. Content Focus
☐ Number/Computation
☐ Geometry
☐ Measurement
☐ Probability/Statistics
☒ Algebra/Precalculus/Calculus

| FIGURE 6.2 | CLASSROOM OBSERVATION INSTRUMENT AND SCRIPT—SAMPLE *(continued)* |

C. Place in Instructional Sequence
- ☒ Introducing new concept   *Minimal*
- ☐ Developing conceptual understanding
- ☐ Applying concept to new situation
- ☒ Reviewing concept or procedure   *9:55–10:50   Equations w/1 variable*
- ☒ Assessing student understanding   *Somewhat w/self-quiz; no monitoring*

D. Grouping Arrangement Used
- ☒ Whole group
- ☐ Small groups working on same task
- ☐ Small groups working on different tasks
- ☒ Individuals working on same task
- ☐ Individuals working on different tasks

The grouping arrangement was appropriate for the apparent instructional goal and activity. ☒ Yes ☐ No

Yes, but only somewhat. Whole-group reviews indicated some understanding, but there was not enough agreement among individuals to determine mastery.

E. Teacher and Student Behaviors Observed

Teacher Behaviors
- ☐ Setting up and guiding students through meaningful problems
- ☐ Moving around the room monitoring/questioning
- ☐ Encouraging students to consider multiple ways to solve/test solutions
- ☐ Guiding students in the use of manipulatives/technology
- ☐ Promoting student use of inquiry/creativity through questioning/group work
- ☒ Facilitating discussions about problem-solving processes efficiency/effectiveness *—only partially*
- ☒ Leading students through discussion/journaling of their understanding *—minimally*

Student Behaviors
- ☒ Interacting with others and working alone
- ☐ Applying math to real-life problems with adopted program
- ☐ Working in groups to test solutions
- ☒ Sharing solution processes and listening to others share their thinking *—minimally; primarily with the teacher*
- ☐ Defending solution processes' efficiency and usefulness
- ☐ Communicating math ideas: demonstrations, models, drawings, and arguments
- ☐ Working in teams to challenge and defend solutions
- ☐ Helping to clarify each other's learning through discussion/modeling
- ☒ Activity in progress was appropriate for the apparent instructional goal *—to a very limited degree*

Activity was
- ☐ ineffective/poor
- ☒ mediocre/minimum impact
- ☐ somewhat effective
- ☐ effective/good
- ☐ exceptionally effective/high quality

FIGURE 6.2	CLASSROOM OBSERVATION INSTRUMENT AND SCRIPT—SAMPLE *(continued)*

F. Inclusion of Open-Response Questions

Students solved one or more nonroutine, or open-response, questions ☐ Yes ☒ No

G. Instructional Design

☐ Established academic focus (e.g., essential question)
☐ Reviewed/connected to previous learning
☐ Included closure

Nothing for the visual learner; no manipulatives. Students solved multistep linear equations w/a single variable on both sides; no real-life connections. Teacher never monitored actual student work by looking at their papers or by having them work a problem. No work taken for a grade.

3. Questioning Strategies   Section Rating __2__

(Mark all that apply.)

☐ Wait Time I   ☐ Wait Time II   ☒ No/limited wait time
☐ Questions were higher-order and stimulated broad student responses
☐ Questions were lower-cognitive and stimulated narrow student responses
☐ No questions were asked by teacher or posed through the activity being conducted
☐ Teacher used strategy to ensure all students had opportunity to respond —*did this for selected students only*
☐ Teacher asked probing follow-up questions
☒ Student(s) asked follow-up questions
☐ Teacher provided specific praise
☒ Teacher provided general praise
☐ Teacher provided no praise

The questioning strategies checked for student understanding of apparent instructional goal. ☐ Yes ☒ No

Only one higher-order question asked. Questions were computation-related . . . did not focus on "the why." Teacher's comments always positive. Responses were generally call-outs, and T did not recognize all student responses.

4. Classroom Climate   Section Rating __4__

A. Student Involvement

☐ Majority of students demonstrated interest
☒ Majority of students were engaged and on task
☐ Majority of students uninterested or apathetic
☐ Majority of students were frequently off task

B. Classroom Management —*Teacher has excellent control.*

☒ Classroom orderly, no student disruptions that impaired learning environment
☐ Classroom generally orderly, but some student disruptions required disciplinary action
☐ Classroom disorderly, frequent student disruptions that seriously impaired the learning environment
☐ The climate was generally positive
☐ The climate enhanced learning opportunities for students.

Students seemed comfortable asking questions and telling where they missed a problem. All students stayed on task.

FIGURE 6.2	CLASSROOM OBSERVATION INSTRUMENT AND SCRIPT—SAMPLE *(continued)*

5. Development of Higher-Order Thinking Skills   Section Rating ___1___

(Check all skills that are introduced and/or developed in the observed lesson.)

A. Basic Process Skills —*What is the principle? What are the rules?*

☐ Observing actions of others
☒ Reciting/recalling facts
☐ Classifying
☐ Measuring/estimating
☐ Collecting/recording data
☐ Constructing charts/graphs

B. Higher-Level Skills —*Very low-level computation*

☐ Interpreting/analyzing data
☒ Computing/calculating
☐ Investigating
☒ Applying theorems/principles —*minimal*
☐ Evaluating relevancy of data
☐ Selecting problem-solving strategy
☐ Creating/formulating patterns/equations
☐ Evaluating logical consistency
☐ Justifying/verifying solutions/strategies

C. Learner Attitudes Demonstrated

☐ Curiosity
☒ Cooperation
☒ Persistence
☒ Responsibility
☐ Confidence
☐ Enthusiasm
☐ Objectivity
☐ Accuracy
☐ Critical Thinking

The students followed the teacher's directions & answered his questions, but they did not demonstrate initiative or confidence.

6. Overall Classroom Observation Rating   ___2___

(Consult criteria in Section 6 of the Classroom Observation Instrument Scoring Rubric.)

FIGURE 6.2	CLASSROOM OBSERVATION INSTRUMENT AND SCRIPT—SAMPLE *(continued)*

Classroom Script

9:55

Today we are going to review our homework about solving equations with variables on both sides and then we will learn how to do identity problems and solve absolute value equations. Absolute value equations have two answers. Turn to page 161.

9:58

(Teacher reviewed each homework problem in turn. Prompted class for feedback on some.)

1. $4x - 3 = 2x + 5$ How may I get it right?

2. $5y + 8 = 2y + 2$ Get what on each side?

5. $-5s - 7 = 3s + 41$ Did you bring the sign with you?

6. $2h + 4 = 25 - h$ Which variable do we move?

10. $4g + 7 - 2g = 5g - 2$ What is the substitution property?

11. $4v - 8 = 8 + 4v - v$ Do you agree with this? (3 times)

12. $3(7 - 2d) = 22 - 8d$ Which is the smallest variable?
                              Does this look correct?

(Teacher worked all of the above problems while calling on John, Rebecca, Cory, Billy, Allison, Amanda, and Dick)

If I throw these at you, can you do them?

13. $-8t = 4(t + 5) + 2t$

Student said answer would be -1.7; then was comfortable with saying he missed it and why. Teacher gave pep talk: it takes practice, use different properties, etc.

FIGURE 6.2	CLASSROOM OBSERVATION INSTRUMENT AND SCRIPT—SAMPLE *(continued)*

1. $-6y + 15 = 3(y - 1)$

2. $1/2 (2x - 5) = -2x$

Let's not go decimal. How do we readjust using distributive? What do we multiply by to get rid of the fraction? (Teacher multiplies by 2 and writes $2x - 5 = -4x$) Look good? What do you think? (Student: "Where did you get the 2?") What goes here? (Teacher writes $2x + 4x = 5$). Always change the sign when you move. (Teacher finishes the problem, $6x = 5$, $x = 5/6$). On a calculator this would be .83 (no calculator is used).

__10:30__

That is how your homework should have looked.
(Teacher puts another problem on the overhead):
$$\frac{2x}{3} - 1 = 5$$

What operations do you use to solve this problem? Addition, multiplication, and division. Do you agree with this? What do you do to get rid of the denominator? Multiply by 3. What does that give us? (Teacher writes 5 problems on the overhead.) These are the types of problems that I will give you in a day or two on a quiz.

__10:35__

1. $6x + 1 = 15 - x$
2. $2x + 3 = 5x - 9$
3. $x + 36 = 1 - 4(x - 5)$
4. $3(2x + 4) = 5x + 12 + x$
5. $3(2x - 5) = 6x + 7$

(Students worked these problems on their own; teacher sat at his desk and carried on casual conversations—not related to assignment—with various students.)

| FIGURE 6.2 | **CLASSROOM OBSERVATION INSTRUMENT AND SCRIPT—SAMPLE** *(continued)* |

<u>10:42</u>

Let's walk through these. Use something besides a pencil. Do them in your head.

1. $6x + 1 = 15 - x$

(Teacher worked through it; no questions from students)

2. $2x + 3 = 5x - 9$

Did you get 4 for the answer? Is the variable on the right-hand side? You could have $x = 4$ instead of $4 = x$.

3. $x + 36 = 1 - 4(x - 5)$

(Teacher doesn't say the answer but calls on three students). I like -3 better. (George got it wrong, but then explained how he "messed up" on the third line.) If I throw one at you, can you handle it?

4. $3(2x + 4) = 5x + 12 + x$

Tell me the answer. That uses the identity property? (Student: "How do you know?")

5. $3(2x - 5) = 6x + 7$
There is no solution to this one. (No questions)
Any questions? Are we good? (Called on George, Dick, Sue, Lee, and Eric while answering the above problems.)

<u>10:50</u>

Turn to Section 4.3 in your text. This deals with absolute value. Absolute value is the distance from zero. The + or − tells the direction.

$x + 2 = 5$
Only one value makes it true.

FIGURE 6.2	CLASSROOM OBSERVATION INSTRUMENT AND SCRIPT—SAMPLE *(continued)*

$|x| + 2 = 5$

What two answers make it right? (Called on Grant.) The operation is done the same way.

$|x| + 3 = -6$ There is no solution. The absolute value can never be negative. (Student: "Why?")
The absolute value can't be negative.

$-2 |x| = -12$
We can see that absolute value of $x = 6$. $|x| = 6$.

$1x + 21 = 5$
Break it into two true statements: $x + 2 = 5$ and $x + 2 = -5$

Then $x = 3$ or $x = -7$.

Now you do $|2x - 3| = 1$.   Rewrite it (he helps). $2x - 3 = 1$ and $2x - 3 = -1$.

$2|2x + 5| = 14$

$|2x + 5| = 7$

$2x + 5 = 7$ $2x + 5 = -7$ Do you agree with this?

$x = 1$ $x = -6$ Did you get 1? Are these correct?

What is the answer to $|-4x| = 12$?

$4x = 12$ or $-4x = -12$

$x = -3$ $x = 3$ Are we good to go?

You will have 8 or 10 homework problems to do on absolute value.

Your homework: p. 61. Do 6 problems like the quiz, 19–24, and p. 63: 1, 11, 14, 15, 16, 23, 29, 30, 31. Tomorrow we will have a 10-problem quiz.

<u>11:15</u>
Let's knock off early and fill out this questionnaire for guidance regarding career days.

The physical environment also gives the first indication of the level of support for the mathematics program and its place in the overall school curriculum. A shortage of mathematics manipulatives, calculators, and adequate numbers of computers for student use can quickly indicate that the mathematics program may not be among the administration's high priorities. Still, a wealth of materials does not necessarily signal strong administrative support for mathematics. Many schools have found themselves with state or federal funds to purchase materials but without the local support to train the teachers in how to use these materials effectively or to purchase appropriate mathematics software for student use.

Even with the advent of No Child Left Behind and its emphasis on mathematics, many schools continue to provide inadequate support for mathematics instruction. Kentucky's Commissioner of Education recently noted that "elementary reading programs are good examples of how grant money (through Reading First and other literary achievements) are paying big dividends in increased literacy skills. We have not provided the same funding for mathematics" (Wilhoit, 2004, p. 3).

Lesson Effectiveness

While the first section of the observation tool helps a reviewer to assess the physical layout and contents of the mathematics classroom, Section 2 helps the reviewer collect data about the effectiveness of the lesson by examining five components:

- The lesson's use of resources
- The lesson's content focus
- The lesson's place in the overall instructional sequence
- How the students are grouped for instruction
- Teacher and student behaviors during the lesson

Each of these areas has several factors to mark as observed or not, but including or not including these components in the lesson is not a measure of high-quality teaching in and of itself. For example, depending on the age level of the students and their knowledge, a teacher may do everything listed under "Place in Instructional Sequence": introduce a new concept, develop conceptual understanding, apply the concept to a new situation, review the concept, and assess student understanding. More commonly, however, a lesson may include only two or three of these elements and still be a very effective lesson.

In MPIR reviews I have conducted, one element in this category that I have rarely observed is "Assessing student understanding." It is surprising, in view of the amount of research on the need for formative assessment and the value of such assessment for learning, that many teachers fail to routinely check for student understanding. As Black & William (1998) note, "innovations that include strengthening the practice of formative assessment produce significant and often substantial learning gains" (p. 140). Time management research has shown that if teachers stop and check for understanding, they will ultimately spend less time going back to reteach. But still, many teachers feel that they must be teaching continuously—without checking for understanding—and they then report that their students do not do as well as they had hoped on the chapter or unit tests.

Observations of teacher and student behaviors gather particularly important data and can be used alone quite effectively for peer observations. Each of the factors listed under "Teacher and Student Behaviors Observed" has been shown in research to be highly effective in increasing student achievement in mathematics (see Grouws & Cebulla, 2000; Marzano, Pickering & Pollock, 2001; Zemelman, Daniels, & Hyde, 1998). As the reviewer checks those behaviors that are occurring, he or she should also be scripting the lesson to use in follow-up sessions (for peer observations) or to summarize within the report (as one component of a complete review).

In my experience, "Inclusion of Open-Response Questions" and "Instructional Design" are, unfortunately, rarely observed. In many schools, an apparent consequence of No Child Left Behind mandates has been an increased use of low-level cognitive questions that require only one-step solutions. The use of open-response questions and questions at higher cognitive levels (analysis, synthesis, and evaluation) is becoming less and less common, even in states that include open-response questions as a part of their state assessment.

The first factor of Instructional Design addresses establishing the instructional focus. Ever since the publications of Madeline Hunter (1982), educators have known the value of what Hunter called an "anticipatory set." Educators now commonly use either the expression "establishing instructional focus" or "incorporating essential questions." Yet many teachers rely entirely on stated textbook objectives, often without even making explicit reference to these objectives. They may teach the lesson exactly as presented in the textbook, with little or no preparation for the students on why they are studying the lesson.

The second factor addresses making relevant connections to prior learning. Despite the calls within the NCTM standards to make connections within mathematics learning clear to students, many teachers apparently continue to depend only on what is contained in text materials. There is seemingly even less effort to make connections to other subject areas through collaborative planning or unit development.

The final factor of Instructional Design is the inclusion of closure, something that I have rarely observed during MPIRs. Typically, a teacher either teaches right up to the class change or gives an assignment—which the students immediately begin working on—without ever checking for student understanding of the lesson. Very often I recommend in review reports that faculty consider adopting the Understanding by Design approach advocated by Grant Wiggins and Jay McTighe (1998). Training in Understanding by Design can aid teachers in the development of their lessons and their units of study.

Questioning Strategies

The "Questioning Strategies" section of the instrument lends itself to separate application by peer groups of teachers or administrators as a focus for self-assessment and improvement.

The first factor considered is the use of "wait time." Although research has long touted wait time as an important part of questioning, I've found few teachers who use it. The instrument prompts the observer to look for both types of wait times: Wait Time I and Wait Time II.

Wait Time I is a pause of 3 to 10 seconds (depending on the age level and maturity of the students) after a question has been asked and before a teacher calls on a student to respond. A special subclass of Wait Time I is Wait Time Extended, which provides an opportunity for students to discuss potential answers with partners before responding.

During Wait Time II, a teacher pauses 3 to 10 seconds to provide all students an opportunity to digest the provided solution and determine the correctness of the answer or other alternatives before the teacher acknowledges whether the provided solution was correct. In some ways, mathematics is unique in that there are almost always different ways to arrive at a correct solution. Wait Time II provides students an opportunity to explore some of these alternatives routes.

Another factor covered under Questioning Strategies is use of praise. The NCTM publication *A Research Companion to Principles and Standards for School Mathematics* provides this example of specific praise:

> Her teacher then publicly validates Riba's work, underlining early in the year a standard for explanation and justification that is more than simple restating of the assertion:
>
> "Do you see the difference in Riba's second explanation? Did you see how she really showed us how it equals ten? The first time you just read it. And the second time you explained it. That was really nice." (Kirkpatrick, Martin, & Schifter, 2003, p. 32)

Teachers generally know the value of specific praise, but general praise has been observed much more frequently. Surprisingly, about 20 percent of the observations have found no praise at all. The teacher merely acknowledges a response and then moves on to the next question or continues with the lesson.

This section of the Classroom Observation Instrument prompts the reviewer to note whether the teacher's questioning checks for student understanding, but the observer should also comment on the pattern that the teacher uses to ask questions. In Question 10 of the student interview (see Figure B.9 in Appendix B, p. 193), students are asked to indicate the pattern their teacher most often uses while asking questions:

- Teacher only calls on students whose hands are raised.
- Some students (generally the same ones) call out the answers each time.
- Teacher calls on students in a predictable pattern, such as by going down the rows.
- Teachers calls on students randomly.

The review also should indicate which of these questioning patterns is used during the observed lesson in order to triangulate with the student data and multiple teacher observations.

Classroom Climate

Classroom climate is an important ingredient of student learning, encompassing student involvement and classroom management. Generally, teachers are professionals and do very well in this area. However, there have been instances, even with the observer present, of the teacher creating a very negative atmosphere. During one elementary school mathematics class observation, the teacher continuously intimidated the students. The students were berated for every response—even responses that were correct. The teacher let it be known that he was the expert on mathematics and the students had a lot to learn before they could ever match his understanding. Needless to say, the achievement results for students of this teacher—a classroom veteran of more than 20 years—were less than stellar. The students met his expectations.

Development of Higher-Order Thinking Skills

The final section addresses the degree of implementation of Bloom's taxonomy as applied to mathematics instruction. Most teachers who provide high-quality instruction also tend to address the higher end of the taxonomy. Low-quality instruction, on the other hand, tends to focus on lower-level, basic process skills (computation is also considered lower level if there is an absence of any other higher-level skills). Again, it is important for the observer to script examples of these as they are used in the instruction so that adequate feedback can be provided in the summary report.

Rubric Scoring

All of the sections of the observation form are graded with the Classroom Observation Instrument Scoring Rubric (Figure B.13 in Appendix B; see p. 205). This rubric provides descriptions of observations that would rate a score of 1, the lowest rating; 3, the middle rating; and 5, the highest rating. In my experience, it is rare that a particular observation will exactly match a rubric description score. Reviewers need to provide the rating that best approximates the score. Scores are not "averaged" but are based on which rubric statement best meets the observed lesson. Scores of 2 and 4 should be given for observations that fall between the provided rubric descriptions. For example, a reviewer setting out to rate Section 5 might note that that the lesson included many of the lower-level, basic process skills listed under element A but decide that the focus of the lesson was higher-level skills, under element B. The reviewer would give an overall rating between 3 and 5, with the final determination made on the strength of the lesson, evidence of learner attitudes (element C), and how much emphasis was included on evaluating logical consistency and other things.

After determining a rating for each section, the reviewer consults criteria in Section 6 of the rubric and decides on an overall rating.

It's important to remember that the classroom observation instruments completed for individual teachers are not included in the MPIR report that is submitted to the school. The report provides only summary data of all classroom observations. Figure 6.3 shows an excerpt of a completed Observation Summary Report. For the complete report form, see Figure B.14. Instructions for completing the Observation Summary Report are provided in Chapter 8.

■ ■ ■

Having discussed the questionnaires, the interviews, and the classroom observations, we will now look at the other data that are collected and analyzed to provide a fullest possible picture of a school's mathematics program.

FIGURE 6.3	CLASSROOM OBSERVATION SUMMARY—SAMPLE

1. Classroom Observation Rating Summary

NUMBER OF CLASSES OBSERVED: 8

Category	# Classes Rating 1	# Classes Rating 2	# Classes Rating 3	# Classes Rating 4	# Classes Rating 5	Average Rating
1. Physical Setting/Classroom Environment	0	1	4	3	0	3.3
2. Lesson Effectiveness	0	1	3	3	1	3.5
3. Questioning Strategies	1	2	2	3	0	2.9
4. Classroom Climate	0	1	2	4	1	3.6
5. Development of Higher-Order Thinking Skills	2	2	3	1	0	2.4
# Observations/Average Rating	.06	1.4	2.8	2.8	.4	**3.1**
						Overall Average

2. Overall Classroom Observation Rating Summary

NUMBER OF CLASSES OBSERVED: 8

# Classes Rating 1	# Classes Rating 2	# Classes Rating 3	# Classes Rating 4	# Classes Rating 5	Average Rating of all Observations
0	0	4	3	1	**3.6**

For information on the overall rating, see the Classroom Observation Instrument Scoring Rubric, Section 6.

3. Summary of Observations of Specific Strategies/Activities (Extract)

NUMBER OF CLASSES OBSERVED: 8

Observations	# Classes Where Observed	% of All Classes Observed
1. Classroom was of adequate size, with appropriate furniture to conduct mathematical investigations.	6	75%
2. Classroom displayed student work.	1	12.5%
3. Classroom mathematics resources were adequate, were used appropriately, and contributed to the quality of the mathematics instruction.	5*	62.5%

Comments:

*All the classrooms had adequate mathematics resources, but not all used the available resources appropriately and effectively.

Other Data Sources

## 7

A FINAL SOURCE OF DATA FOR THE MPIR IS A COLLECTION OF PRINTED materials that the school supplies to the review team. The notification letter to the principal (see Figure 2.3) includes the request that that these materials be collected and ready for the team to take with them on the day of the site visit. For the school under review, collecting the materials can be a learning process in itself. As they gather the items, school administration and faculty members often gain new understanding of the elements needed to have an effective, well-supported, high-quality mathematics program.

The additional data sources examined for the MPIR always include the following:

- Mathematics curriculum guide(s).
- Samples of lesson plans and assessments from each mathematics teacher (in a separate folder for each teacher).
- Mathematics assessment data (national, state, and local if available), including trend data and disaggregated data.
- Parent information and communications regarding the mathematics program (e.g., newsletters, a list of grade-level expectations).
- Memos or e-mail messages regarding instructions sent by the principal to the teachers.
- Information related to professional staff development for improving mathematics instruction (number and type of sessions that have been presented and teachers who have attended).
- The school report card issued by the state department of education.
- The school improvement plan (particularly pages that relate to the mathematics program).
- A copy of the school floor plan identifying teacher workstations, library location, computer lab locations, and so forth.
- A listing of computer software available for instructional use in mathematics classrooms indicating whether the software is stand-alone or on the school network.

- An inventory of the school's math-related books, periodicals, and videos that are available to teachers or students.
- Any other materials that would help outside personnel understand the mathematics instructional program within the school, especially the mathematics department budget and the URL of the school Web site.

Let's examine the importance of each item to the review, along with examples of what each has told review teams about particular schools.

The Mathematics Curriculum Guide

Mathematics curriculum guides are needed to help reviewers evaluate the curriculum standard. As pointed out during the standard's discussion in Chapter 3, good curriculum documents should be teacher friendly and should include more than a scope and sequence built around objectives. A curriculum that can be used by classroom teachers, substitute teachers, and administrators should *also* do the following:

- Align the school's objectives with state and national objectives and standards.
- Align the school's objectives to the adopted program (textbook, kit, etc.).
- Indicate the mastery level expected. For example, some objectives may be introduced at one grade level or within one course, but mastery may not be expected until a subsequent grade level or course. Similarly, some objectives may have been mastered earlier, but are reinforced within a particular grade or course through further applications.
- Estimate instructional time to be given to each of the objectives.
- Give the anticipatory set or essential questions to be used with each objective.
- Provide activities to be used within the lessons to teach the objectives, including closure activities.
- Specify resources such as Web quests, supplemental materials, or manipulatives that will be used within lessons to teach the objectives.
- Determine assessments—both formal and informal checks for understanding—that will be used to evaluate student success in accomplishing the objectives.

The first MPIRs completed throughout the six-state ARSI region found that most of the schools under review lacked a school or district mathematics curriculum. These schools were using a state framework, or an adopted textbook series' scope and sequence, or a combination of these and other sources. Reviewers at one elementary school discovered that the teachers were not using *a* mathematics curriculum—they were using *three* of them. Some teachers used the state curriculum guidelines and nothing else to support the content they were teaching. Some teachers used a copy of a mathematics curriculum from another district in the state without determining beforehand if it met their school's goals or had been modified in any way. Most teachers used a curriculum that had been developed based upon the input of a district committee. Some teachers attempted to refer to each of these three documents as they developed their lesson plans, even though there was little correlation among them. The lack of a consistently developed and used curriculum led to a lack of consistent instruction in important mathematics concepts, and student achievement results were less than noteworthy.

Lesson Plans and Assessments

Because review teams cannot observe all classes (and sometimes, especially in elementary school, they can't even observe all teachers), copies of lesson plans provide another means for team members to collect data about instruction. As the review team goes through the plans, they should ask these questions:

■ Did the teacher include class openers that provided either the objective for the lesson, an essential question, or some type of "hook" to motivate the students to want to learn the lesson content?

■ Did the teacher script several key questions to be asked during the lesson to check for student understanding?

■ Did the teacher make connections to previous learning as well as to upcoming lessons, including connections to other subject areas?

■ How was the teacher proposing to teach the lesson—through cooperative learning, lecture, computer simulation, or some other approach?

■ Was closure built into the lesson?

■ Were the formal assessments (quizzes, chapter tests, etc.) proposed exclusively paper-and-pencil?

■ Did the formal assessments measure only computational proficiency?

■ What role did higher-order thinking as reflected in problem solving have in the assessment? For example, did the assessment include open-response questions or constructed-response questions?

■ Were the assessments related to the ways in which the skills or concepts were taught? In other words, did there seem to be an alignment between the lesson plan and the assessment?

Review teams should also examine lesson plans and teacher assessments for information about the curriculum. Teams often find that lesson plans are heavily dependent upon adopted textbooks and that assessments are usually the tests provided by the textbook publishers. Teachers use the textbooks as prescribed but often without seeing "the big picture": where the students are going with the content.

Lesson plans and assessments revealed some of these issues at Foster Elementary School. Chiefly, lesson plans were being presented as a series of isolated facts without the connections that are called for in the NCTM standards—the kind of connections necessary to help students achieve proficiency with state standards on the accountability tests. There was no curriculum that provided links between the various topics that were being introduced in the daily lessons.

State and National Mathematics Assessment Data

Examining the trend data is the most critical element of interpreting assessment results. A single year's data is important in that it can show that a school is capable of producing outstanding results. However, the trend data may paint a different picture. Often, multiple annual data reports can reveal whether or not there is a continuous pattern of improvement in mathematics achievement.

In the United States, No Child Left Behind is making this pattern a critical measure for students. Now school test data must show "adequate yearly progress" not only for the school overall, but also for disaggregated groups (gender, special education, non-English–speaking, etc.). This is a change from the traditional way of determining success, when a school average that was improving was all that was necessary. "Our students are above the 50th percentile" was a popular statement, even if it meant that perhaps at least a quarter of the school's population was below the 30th percentile.

When review teams analyze assessment data, they are often able to detect trends that school faculties have missed. For example, testing companies can present gender data in ways that can obscure the reality that may exist in a school's mathematics program. Further analysis by an MPIR review team, particularly when the data is presented graphically, can be a dramatic eye-opener to a school staff. Let's see how a review team analyzed test data from Foster Elementary School to learn about gender differences in achievement.

Foster had 200 students in the 5th grade (the state-tested grade). The gender makeup was 106 males and 94 females. The 2003 test report issued by the testing company seemed to indicate that there were no major gender differences: 20 percent of the females and 20 percent of the males received a "novice" score. In addition, 50 percent of the females and 57 percent of the males scored "proficient" or "distinguished."

The MPIR review team's analysis of the novice scores is shown in Figure 7.1. The team calculated that 20 percent of 94 females equaled 19 students, and 20 percent of 106 males equaled 21 students. Thus, a total of 40 students (19 + 21) scored at the novice level. Nineteen of these 40 students (47.5 percent) were female and 21

FIGURE 7.1	GENDER DIFFERENCES IN MATHEMATICS SCORES

Foster Elementary School: State Assessment in Mathematics 2003

Descriptors	% Female	% Male
Students in Grade 5	47	53
Scoring "Novice"	47.5	52.5
Scoring "Proficient" or "Distinguished"	38.8	61.2

of the 40 (52.5 percent) were male. This 5 percent difference between girls and boys didn't show up in the initial data.

The analysis of Foster's proficient and distinguished scores did show a significant difference that was not seen in the original report. Thirty-eight of 94 females (40 percent) scored proficient or distinguished, and 60 of 106 males (57 percent), scored proficient or distinguished. Thus, a total of 98 students scored in the two top achievement levels. Females made up 38.8 percent (38 of 98), and males made up 61.2 percent (60 of 98), revealing a considerable gender difference that favored males. Examination of the released test data from previous years indicated that this gender pattern among students scoring proficient or distinguished had been in existence for a number of years. However, the Foster faculty had never noticed the discrepancy.

Communications Between School and Home

Reviews have consistently found that most schools that have high parental and community involvement have higher than average achievement results. Unfortunately, it seems that the most neglected aspect of the school community is the communication between the school and home. During MPIR interviews, principals often report that their parent organization is very small and, outside of fund-raising activities, is minimally involved with school functions. This has been especially true for middle schools and high schools. Principals also typically report that attendance at parent–teacher meetings is sparse unless students are performing. Yet school staffs could encourage parent participation and involvement simply through better communication.

Abbott Elementary School is a case in point. Although Abbott had a high percentage of students who received free or reduced-price lunch, its staff had made numerous efforts to involve parents in school activities. The principal regularly sent "principal newsletters" home to parents, informing them of upcoming events, reporting test results, and making suggestions about how parents could be involved in their children's education. She also maintained a parent link on the school Web site that provided information about the school program. The parent page also linked to Abbott's school improvement plan. The parent–teacher organization was active in fund raising, but it also sent regular newsletters and e-mails to parents informing them of upcoming school events, units of study, and school needs.

Parents of Abbott students had responded by becoming members of most school committees (curriculum, professional development, safety, etc.) and by regularly volunteering in classrooms, where they assisted with reading groups, basic fact drills, and other areas of student learning. Parents also attended school functions, many of which were held off campus at businesses and churches within the community. (Abbott's staff had noticed that some parents were reluctant to attend school functions at the school.) Communicating with parents had led to parent involvement and to students knowing that their parents cared about their learning. Achievement results at Abbott testified to the success of this joint effort.

Internal Communication Between Principal and Faculty

Memos (or copies of e-mails) from principals to teachers on the topic of instruction in general and mathematics instruction in particular can be a valuable source of information about school leadership. These communications can answer many of the review team's questions:

- What expectations does the principal have for the faculty?
- Does the principal act independently in setting these expectations or does the principal work collaboratively with all faculty members or a committee of faculty members to develop expectations?
- Does the principal provide encouragement, suggestions, Web sites to visit, and so forth?
- Does the principal show an interest in the mathematics program? For example, do all of the e-mails relate to reading or another content area, or is each subject area given equal treatment?
- Does the principal inform the faculty of professional development opportunities in mathematics?
- What process does the principal communicate to the faculty about how formal observations and informal, walk-through observations will be conducted?
- Do the messages seem to indicate that the principal is a more of a colleague in the learning process or more of a plant manager?

The review team at Abbott found that the e-mail messages provided by the principal were a helpful indicator. This principal sent e-mail messages to each staff member weekly. The e-mails were both informative and supportive. She regularly commended those grade levels that were involving students in activities that supported the school curriculum and also made it obvious that the activities were not just "activity-mania," but had a clearly defined purpose.

Professional Development

Just as it is important to determine how the principal has communicated professional development opportunities to staff, it is also important to gather data about the professional development that has been provided. Teams should look through the school's information with the following questions in mind:

- Has the school or district provided professional development based on a needs analysis or on the school or district improvement plan?
- Have teachers been trained on the adopted materials for teaching mathematics beyond a cursory overview of the textbook resources from the publisher's salesperson?
- Has mathematics professional development, if provided at all, been grade-level or subject specific (such as training for algebra teachers or training in the use of manipulatives for primary grade teachers)?

■ Did the school or district set aside professional development days for all teachers to be involved in the alignment of its curriculum?

■ Were professional development time and resources used to analyze state or national test results?

■ Was the principal involved in mathematics professional development activities—either with the teachers, with other administrators, or individually?

■ What format has the mathematics professional development taken? For example, has it been a large, one-shot event in which all teachers in the school or the district attended a presentation? Has it been a study group? Has it involved lesson analysis in which peers observed each other and provided critical analysis? Has it included provision for teachers to attend graduate classes for professional development credit?

Despite current literature that indicates the importance of teacher involvement in choosing the areas of professional development (see Figure 7.2), many schools continue to base their offerings on a "one size fits all" mentality, with little,

FIGURE 7.2	EFFECTIVE PROFESSIONAL DEVELOPMENT

The National Partnership for Excellence and Accountability in Teaching (1999) has identified nine general principles for effective professional development:

1. The content of professional development focuses on what students are to learn and how to address the different problems students may have in learning the material.
2. Professional development should be based on analyses of the differences between (a) actual student performance and (b) goals and standards for student learning.
3. Professional development should involve teachers in the identification of what they need to learn and in the development of the learning experiences in which they will be involved.
4. Professional development should be primarily school based and built into the day-to-day work of teaching.
5. Most professional development should be organized around collaborative problem solving.
6. Professional development should be continuous and on-going, involving follow-up and support for further learning, including support from sources external to the school that can provide necessary resources and new perspectives.
7. Professional development should incorporate evaluation of multiple sources of information on (a) outcomes for students and (b) the instruction and other processes that are involved in implementing the lessons learned through professional development.
8. Professional development should provide opportunities to gain an understanding of the theory underlying the knowledge and skills being learned.
9. Professional development should be connected to a comprehensive change process focused on improving student learning.

Source: National Partnership for Excellence and Accountability in Teaching (1999, p. 3).

if any, input from classroom teachers. The MPIR process generates data that can turn schools in the direction of meeting their staff's actual development needs. There is no reason for mathematics teachers to be left behind in planning and conducting their own professional development.

Reviewers of the program at Foster Elementary School hoped their recommendations would help teachers become part of the process of choosing professional development offerings. The review team found that Foster's teachers had had no input into the determination of the professional development required of them. The central office instructional supervisor and assessment coordinator had examined the previous year's state assessment results and had made a determination that upcoming professional development would focus on reading strategies. The central office purchased a reading package from a software vendor, and the first two days of teacher inservice training were devoted to the vendor instructing them on the use of this software. The remaining inservice training days for the school year continued the focus on reading strategies. This had been a consistent pattern with the district—that is, the professional development programs each year were determined by a central office staff that identified which content strand had the lowest test scores the previous year. This meant there had been no consistency in the professional development offerings and little or no effort at making the professional development classroom-based with teacher input.

School Report Cards

Most state departments of education now publish annual "school report cards" for each of their public schools. Typically, these reports are sent to parents and communities and provide information about achievement scores, at least in mathematics and reading. They also often include other data that can be useful in the MPIR process, such as the percentage of students on free or reduced-price lunch, attendance and retention percentages, number of teachers teaching out-of-field, and extracurricular programs offered by the school. If seen before or early in the day of the site visit, the report card can lead review team members to ask relevant follow-up questions during principal, teacher, and parent interviews. Reviewers at Foster used the report card in this way.

Foster's report card indicated that 38 percent of the students were on free or reduced-price lunch. The average scores on the previous year's standardized test were in the 47th percentile for reading and the 48th percentile for mathematics; both of these marks fell below district and state averages. The report card also noted that all of Foster's teachers were certified to teach in their assigned grades, and that the school provided several extracurricular programs including an after-school Title I reading program, an academic team that competed against other elementary schools in the region, and a gifted and talented pull-out program. This information led the review team to ask the following questions:

- What are the teachers doing to assist with the needs of low-income students who may not have access to resources (calculators, newspapers, Internet, etc.) that other students have available within their homes?
- Does the gifted and talented program include a mathematics component?
- Are parents concerned that their children are performing below the level of other students in the district and state? If so, what services has the school provided to parents? For example, has the school established a Family Math program or a similar outreach effort to involve parents in understanding their child's mathematics curriculum?

School Improvement Plan

All states now require that schools (and usually districts) develop and implement school improvement plans. The names of these plans vary from state to state, and may be known instead as "consolidated improvement plans," "unified improvement plans," or "continuous improvement plans." Although the names may be different, these plans all serve a similar function: to help schools develop goals for their improvement and to hold schools accountable for the accomplishment of these goals. That sounds reasonable and indeed it is, *if* the emphasis remains on substantial and sustained improvement.

Unfortunately, school improvement plans are often patterned on state models, and these tend to emphasize improving test scores, because state departments of education and central office administrators are most in tune with the accountability legislation. This focus can lead schools to adopt methods that bring about superficial change but not sustained improvement. For example, MPIRs have found that schools that can demonstrate dramatic improvement in scores have usually accomplished this feat through short-term measures, such as teaching test-taking strategies. Without systemic change, it's rare that a school is able to show continued improvement or even maintain improvement gained.

MPIRs have found that those schools that have identified instructional goals and have made changes to their instructional strategies through systemic efforts—such as appropriate professional development, administrative support (e.g., released time for peer evaluations), the development of aligned curricula that include references to appropriate strategies and resources—do experience continuous improvement in student achievement. Let's look at the school improvement plan of Abbott Elementary School, which experienced this kind of sustained success.

Abbott's improvement plan had a clearly stated instructional goal. Furthermore, the plan included strategies for the goal's implementation as well as benchmarks for measuring success. Among the strategies that the faculty had written into their plan was that all teachers would receive training in effective instructional strategies (Marzano, Pickering, & Pollock, 2001) and classroom management (Marzano, 2003). All teachers agreed to articulate and enforce common classroom rules and procedures for reward and punishment based on the research analysis presented by Marzano, and teachers of each grade level selected an instructional strategy from the training to be developed and used throughout the year. For example, 4th grade teachers selected "questions, cues, and advance organizers" and helped students to recognize and use this strategy in all content areas.

School Floor Plan

Providing the review team with copies of the school floor plan serves several purposes. First, the plan helps to orient team members as they travel through the school during the site visit, observing and interviewing teachers, students, and parents. The floor plan also helps team members to locate support areas, such as the school library and media center. Stopping by these areas may give teams more than a chance to see what resources are available.

For example, a review team member at Cartwright Middle School gleaned valuable information about receptive learning environments by observing an activity in the library. One of the mathematics teachers had chosen to conduct an investigation in the library because it had a much larger space. The investigation was for students to design and fly paper airplanes to develop a hypothesis about their properties. However, when a student launched the first airplane, the librarian came running from her office area, screaming at the student that the library was no place for such activities. Although the teacher perhaps should have prepared the librarian for what to expect during the lesson, the reaction provided a quick insight into the librarian's viewpoint on library usage. To her, the library was a place for quiet reading and study, not a place for active learning. If this was a common viewpoint within the school, then mathematics teachers might be hesitant to involve students in "noisy" activities that would disturb other classes.

Mathematics Software Listing

An inventory of software available to support mathematics instruction can provide insight into the capabilities of the school's hardware and the overall role that technology plays in instruction. Based on inferences made from the inventory, the review team can explore these issues further during classroom observations and interviews of students, parents, and teachers and during a visit to the school's computer labs. Reviewers should keep the following questions in mind while evaluating lab use and the list of software:

- Must the computer lab be scheduled? If so, how far in advance? Can a teacher be "bumped" by another teacher or administrator?
- How often do teachers use the computer lab for mathematics instruction?
- What types of software (simulation, computer-assisted instruction, etc.) are available?
- Does the software involve problem solving, concept development, applications, or computational drill?
- Is the mathematics software stand-alone, so that it must be loaded on each computer each time the lab is used, or is it on the school network?

Despite the evidence of the benefits that result from using computers (Sutton & Krueger, 2002), MPIRs have shown that many schools hinder computer use for mathematics instruction. If labs are available, scheduling may be difficult, because other content areas are given priority. For example, in Kentucky, writing portfolios are a component of state assessments, and schools typically reserve large blocks of computer lab time for their portfolio development and revision. Funding to maintain computers may be an additional issue. Oftentimes, using the latest software requires equipment upgrades; schools may either be reluctant to invest their funds in technology (when achievement is their top priority) or lack funds altogether.

Bibliography of Mathematics Media Resources

Many times the bibliography of mathematics books, periodicals, and videos prepared for the review team is the first such compilation that a school has made. In these instances, the bibliography can make teachers aware of resources that have been available to them and their students. Even when resource lists have been routinely provided to teachers before the review of the school, the lists usually are not annotated as to possible use. For example, elementary school teachers may have a listing of trade books, but the books aren't correlated to counting, to measurement, to two-dimensional geometry, and so forth.

Reviewers do find that many schools lack sufficient professional materials (books and periodicals) to support mathematics instruction or lack sufficient guidance about which resources might be appropriate for specific purposes (personal professional development, applications of right triangle trigonometry that could be used in lessons, etc.). In some schools, the mathematics faculty is perceived as not using and so not needing library resources. This was the case at Collingwood High School.

The librarian at Collingwood provided the team with a comprehensive bibliography of all of the mathematics-related books (fiction and nonfiction), periodicals (*Mathematics Teacher*, *The Physics Teacher*), and stand-alone mathematics software that could be checked out by teachers or students. She indicated that she had a fairly sizable budget to purchase additions to the library's inventory each year and sent out annual requests to teachers for suggestions for purchase. She noted, however, that none of the mathematics teachers ever provided any suggestions, and because they also did not seem to make assignments that required the use of mathematics history or other books in the discipline, it had been several years since she had made any additional purchases.

Financial Support of the Mathematics Program

Data related to financial and material support of the program are gathered through the principal questionnaire and teacher interviews, but a copy of the budget is indispensable in giving the review team an accurate picture of financial support. The budget may reveal that there is a lack of funding, or that despite adequate funds, there is a resource issue. The review team analyzing the budget at Foster Elementary School discovered funds were available for teachers, but their purchases of resources had not been coordinated.

Foster had received an additional supplement of funds to support its mathematics program because the school's mathematics scores showed a decline on the most recent state test. The teachers had been given a free hand to order materials that they felt they needed in their classrooms. As a consequence, a substantial number of selected materials (such as unifix cubes, rulers, place value charts) were in the school. However, some items had been overstocked, and other items that could have been beneficial (such as more primary balances) had not been purchased. The faculty had not examined the curriculum objectives to see which needed added support through resources and which were being met adequately with existing resources.

The School Web Site

A school's Web site (if it has one) can reveal much about the school's communication with parents and the community. It is often the only avenue available for these groups to evaluate the school's programs and can be a window to the soul of the school. Answers to many review questions can be found there:

- What does the school faculty determine to be important?
- Does the athletic program seem to be the featured component of the school?
- What part do academics play in the school?
- How effectively does the school communicate its mission?

■ Can parents quickly determine what the objectives are for mathematics for their child's grade level?

■ Do individual teachers or grade levels have links that communicate updated information about classroom events or lessons?

■ ■ ■

With the overview of other resources complete, we have addressed all the data that are collected by a review team for an MPIR. In the next chapter, we will move on to examine how the data are assimilated for the report issued to the school.

The Final Report

## 8

THE WRITING OF THE FINAL REPORT IS AS IMPORTANT TO THE MATHEMATICS Program Improvement Review process as the collection of data is. Compiling the data, assigning scores, and presenting findings and recommendations in a sensitive way require considerable effort and skill. An effective report must be well balanced. It must honestly reflect the review findings about the school, but at the same time, it must not be too discouraging. If the report does not address issues that teachers know exist at the school, the review will lose credibility and not effect change. If the report is too negative, it may be perceived as personally critical to the school principal (and never see the light of day) or as too overwhelming to act upon. The acceptance or rejection of the review team's recommendations can depend on how well the report is written.

In most cases, a report that is done well does not contain any findings that are surprising to the principal or faculty. Many times a principal or instructional supervisor has told me that a review report contained nothing new to them; however, they were appreciative of the supporting evidence that they could then present to teachers or district leaders to bring about change. For example, a principal may have felt the school was not receiving the degree of financial support needed for the mathematics program, and the report provided the documentation to take to the administration.

Collingwood High School used its review report in this way. The MPIR report for this school confirmed that teachers were providing their students with the highest-quality mathematics instruction that they could. Teachers had gone to a local bank to obtain a financial grant to purchase graphing calculators. They had attended professional development training in mathematics, even traveling 50 to 70 miles at the end of a school day to attend training that was not available in their home district. Yet despite these and other efforts, the teachers and the principal felt there had been no major improvements in mathematics achievement due to large class sizes.

One of the recommendations of the review report was for the district to provide funding for the employment of an additional mathematics teacher at Collingwood.

The principal and the mathematics chair took a copy of the report to a meeting they requested with the district superintendent. After reviewing the entire report, the superintendent agreed to provide support for several of the recommendations, including the employment of an additional mathematics teacher.

MPIR reports can also support changes already underway. During a review of one school, teachers were observed presenting very effective lessons that were part of an ongoing unit. However, interviews and questionnaires revealed that some teachers were not convinced that the instruction methods were beneficial. The staff had just begun a transition from traditional instruction, in which each lesson introduced new skills or concepts, to an instruction model that allowed students to develop many of the concepts for themselves. Teachers felt the new method took more time, and they weren't sure it would allow them to cover all of the content they were required to cover. In this instance, the review team was able to support and encourage these teachers in their use of the new model and to validate the effort as one that would bring about substantial improvement in learning.

Review Team Responsibilities

Review teams typically use one of two methods to write the report. Either one person (usually the team leader) writes the report with input from the team, or the team divides the writing. When multiple members write the report, each usually has responsibility for several standards, and then the team leader compiles all of the subsections and edits for a consistent format. In my experience, having one writer usually results in the most successful reports. With this method, all team members compile data, and the whole team meets to agree on ratings and recommendations, but just one team member does the actual writing. This person submits a draft of the report to the rest of team for approval and possible revision, and then makes final changes.

Data Compilation

Preparing the report can be very time-intensive. Whereas completing all the interviews and observations during a site visit will often take just eight to nine hours, compiling all the data and writing the report can take days. The process goes more quickly as team members become familiar with the review instruments and where to locate the triangulated data. But initially, all of the accumulated data can be overwhelming.

Teams should start by compiling data from each teacher tool. Since the teacher questionnaire is typically and ideally completed and collected before the site visit, a team member may have had an opportunity to compile the data before the visit. Figure 8.1 shows a summary of teacher questionnaire data for a school.

FIGURE 8.1	SAMPLE SUMMARY DATA FROM TEACHER SELF-PERCEPTION QUESTIONNAIRES†

SCHOOL Cartwright Elementary School (Submitted by 21 of 22 mathematics teachers)

Your school leadership has requested that a team visit your school to conduct a Mathematics Program Improvement Review. This review will use self-reported data from this questionnaire as well as interviews and observations on the day of the visit. None of the collected data will be used to identify or single out any teacher. The report issued as a result of the visit will be an analysis of the overall mathematics program. After completing this form, return it to your school secretary to be placed anonymously in an envelope.

Compiler's Use

Professional Background and Affiliation

a. I have _____ total years of classroom teaching experience.

0–4 yrs: 4; 5–10 yrs: 6; 11–20 yrs: 6; 21–30 yrs: 5

b. I have a certification to teach mathematics in the following grade-span (circle one):

K–4   K–6   K–8   5–8   7–12   9–12

[6.5] c. I am a member of a state mathematics organization and/or NCTM.

[3] Yes   [17] No

[6.5] d. I have attended a state, regional, or national mathematics conference in the past three years.

[5] Yes   [15] No

Instructional Approaches

How often do you use each of the following techniques to teach math in your classes?

		Daily	Weekly	Monthly	Rarely	Never
[5.4]	a. Students solving real-life problems		18	1	2	
[2.2c]	b. Library research			1	13	7
[2.2c]	c. Mathematical writing (reflections)	1	6	3	7	4
[2.1]	d. Demonstrating/modeling	18	3			
[2.2d]	e. Students using manipulatives*	9	12			
[2.2b]	f. Students in groups or teams	7	12		1	
[2.2b]	g. Group projects	2	7	6	4	2
[1.4]	h. Workbooks	5	10		4	2
[2.3]	i. Calculator problem solving		4	7	7	3
[2.3]	j. Computer drill and practice	1	3	7	5	5
[2.4]	k. Review of skills and procedures	7	12	2		
[2.4]	l. Individual projects	1	1	5	9	5
[2.5]	m. Math-related field trips			1	9	11
[1.3]	n. Computer problem solving		1	7	6	7
[2.4]	o. Lecture with student note taking		2	3	7	9

*Note: *Manipulatives* are items like geoboards, counters, algebra tiles, base-10 blocks, and so on. *Math tools* are single-purpose items like calculators, graph paper, rulers, compasses, and protractors.

†Data reflect actual questionnaire responses; some items were left blank by some respondents.

FIGURE 8.1	SAMPLE SUMMARY DATA FROM TEACHER SELF-PERCEPTION QUESTIONNAIRES *(continued)*

Compiler's Use

		Daily	Weekly	Monthly	Rarely	Never
[2.4]	p. Whole-class discussion	12	5	2		2
[1.4]	q. Student-led discussion	5	9	3	2	2
[2.4]	r. Individualized assignments	6	11	3		1
[2.5]	s. Guest speakers				11	10
[5.3]	t. Interdisciplinary lessons	1	4	4	5	2

Concerns

To what extent is each of the following a problem that limits students' mathematics learning in your school?

		Not a Problem	Slight Problem	Moderate Problem	Major Problem
[10.1]	Availability of funds for mathematics materials and supplies	5	4	7	5
[1.8]	Availability of appropriate curriculum materials (texts, calculators, software, etc.)	4	7	7	3
[10.5]	Availability of and access to computers and other technology	6	2	9	4
[9.1b]	Pressure to prepare students for state assessment	6	8	6	1
[8.2]	Availability of inservice opportunities for math teachers	6	8	4	3

Training

Reflect on the inservice training you have received and evaluate how prepared you feel to perform the following activities.

		Not Well Prepared	Somewhat Prepared	Well Prepared	Very Well Prepared
[1.3]	Develop lessons with a problem-solving focus	1	16	4	
[1.6]	Use an approach that provides mathematical connections	3	14	4	
[2.1]	Develop lessons that provide opportunities for students to actively construct their own mathematical knowledge	7	12	2	
[2.2d]	Provide opportunities for students to use manipulatives to verify mathematical reasoning		8	11	2
[2.2b]	Use cooperative learning groups		6	14	1
[2.2a]	Model multiple problem-solving strategies and have students apply what they have learned	3	13	5	
[2.2e]	Have students pose their own problems	4	14	3	
[3.1]	Teach classes containing students of heterogeneous abilities	4	7	9	1
[3.3]	Use appropriate techniques for students with special needs	4	10	5	2
[3.1]	Teach classes containing students with different learning styles	2	10	8	1
[5.4]	Connect math to real-life contexts and careers	1	13	7	
[9.3]	Use a variety of assessment strategies to measure students' success	4	12	4	1

FIGURE 8.1	SAMPLE SUMMARY DATA FROM TEACHER SELF-PERCEPTION QUESTIONNAIRES *(continued)*

Compiler's Use

Preparation

Do you feel well prepared—either through professional development or coursework—to do the following?

		Not Well Prepared	Somewhat Prepared	Well Prepared	Very Well Prepared
[3.1]	Encourage participation of males in mathematics	2	6	12	1
[2.2c]	Listen/ask questions as students work in order to gauge their understanding.	3	5	12	1
[5.1]	Encourage students' interest in mathematics		11	9	1
[2.1]	Develop students' conceptual understanding of mathematics.		14	7	
[3.1]	Encourage participation of minorities in mathematics	3	7	10	1
[2.2f]	Take students' prior understanding into account when planning curriculum and instruction	1	8	12	
[2.2d]	Manage a class of students engaged in hands-on/project-based work	1	7	13	
[1.8]	Use the textbook as a resource rather than the primary instructional tool.		10	11	
[3.1]	Recognize and respond to student cultural diversity	1	8	12	
[2.3]	Use calculators/computers for mathematics learning games	2	14	3	
[7.2]	Involve parents in the mathematics education of their children	4	10	7	
[2.1]	Lead a class of students using investigative strategies	3	11	7	
[2.3]	Use calculators/computers for drill and practice.	1	13	5	2
[2.3]	Use calculators/computers to demonstrate mathematics principles	4	12	4	1
[2.3]	Use calculators/computers to collect and analyze data	3	12	5	1
[2.3]	Use calculators/computers for simulations and applications	4	14	2	
[2.3]	Use the Internet in your mathematics teaching for general reference	8	8	5	
[2.3]	Use the Internet in your mathematics teaching for data acquisition	9	9	3	
[2.3]	Use the Internet in your mathematics teaching for collaborative projects with classes/individuals in other schools	8	10	3	

[6.4]   In the past three years, how many hours of professional development have you had in mathematics or mathematics education?

☐	None
10	6 hours or less
7	7–15 hours
3	16–35 hours
1	More than 35 hours

FIGURE 8.1	SAMPLE SUMMARY DATA FROM TEACHER SELF-PERCEPTION QUESTIONNAIRES *(continued)*

Compiler's Use

[6.4] If you have had professional development related to your mathematics teaching in the past three years, what was the format? (Check all that apply.)

- [ ] N/A
- [17] Attendance at a workshop on mathematics teaching
- [7] Observation of other teachers teaching mathematics as part of your own professional development (formal or informal)
- [12] Study group of teachers on mathematics teaching issues
- [5] A formal college/university course in the teaching of mathematics (math ed)
- [2] A formal college/university mathematics course
- [1] Service as a mentor and/or peer coach in mathematics teaching as part of a formal arrangement that is recognized or supported by the school or district
- [4] Attendance at a national or state mathematics teacher association meeting
- [ ] Collaboration on mathematics teaching issues with a group of teachers at a distance using telecommunications (distance learning)

Instruction

How much emphasis does your instruction place on each of the following elements?

Compiler's Use		Not Much	Some	Moderate	Extensive
[2.1]	Mathematical concepts			8	13
[2.2a]	Problem solving			11	10
[2.1]	Mathematical reasoning		3	12	6
[1.7a]	Computational skills		1	11	9
[1.6]	How mathematics ideas connect with one another		4	10	7
[5.1]	Increasing interest in mathematics		3	13	5
[5.1]	Preparing for further study in mathematics	2	4	12	3
[1.7a]	Mathematical algorithms/procedures	4	6	8	3
[1.7a]	Ability to perform computations with speed and accuracy	3	4	10	4
[9.1b]	Standardized test preparation	4	6	8	3
[1.4]	Expression of mathematical ideas (orally and in writing)	3	5	10	3
[1.6]	The logical structure of mathematics	1	2	13	5
[5.4]	Applications of mathematics in business and industry	9	7	3	
[5.4]	The history and nature of mathematics	11	7	3	

[2.4] How much homework do you assign in an average school <u>week</u>?

- [7] 0–10 minutes
- [5] 11–20 minutes
- [8] 21–40 minutes
- [1] 41–90 minutes
- [ ] 91–120 minutes
- [ ] More than 120 minutes

FIGURE 8.1	SAMPLE SUMMARY DATA FROM TEACHER SELF-PERCEPTION QUESTIONNAIRES *(continued)*

Compiler's Use

[2.3]

Technology Use

In which of the following ways do students use calculators or computers in your math class?
(Check all that apply.)

- [13] Do drill and practice
- [5] Demonstrate mathematics principles
- [14] Play mathematics learning games
- [2] Do probability simulations
- [ ] Collect data using sensors or probes
- [ ] Retrieve or exchange data
- [5] Solve problems using simulations
- [4] Take a test or quiz

Resources/Equipment

[1.8]

Indicate the degree of use of each of the following in your math instruction.

	Do Not Use (Not Needed)	Do Not Use (Not Available)	Use
Overhead projector	5		16
Videotape player	7	1	10
Videodisc player	13	2	3
DVD player	9	3	7
Four-function calculator (class set)	6	2	10
Fraction calculators (class set)	13	4	
Graphing calculators (class set)	13	4	
Scientific calculators (class set)	12	3	2
Computers		6	13
Calculator/computer lab interfacing devices	10	2	7
Computers with Internet connection	6	3	10

Use of Textbooks/Commercial Programs

[1.8]

Which of the following best describes your use of textbooks or alternative commercial programs in your math classes?

- [10] Use one textbook or program all or most of the time
- [10] Use multiple textbooks or programs
- [1] Do not use a textbook or commercial program

Data from teacher interviews and classroom observations must also be compiled for analysis by standard and indicator.

You will remember that the format for presenting observation data is the Classroom Observation Summary, first seen in Figure 6.3. (The complete template is provided in Appendix B as Figure B.14.) The completion of this three-part form requires several calculations.

Part 1 of the form is the Classroom Observation Rating Summary. Tallies are made of the scores given for each of the five sections of the filled-in Classroom Observation Instruments. Average ratings for each category are then computed to give an overall view across the classes observed. To illustrate the calculation process, let's look at the data in the Classroom Observation Rating Summary shown in Figure 8.2. On Section 1 of the instrument (Physical Setting/Classroom Environment), one of the eight classes observed received a rating of 2, four received a rating of 3, and three received a rating of 4. For calculation purposes, the one 2 contributes 2 points (1 x 2), the four 3's contribute 12 points (4 x 3), and the three 4's also contribute 12 points (3 x 4). Thus, the school earned a total of 26 points in this category (2 +12 +12 = 26). Dividing this point total (26) by the number of classrooms observed (8) produces an average Physical Setting/Classroom Environment score of 3.3, which appears in the far right "average rating" column.

After calculating averages for each of the sections, the row indicating the number of class observations/average is filled in by adding the number of observations within each column and dividing each of those sums by 5, the number of sections. The Overall Average is reached by calculating the average of the "average rating" column. In this example:

$$\frac{3.3 + 3.5 + 2.9 + 3.6 + 2.4}{5} = \frac{15.7}{5} = 3.1$$

Part 2 of the form, the Overall Classroom Summary (see Figure 8.3) displays the overall ratings given for all observations and presents a single averaged rating to represent the average overall rating of all the classes observed. For example, and as shown in Figure 8.3, four of the eight classes observed received an overall rating of 3 (12 points), one of the eight classes received an overall rating of 2 (2 points), and three received an overall rating of 4 (12 points). The review team divided the point total (26) by the number of classes (8) to arrive at a rating of 3.3. This rating should be—and is—close to the overall average found in the Classroom Observation Rating Summary.

Finally, the findings of the individual classroom observations are compiled in the third table, the Summary of Observations of Specific Strategies and Activities. Figure 8.4 illustrates a completed sample of a portion of this form. (For the complete template, see Figure B.14.) Of the eight classrooms observed, six classrooms were of

FIGURE 8.2 | CALCULATIONS FOR A SAMPLE CLASSROOM OBSERVATION RATING SUMMARY

1. Classroom Observation Rating Summary

NUMBER OF CLASSES OBSERVED: 8

Category	# Classes Rating 1	# Classes Rating 2	# Classes Rating 3	# Classes Rating 4	# Classes Rating 5	Average Rating
1. Physical Setting/ Classroom Environment	0	1	4	3	0	$\frac{(1\times2)+(4\times3)+(3\times4)}{8}$ $\frac{2+12+12}{8}=\frac{26}{8}=3.3$
2. Lesson Effectiveness	0	1	3	3	1	$\frac{(1\times2)+(3\times3)+(3\times4)+(1\times5)}{8}$ $\frac{2+9+12+5}{8}=\frac{28}{8}=3.5$
3. Questioning Strategies	1	2	2	3	0	$\frac{(1\times1)+(2\times2)+(2\times3)+(3\times4)}{8}$ $\frac{1+4+6+12}{8}=\frac{23}{8}=2.9$
4. Classroom Climate	0	1	2	4	1	$\frac{(1\times2)+(2\times3)+(4\times4)+(1\times5)}{8}$ $\frac{2+6+16+5}{8}=\frac{29}{8}=3.6$
5. Development of Higher-Order Skills	2	2	3	1	0	$\frac{(2\times1)+(2\times2)+(3\times3)+(1\times4)}{8}$ $\frac{2+4+9+4}{8}=\frac{19}{8}=2.4$
# Observations/Average Rating	$\frac{0+0+1+0+2}{5}$ $=\frac{3}{5}=0.6$	$\frac{1+1+2+1+2}{5}$ $=\frac{7}{5}=1.4$	$\frac{4+3+2+2+3}{5}$ $=\frac{14}{5}=2.8$	$\frac{3+3+3+4+1}{5}$ $=\frac{14}{5}=2.8$	$\frac{0+1+0+1+0}{5}$ $=\frac{2}{5}=0.4$	$\frac{(3.3+3.5+2.9+3.6+2.4)}{5}$ $=\frac{15.7}{5}=\textbf{3.1}$
						Overall Average

FIGURE 8.3	CALCULATIONS FOR A SAMPLE OVERALL CLASSROOM OBSERVATION RATING SUMMARY

NUMBER OF CLASSES OBSERVED: 8

# Classes Rating 1	# Classes Rating 2	# Classes Rating 3	# Classes Rating 4	# Classes Rating 5	Average Rating of all Observations
0	1	4	3	0	$$\frac{(1 \times 2) + (4 \times 3) + (3 \times 4)}{8}$$ $$= \frac{2 + 12 + 12}{8}$$ $$= \frac{26}{8}$$ $$= 3.3$$

For information on the overall rating, see Section 6 of the Classroom Observation Instrument Scoring Rubric (p. 209).

adequate size with appropriate furniture to conduct mathematical investigations. Thus, 6/8 (75 percent) of all classrooms met this indicator. Similarly, 1/8 (12.5 percent) of the observed classrooms had student work displayed, and 5/8 (62.5 percent) had adequate mathematics resources that were used appropriately and contributed to the quality of the lesson.

The comments section of this table allows further explanation of the ratings. For example, the third summary statement in the sample in Figure 6.3 (see p. 80) includes an asterisked item: five classrooms in which mathematics resources were adequate, were used appropriately, and contributed to the quality of the mathematics instruction. This item is further clarified in the comments section: All of the classrooms had adequate mathematics resources, but only five of the classrooms used the available resources appropriately and effectively.

The three-part Classroom Observation Summary has proven to be an effective means of presenting data about classrooms without targeting individual teachers. If overall patterns emerge, the mathematics teachers will be able to identify strengths in their program as well as areas that might need additional professional development or college coursework. For example, if an average score of 2.5 was given on questioning strategies, it should be clear that this area needs additional emphasis.

After the data from teacher tools have been compiled and team members have had an opportunity to read the supplemental documents (test data, curriculum documents, principal memos, etc.), the team meets to assign scores for each standard indicator using the scoring rubric (see the Guide for Rating MPIR Indicators and Standards, Figure B.2 on page 153). As the scores are agreed upon, the team leader makes note of the evidence supplied by team members that supports that score. For example, if a team agrees that a score of 1 should be given for Indicator 2.2d ("Instructional strategies include the use of manipulatives to introduce concepts, practice

FIGURE 8.4	CALCULATIONS FOR A SAMPLE SUMMARY OF OBSERVATIONS OF SPECIFIC STRATEGIES AND ACTIVITIES

NUMBER OF CLASSES OBSERVED: 8

Observations	# Classes Where Observed	% of All Classes Observed
1. Classroom was adequate size with appropriate furniture to conduct mathematical investigations.	6	$\frac{6}{8} = 75\%$
2. Classroom displayed student work.	1	$\frac{1}{8} = 12.5\%$
3. Classroom mathematics resources were adequate, were used appropriately, and contributed to the quality of the mathematics instruction.	5	$\frac{5}{8} = 62.5\%$

skills, provide for problem solving, and verify mathematical reasoning"), then the review team must cite supporting evidence documented during teacher interviews, student interviews, and classroom observations.

Again, the various data-collection tools are designed to facilitate triangulation. Each question, whether it is on a questionnaire or in an interview, is cross-referenced to the appropriate indicator and standard. For example, evidence to support a rating for Standard 5.1 can be found in two sections of the teacher questionnaire, in the teacher interview, in the principal's checklist, and in the student interview (see Figure 8.5).

The team assigns each indicator a rating, which it records on the standard rating form, Figure B.1 in Appendix B. Even though the school will receive a copy of the scoring rubric (Figure B.2) with the report, the rating numbers by themselves can be rather stark and initially upsetting if there are a quite a few low scores. The team can relieve some of this anxiety by including sufficient evidence for the scores. Although the team should cite evidence for the rating of each indicator, an extended discussion for each is not necessary. In general, the report should include complete support for scores of 1, 2, or 5 to document the reasons for these ratings.

The MPIR process has been designed to be as accurate as possible, but I have found it wise to communicate to the principal and staff that there can still be errors in rating individual indicators. The reviews are generally completed in one day, and this "snapshot" may not always be indicative of what happens on a regular basis.

Tips for Report Recommendations

Review team members should remember that ratings reflect the evidence, or data gathered, but recommendations are guides for taking action. They should be based on the evidence but chosen and presented in a way that is most helpful to the school.

FIGURE 8.5	CROSS-REFERENCED DATA SOURCES FOR INDICATOR 5.1

5.1   *Teachers relate mathematics to individual student interests and to subsequent mathematical studies.*

Group	Data Source	Item
Teachers	Teacher Self-Perception Questionnaire (Preparation)	■ Do you feel well prepared—either through professional development or coursework—to encourage students' interest in mathematics?
	Teacher Self-Perception Questionnaire (Instruction)	■ How much emphasis does your instruction place on increasing interest in mathematics? ■ How much emphasis does your instruction place on preparing for further study in mathematics?
	Teacher Interview Questions	■ What process do you have to relate lessons to student interests or subsequent mathematics topics?
Principal	Principal's Checklist for the Mathematics Program (Program Materials)	■ Do the materials draw upon the students' own interests and experiences?
Students	Student Interview Questions	■ Does your teacher ever ask you what you are interested in and then find problems related to your personal interests?

After a review team has rated the standards, it should make recommendations to address all the standards in need of improvement. But before including this list in the report, the team should consider these hints for successful recommendations:

■ Winnow the number of recommendations to 10 or fewer. If there are more than 10, the faculty is more likely to react unfavorably to the overall report.

■ Include both recommendations that can be accomplished fairly easily and recommendations that may take some time to enact.

■ Do not prioritize recommendations in the report. Leave it for the school staff to decide which recommendations are most important to the school.

■ Support recommendations. Use triangulated data when possible, but keep the evidence general. Quotations should be used diplomatically, if at all, to protect the anonymity of sources. Make sure that recommendations are distinguished from the evidence, or data.

■ Make recommendations as specific as possible. Recommendations that are too general or nebulous are hard to act on. If the team doesn't know what specifically to recommend to address a problem, consult the national standards or a colleague well versed in current practices and in what the research considers exemplary strategies and techniques.

■ Encourage schools to explore alternative professional development models in implementing the recommendations. Attempt to match the models to the recommendations.

■ Seek assistance from a colleague in editing and proofreading the report. The colleague must understand that the material is confidential.

■ Include as many commendations as recommendations. The school faculty can easily be discouraged if all they see in the report are recommendations. Even the lowest-achieving schools have positive aspects that should be noted.

Elements of the Final Report

The final report typically includes these elements:

■ Commendations for strengths of the program.
■ The rating form for the standards and indicators, with scores for each.
■ Evidence and discussion to support these scores.
■ Recommendations for standards most in need of improvement.
■ Suggested resources and materials for consideration for use.
■ Summary of school-reported strengths and weaknesses.
■ Classroom observation summary.
■ Summary of the mathematics teacher self-perception questionnaires.

The report may also include appendixes of research or other supporting articles (professional development readings, explanatory discussions, etc.). These should be included only when appropriate and high-quality resources are known to the team. If team members are not aware of the most effective resources or research to recommend, it is best to consult with other colleagues who can contribute this information or omit it all together. Supplying inferior resources or articles is not beneficial to schools.

I've included samples of some of the other report elements. A list of commendations from a report is given in Figure 8.6. Teams should try to include equal numbers of commendations and recommendations. Figure 8.7 shows a sample summary of school-reported strengths and weaknesses, compiled from the principal questionnaire and interviews with teachers, parents, and students. Figure 8.8 shows a sample list of recommendations for a targeted standard. To review a compilation of data from teacher questionnaires, refer to Figure 8.1. Inclusion of this summary is another way to show the school faculty that their responses were noted and used in the review. These data may also help faculty recognize strengths or weaknesses within particular areas (instructional approaches, training, etc.) that were not targeted in the report's recommendations.

FIGURE 8.6	SAMPLE SUMMARY OF COMMENDATIONS

- The success of the students on the state assessments is a tribute to the excellent work of the faculty and staff.
- The school has a staff of teachers who are caring and supportive.
- The teachers are very willing to incorporate various grouping patterns within their classrooms to facilitate learning.
- The students have obvious strengths in problem solving.
- The faculty is composed of a good blend of veteran and beginning teachers—bringing both excitement and experience to teaching.
- The use of study groups has been a successful component of the school's professional development model.
- There is a consistent method of introducing students to the need for and method of demonstrating understanding of mathematics—using words, numbers, and pictures to explain their work.
- The faculty attempt to provide numerous methods to recognize students for achievement.
- Some (perhaps all) of the teachers have recognized that mathematics instruction is best served by in-depth development rather than overly broad coverage without sufficient development of understanding.
- Teachers are beginning to analyze student work based on standards of performance.

Submitting the Report

Two copies of the completed final report should be mailed to the school principal, along with a copy of the scoring rubric and a cover letter. In the cover letter, it's advisable to note that although the report contains a number of recommendations, the mathematics faculty should prioritize the recommendations based upon their own perceived needs. The faculty should select no more than two recommendations to address during the upcoming year. One of these should be an action that can be completed in a relatively short time so that the teachers can recognize a quick benefit. The other recommendation may be one that may take an extended period to complete but will have a major sustained effect.

A mistake I made during the first year of conducting MPIRs was to give copies of the reports to the instructional supervisors of the reviewed schools if these individuals had provided the review funding. (I let the principals know that a copy of the report would also be sent to the instructional supervisor, and the principals agreed because supervisors did work closely with the instructional program.) In one school district, the instructional supervisor took the submitted reports of three elementary schools to a school board meeting and made a presentation about the reports to the board without notifying the school principals or inviting them to be present. The principals and teachers felt the supervisor had violated confidentiality and showed a lack of professionalism. They blamed me as well. Even though I had been working closely with the schools in this district, one principal banned me from his building for the next two years—until he retired. After this incident, I made it a point to give review reports to the reviewed school's principal only. It's a practice I strongly recommend.

FIGURE 8.7	SAMPLE SUMMARY OF SCHOOL-IDENTIFIED STRENGTHS AND WEAKNESSES	
Group	**Strengths Identified**	**Weaknesses Identified**
Teachers	■ Interested students ■ The program focuses on going "deeper and slower" rather than trying to "cover it all" ■ Students are asked to prove why—and to use numbers, words, and pictures to do so ■ Student work is analyzed based on standards ■ Manipulative use gives students the opportunity to explore concepts ■ Caring teachers who individualize and don't just have students do pencil-and-paper assignments ■ Teachers are willing to go the extra mile to challenge students	■ Not enough training to be able to explain problem solving ■ Not enough applications to use with students ■ Professional development often consists of teachers modifying a set of ready-made activities to their own grade levels ■ Curriculum is inconsistent between grades ■ Curriculum is just bits and pieces: needs to be comprehensive, clear, organized program ■ Review is not built into the lessons within the program ■ Weak home/school connections and parent communication ■ Not enough conceptual learning ■ Not enough knowledge or use of best practices ■ Students' math vocabulary insufficient ■ Not enough opportunities to see others teach ■ Technology is incomplete
Principal	■ Teachers are talented and dedicated ■ Good parent interest and support ■ Resources	■ Need more math professional development ■ Need more team meetings ■ Need to purchase more math manipulatives
Parents	■ Teachers are willing to work with parents to boost student math achievement	■ Not enough challenge for higher-achieving students; ability grouping needed? (one parent)
Students	■ Math centers ■ "Say why" training ■ Use of manipulatives	■ Classrooms are crowded ■ Too much cheating ■ Not enough experiments ■ Have to switch teachers for different subjects (i.e., departmentalizing is a weakness) ■ Switching teachers is good, but creates too many logjams (one student) ■ Need to play games more

Presenting the Report

The letter that accompanies the final report should also remind the principal that a team member will be available to return to the school to present the report to the faculty. If the principal requests an oral presentation, the selected team member should prepare highlights of the report using either overhead transparencies or presentation software such as PowerPoint. If software is used, the team member needs to remember to confirm the availability of a computer and projector with the principal.

The team member should be prepared to answer questions during the presentation; however, he or she should not provide any information that is not contained

FIGURE 8.8	SAMPLE REPORT RECOMMENDATIONS (EXTRACT)

Recommendations for Improving Professional Development

1. Provide focused teacher participation in professional development opportunities, particularly regional or national math conferences, to enable teachers to become more aware of resources, materials, and applications of mathematics.

2. With the help of teachers, administrators, and district personnel, develop a progressive 5-year plan for professional development. This plan can provide professional development in some or all of the following areas:
   - Use of inquiry/constructivist strategies in mathematics instruction
   - Methods for using models (including, for example, software and manipulatives) to enhance concept development and understanding
   - The best uses of calculators designed to meet the middle school mathematics curriculum
   - Use of higher-order questioning strategies (wait time, specific praise, Bloom's taxonomy, etc.)
   - "Best practice" instructional strategies
   - Meeting the needs of gifted students within the heterogeneous classroom
   - Developing higher-order thinking through problem solving (including regular use of problem-solving heuristics and/or investigations)
   - Use of computer technology (including spreadsheets, Web sites, simulation software, problem-solving software, etc.) in mathematics instruction
   - Developing and using essential questions within lesson and unit planning
   - Differentiated instruction in mathematics

3. Locate a provider, conference, or study group resource for professional development for the highest priority needs.

within the written report. In particular, the presenter should not refer to any specific teacher or classroom. At the conclusion, the presenter needs to make the same comment that was made in the cover letter to the principal about the school choosing which recommendations are a priority and selecting two to start with. I like to make sure the last screen presented to the assembled mathematics teachers and administrators shows the list of commendations. This ends the meeting on a high note.

Another useful practice is for the presenter to bring copies of some of the recommended reference or supplemental materials. The teachers can individually review these materials at the conclusion of the meeting, and to facilitate further reference, a teacher or librarian might record the ISBNs (International Standard Book Number, a unique identifier) of materials that appear to be particularly beneficial to the mathematics program.

Acceptance of the Report

Ultimately, the review team cannot control whether the school accepts or rejects the recommendations in the final MPIR report. Even a well-written and well-presented report is not always acted upon. Review reports that have clearly detailed deficiencies in a mathematics program and made clear recommendations sometimes have not been adopted. This may be due to factors outside of the review process that prevent or defer the school taking action.

Happily, though, I have found that MPIRs are almost always seeds for change, and that even if there *seems* to be no response to a report, change may be taking root and spreading. One time, I conducted reviews for a university project that had obtained a federal grant to work with the mathematics programs of schools within its geographic service area. The director of the project had heard of the successful use of MPIRs in other school districts, and he decided to use some of the funds to have review teams visit the schools served through his grant. He met with the superintendents of the districts, and they all approved his proposal.

Subsequently, reviews were scheduled for each of the schools in the project districts. The reviews were completed and the reports sent back to the school principals. I didn't hear any more from the director of the project or the schools for several years. Then one fall, I had another call from the director. He asked if return visits could be scheduled for the schools previously reviewed and first reviews scheduled for additional schools.

Apparently, a meeting of all of the superintendents in the project's service area had taken place. One school in the area had been singled out by the state department of education because it had made exemplary improvement in its mathematics achievement results. Once among the lowest-scoring schools in the state for mathematics, the school was now scoring among the highest. The superintendents asked the school's principal what he attributed the improvement to. He replied that he had merely enacted each of the recommendations of the MPIR report for his school over the course of the last three years.

The other principals had ignored the reports they had received because they had been initiated not within their school by the superintendent and the university in a top-down manner. Now those principals wanted the Mathematics Program Improvement Reviews because they saw their value. In the intervening years, however, there had been many changes at all the schools reviewed—changes in principals, teachers, and facilities. "We need new MPIRs," the principals told me. I was happy to schedule these. The cycle began again.

■　■　■

APPENDIX A

TRAINING

This appendix provides step-by-step instructions for training teachers and administrators to conduct Mathematics Program Improvement Reviews. I have included the agenda I use for training and most of the tools needed; these begin on page 145. Schools that would like to train staff to conduct reviews should remember that it may not be an effective practice to have a team evaluate a school in its own district. A better option is to have trained staff members from one district evaluate schools in another district, and then have teams from that district evaluate your schools—the exchange review system. However, the best use of this training may be to help your school's mathematics faculty and or your district's building-level administrators learn what factors contribute to a high-quality mathematics program. This training, together with the handbook, can be a valuable professional development model to better understand your mathematics program.

When I train teachers and administrators, I schedule the program over two days. The focus of the first day is collecting and using data, and the focus of the second day is writing a review report. All participants are involved in the first day of training, but only those who are interested in actually serving on teams and writing reports are included in the second day of training.

Figure A.1 is the agenda I use for training, and I will follow it as I discuss each day's activities. The training involves using sample data from actual school reviews as well as collecting data by performing mock interviews and observing taped classes. Participants are also given experience summarizing data, using data to rate indicators and standards, and making recommendations for schools. The trainer should provide each participant with copies of all the MPIR tools in Appendix B; figures A.2 through A.11, which begin on page 123; and a few figures from other chapters, as noted.

Day One

Introduction

The first day begins with an introduction to MPIRs: how a school or district determines if it would like to pursue a review, the standards and indicators for a review, and the objectives that would be achieved by completing a review. This information is covered in Chapters 1, 2, and 3 of this handbook. The trainer should use the following handouts to accompany the discussion:

- Figure 2.2: Does Your School Need a Mathematics Program Improvement Review?
- Figure B.1: Rating Form for the MPIR Standards
- Figure B.2: Guide for Rating MPIR Indicators and Standards

FIGURE A.1	AGENDA FOR MPIR TRAINING

Day One

9:00   Introduction to the Mathematics Program Improvement Review Process
- Do you need a review? Should the school have external or internal reviewers?
- What are the objectives, expected outcomes, and potential uses of a review?
- What are the mathematics program standards and indicators?

9:40   Analyzing Assessment Data
- Aggregated and disaggregated results
- Trends in the data

10:15   Data Collection
- Questionnaires
- Interviews (mock and sample for parents, teachers, principal and students)

12:00   Lunch

1:00   Complete Interviews

1:45   Classroom Observations (2 Videotaped Lessons)

3:00   Discussion of Observed Lessons
- Whole group
- Small group

3:20   Small Groups: Assigning and Supporting Rubric Scores

3:35   Reporting by Small Groups

3:55   Closing Comments

Day Two

9:00   Review of Collected and Additional Data

9:30   Third Classroom Observation

10:30   Assignment of Classroom Observation Scores

10:45   Completion of Classroom Observation Summary

11:15   Tips for Writing Effective Program Review Reports

12:00   Lunch

1:00   Small-Group Work: Writing the Report

3:00   Reporting and Selecting Final Recommendations

3:50   Evaluation and Closing Comments

Analyzing Assessment Data

The second session in the training is used to analyze local testing data. The trainer will need to obtain copies of school or district test data before the training to make transparencies of the mathematics portion of the results as well as printed copies to hand out to each participant. The trainer will explain how the testing data can be analyzed to examine trend data among the entire school or district population and discuss all other relevant data pertinent to mathematics—for example, discrepancies among various subpopulations. Much of the allocated 30 minutes is usually used for discussion of the data on the subgroups (ethnic populations, socioeconomic levels, gender, special education populations, etc.).

Near the end of the session, the trainer reminds the participants that a review team not only collects copies of test data from the school but also takes other printed material home from the site visit. These documents are listed and discussed in Chapter 7. Later in the training, the participants will look at a sample school improvement plan to practice collecting data from these sources. The other materials are not used during the training but are important in writing the final report because they provide additional triangulated data for many of the indicators.

Data Collection

The rest of Day One is devoted to data collection. The trainer provides some sample data but also allows participants to gather data, using mock interviews and classroom observations. Participants are divided into groups of no more than five. Each group is assigned a standard for which members will collect data. At the end of the day, each group will give a summary of its findings for each standard.

Questionnaires

The trainer hands out completed questionnaires from constituent groups at "Harder-Not-Smarter Middle School." The handouts are

- Figure A.2: Summary Data from Teacher Self-Perception Questionnaires, which shows compiled results from the school's six mathematics teachers
    - Figure A.3: Principal's Self-Perception Questionnaire
    - Figure A.4: Principal's Checklist for the Mathematics Program
    - Figure A.5: Class Description Questionnaire

Each of these is documents is reviewed in turn. (The questionnaires are discussed in detail in Chapter 4.) The trainer then asks participant groups to begin compiling data from the questionnaires for the standard their group has been assigned. This data is collected in reference to specific indicators. For example, if a group has the responsibility for Standard 1 (Curriculum), the following would be collected for Indicator 1.3 dealing with problem solving.

Teacher Questionnaire: Instructional Approaches
[1.3] n. All six teachers reported that they never do "computer problem solving."

Teacher Questionnaire: Training
[1.3] All six teachers reported that they feel they are "not well prepared" to develop lessons with a problem-solving focus.

Principal's Checklist: D. Program Materials
[1.3] 2. The principal reported that he does not know if the processes of math—including reasoning, communications, representations, connections, and problem solving—are an integral part of the materials used in math.

The sample Class Description Questionnaire (Figure A.5) is representative of descriptions provided by Harder-Not-Smarter's six mathematics teachers. Although I developed this questionnaire primarily to aid the classroom observer in quickly identifying features in the classroom, it can also help in triangulating data. For example, this sample questionnaire indicates that Harder-Not-Smarter's teachers use traditional methods of instruction and have adopted a textbook that adheres to this philosophy. The teachers also appear to have students with individual education plans (IEPs) in their classrooms, and a review team would need to assess the type of training the teachers have had in accommodating these students.

Interviews

In the interview portion of the training, participants conduct mock interviews to gain experience in the process. For the mock interviews, some participants are reviewers and some take on the roles of parents, teachers, and the principal. Each mock interview lasts 15 to 20 minutes. Not all interview questions are asked, but the participants should be able to develop an understanding of the process and should be able to focus on specific questions that are relevant to their assigned standards.

Parent Interview. The trainer chooses two male and three female participants to "play" parents. The trainer gives each an index card that describes the parent that he or she will be playing. These descriptions are provided in Figure A.6. The trainer briefs the "parents," letting them know that they will need to represent the character traits that are described on their cards. These descriptions are based on actual parents interviewed during a school review.

The rest of the participants are given 15 minutes to interview the "parents" using questions in Figure B.10 in Appendix B. Not all of the questions in the figure can be asked during this short period, so the "reviewers" need to focus on questions relevant to their standards.

Teacher Interviews. The trainer selects a different group of five participants to play the mathematics teachers of Harder-Not-Smarter Middle School. The trainer gives each an index card that describes the background, practices, and attitudes of the teacher to be portrayed during the interviews. These descriptions given in Figure A.7 are based on five mathematics teachers interviewed at a middle school that went through the review process.

The trainer gives remaining participants the Elementary and Middle School Teacher Interview Questions (Figure B.7) and 20 minutes to interview the mathematics teachers as a group. This is usually the most popular part of the training. Some of the teachers really get into their roles and play them to the hilt.

Principal Interview. When I conduct training sessions, I always play the principal for this mock interview because I can use features of various principals that I've interviewed over the years to make a composite personality. The trainer may opt to play this role or select a "principal" from among the participants. The trainer should tell the person selected to play a principal who lacks a strong understanding of the mathematics program. The principal should be someone who has left much of the decision making for the mathematics program up to the department chair. The reviewers should complete the interview in approximately 10 minutes using the Principal Interview Questions in Figure B.11.

Student Interview. Time constraints preclude mock interviews of students. Instead, the trainer provides sample responses from students of Harder-Not-Smarter Middle School, given in Figure A.8.

Classroom Observations

To give participants experience in making classroom observations, the trainer will need videotaped lessons of three different classroom teachers. The trainer should be able to obtain videotapes either from a source such as a university or state department of education, or by requesting a teacher's (and principal's and students') permission to videotape a lesson.

I've used both methods to obtain videotapes for MPIR training. The Kentucky Department of Education requires that principals, supervisors, and supervising teachers receive regular training on evaluation of interns, and for that, training videotapes of lessons are used. I have used one of these tapes for the MPIR training. The tape shows a middle school math lesson in geometry and includes many examples of ineffective practices and of some practices that could have been effective if they had been more carefully planned.

Another videotape I use in training is of a master teacher working with a heterogeneous classroom. The class includes five special education students as well as several students gifted in mathematics. The algebra lesson incorporates both calculators and manipulatives to teach skills and concepts.

I recorded the videotape of the master teacher, and taping the lesson myself gave me an advantage: I could make sure all indicators were included. For example, I made it a point to walk around the classroom to record the layout of the room, storage facilities, student awards, student work, and other elements of the environment. I did this before the students entered the classroom and the lesson began. During the lesson, I was able to focus on aspects of the lesson that made it effective.

Videotapes made by others may not show all the elements that reviewers should observe during a lesson. In the videotape from the state department, some elements are not as evident as they could be. For example, the camera focuses primarily on the teacher and his students; the classroom environment is not as discernable. There are some papers on the wall, but it isn't possible to determine if any are student work. Two of the walls are never shown. And there isn't any evidence of the presence or lack of storage space for calculators, manipulatives, and other indicators of the physical environment.

Whatever the source of the videotaped lessons, the trainer should allow adequate time for the participants to observe the lessons, take notes, and discuss their observations as a group. On this day of training, the participants will watch two of the tapes (the third tape is shown on the second day of training). Each participant is given two copies of the Classroom Observation Instrument (Figure B.12), one to fill out for each lesson. Directions to the participants include two primary stipulations: (1) MPIR observations note aspects of an effective or ineffective lesson, and (2) observations do not target individual teachers or their idiosyncrasies. Consequently, participants should note general observations about practices and should particularly concentrate on those relevant to their assigned standard.

Discussion of Observed Lessons

The follow-up discussion to the observed lessons is conducted in two parts. First is the general discussion, in which participants cite examples from the lessons that they felt were effective or ineffective in achieving the perceived or stated objectives. These could be related to any of the review standards. Second is the discussion within each small group about observations relating to the assigned standard. During this discussion period, the trainer should remind the groups to record all evidence that is cited for the various indicators.

For example, the group of participants that is working on the curriculum standard may observe instances in which the students appear to use communication skills similar to Indicator 1.4 ("Students understand that communicating mathematically requires a variety of processes—observing, representing, discussing, analyzing, thinking creatively, reading, writing, and listening"). Each of these instances needs to be documented in writing. Even though the specific teacher will not be referenced in the final report, the accumulation of documentation from all of the teacher observations will be used as at least one source of data for the score that will be given for Indicator 1.4.

Small-Group Work: Scoring and Rationales

Each participant group is given 15 minutes to review all the data and to assign rubric scores for all the indicators for its assigned standard using the Guide for Rating MPIR Standards and Indicators (Figure B.2). Trainers should emphasize that scores should be based on at least three distinct sources of data chosen from interviews, observations, questionnaires, test results, and other materials. If for any reason inadequate data are collected for a specific indicator, then the group does not assign a rubric score. Instead, the indicator is marked with an N/O (not observed) or, in rare instances, N/A (not applicable). Each group then selects one indicator that received a high score and one that received a low score and writes an explanation for why each score was assigned.

Reporting

As time permits, each group reports to the others on their high- and low-scoring indicators, giving the rationales for the scores. The groups may also want to describe any problems that they may have encountered in collecting data, since there may have been insufficient data to assess the indicators due to the abbreviated schedule of the day.

Closure for Day One

Most participants in the training are only interested in learning about the review process. Either their school will be undergoing a review or they plan on using the information from the review tools (scoring guide, rubric, questionnaires, etc.) to make self-improvements to their mathematics program. In either case, most are not interested in training on how to write a report. With this in mind, after the discussions of the sores for indicators and standards, I mention briefly that review teams compile reports for schools in a similar manner, triangulating data for each indicator and standard and basing recommendations for the school on the results. Then I conclude the day with comments from the participants.

Usually, at least one participant has been on the receiving end of a review. If so, then I call on this individual to describe whether or not the review process and final report were valuable to the school's mathematics faculty. If there is no one in the group who has been through a review, then I share some of my experiences and note that, in general, reviewed schools have been very positive about both the process and the report that they have received. The trainer should always try to end the day on a high note and remember to thank participants for being actively involved in the training. I also remind participants that the second day of training will focus on the writing of the report.

Day Two

Review of Collected and Additional Data

The second day begins with a summary of all of the data collected on the first day by each small group. Most of the day's activities call for the participants working in their groups, so the trainer should arrange the seating so that each group collecting data for a specific standard is seated together. The trainer provides everyone with some additional data that will be needed for the groups to write their reports. The additional handouts provided to the participants include the following:

- Figure A.9: Additional Information from Parent Interviews
- Figure A.10: Additional School Information Collected
- Figure A.11: School Improvement Plan for Mathematics
- Figure 6.2: Classroom Observation Instrument and Script—Sample

The trainer should review with the participants the significance of these additional data for the report.

Third Classroom Observation

The participants then view the third videotaped lesson and note teacher practices using the Classroom Observation Instrument (Figure B.12). Together with the handout of Figure 6.2, which is the sample classroom observation for teacher Trey Ditional, and the two assessments of the lessons viewed on the first day of training, the participants now have four completed classroom observation forms to use for their reports.

Summarizing Classroom Observation Data

The next session focuses on summarizing observation data using the Classroom Observation Summary form, Figure B.14. This form has three tables, and the trainer should use a completed sample of the form to walk participants through the calculations (see Figure 6.3, p. 80).

After explaining the calculations for these forms, the trainer should ask participants to fill out the three tables in a blank Classroom Observation Summary form (Figure B.14), using data from the four observation instruments from the training. Typically, I provide calculators for those participants who need them to complete the form. The trainer should check the math on the forms and answer related questions.

Small-Group Work: Writing the Report

With the summary observation data completed, the training moves on to the writing process for the report. Each participant is given a list of tips for writing effective program review reports (see p. 106). The work of the entire MPIR and all that the school's faculty and students could gain from it can be destroyed by a poorly written report.

The remainder of the day is devoted to each small group, or "team," writing a report on its assigned standard. Each team must use the scoring rubric (Figure B.2) to assign numeric ratings for each indicator within its assigned standard. The narrative must justify scores of 1 or 2 and also indicate a rationale for assigning a score of 5. The trainer explains that the rationale for scores of 5 will be rephrased and included in the commendations portion of the final compiled report. Each team must also write one—and only one—recommendation for its assigned standard.

Reporting and Selecting Final Recommendations

In the last session of the day, each team presents its report on the team's assigned standard, including its recommendation, which is written on large easel paper. After all teams have made their presentations, the group decides as a whole which recommendations they want to include in the final report. The trainer should give the following instructions:

- At least one recommendation should be one that can be readily completed with near-immediate results.
- At least one recommendation should be feasible, even though it may take some time to achieve the desired change.
- Although all serious concerns should be addressed, the fewer the recommendations, the better.

Evaluation and Closing Comments

After selecting their recommendations, participants are asked to evaluate the training using a standard evaluation form provided by the district, school, or agency. The trainer should end the session with closing comments appropriate for the participants. For example, some participants may want to be part of a review team. In such instances, the trainer may want to state his or her willingness to serve as an intermediary to facilitate teams from one district performing a review for another district. The trainer can also encourage participants as individual educators or as a faculty or district to use the handbook and tools to informally evaluate practices and make improvements to the quality of their own mathematics programs.

FIGURE A.2	SUMMARY DATA FROM TEACHER SELF-PERCEPTION QUESTIONNAIRES

SCHOOL _Harder–Not–Smarter Middle School_

Your school leadership has requested that a team visit your school to conduct a Mathematics Program Improvement Review. This review will use self-reported data from this questionnaire as well as interviews and observations on the day of the visit. None of the collected data will be used to identify or single out any teacher. The report issued as a result of the visit will be an analysis of the overall mathematics program. After completing this form, return it to your school secretary to be placed anonymously in an envelope.

Compiler's Use

Professional Background and Affiliation

a. I have ____ total years of classroom teaching experience.

   Responses range from 0 (3 mos.) to 30 years

b. I have a certification to teach mathematics in the following grade-span (circle one):

   K–4   (K–6)   (K–8)   (5–8)   7–12   9–12

[6.5] c. I am a member of a state mathematics organization and/or NCTM.

   [0] Yes   [6] No

[6.5] d. I have attended a state, regional, or national mathematics conference in the past three years.

   [1] Yes   [5] No

Instructional Approaches

How often do you use each of the following techniques to teach math in your classes?

		Daily	Weekly	Monthly	Rarely	Never
[5.4]	a. Students solving real-life problems		6			
[2.2c]	b. Library research					6
[2.2c]	c. Mathematical writing (reflections)					6
[2.1]	d. Demonstrating/modeling	6				
[2.2d]	e. Students using manipulatives*			0	2	1
[2.2b]	f. Students in groups or teams		6			
[2.2b]	g. Group projects				5	1
[1.4]	h. Workbooks	4	2			
[2.3]	i. Calculator problem solving					6
[2.3]	j. Computer drill and practice					6
[2.4]	k. Review of skills and procedures	6				
[2.4]	l. Individual projects					6
[2.5]	m. Math-related field trips				4	2
[1.3]	n. Computer problem solving					6
[2.4]	o. Lecture with student note taking	5	1			

*Note: *Manipulatives* are items like geoboards, counters, algebra tiles, base-10 blocks, and so on. *Math tools* are single-purpose items like calculators, graph paper, rulers, compasses, and protractors.

FIGURE A.2	SUMMARY DATA FROM TEACHER SELF-PERCEPTION QUESTIONNAIRES *(continued)*

Compiler's Use

		Daily	Weekly	Monthly	Rarely	Never
[2.4]	p. Whole-class discussion	6				
[1.4]	q. Student-led discussion		6			
[2.4]	r. Individualized assignments				6	
[2.5]	s. Guest speakers					6
[5.3]	t. Interdisciplinary lessons				4	2

Concerns

To what extent is each of the following a problem that limits students' mathematics learning in your school?

		Not a Problem	Slight Problem	Moderate Problem	Major Problem
[10.1]	Availability of funds for mathematics materials and supplies	5	1		
[1.8]	Availability of appropriate curriculum materials (texts, calculators, software, etc.)	4	2		
[10.5]	Availability of and access to computers and other technology	6			
[9.1b]	Pressure to prepare students for state assessment			5	1
[8.2]	Availability of inservice opportunities for math teachers	5	1		

Training

Reflect on the inservice training you have received and evaluate how prepared you feel to perform the following activities.

		Not Well Prepared	Somewhat Prepared	Well Prepared	Very Well Prepared
[1.3]	Develop lessons with a problem-solving focus	6			
[1.6]	Use an approach that provides mathematical connections	3	3		
[2.1]	Develop lessons that provide opportunities for students to actively construct their own mathematical knowledge	6			
[2.2d]	Provide opportunities for students to use manipulatives to verify mathematical reasoning		3	3	
[2.2b]	Use cooperative learning groups				6
[2.2a]	Model multiple problem-solving strategies and have students apply what they have learned	1	3	2	
[2.2e]	Have students pose their own problems	6			
[3.1]	Teach classes containing students of heterogeneous abilities			1	5
[3.3]	Use appropriate techniques for students with special needs	4	2		
[3.1]	Teach classes containing students with different learning styles	6			
[5.4]	Connect math to real-life contexts and careers	6			
[9.3]	Use a variety of assessment strategies to measure students' success			6	

FIGURE A.2	SUMMARY DATA FROM TEACHER SELF-PERCEPTION QUESTIONNAIRES *(continued)*

Preparation

Do you feel well prepared—either through professional development or coursework—to do the following?

Compiler's Use		Not Well Prepared	Somewhat Prepared	Well Prepared	Very Well Prepared
[3.1]	Encourage participation of males in mathematics			5	1
[2.2c]	Listen/ask questions as students work in order to gauge their understanding.				6
[5.1]	Encourage students' interest in mathematics			6	
[2.1]	Develop students' conceptual understanding of mathematics.		2	4	
[3.1]	Encourage participation of minorities in mathematics	5	1		
[2.2f]	Take students' prior understanding into account when planning curriculum and instruction			4	2
[2.2d]	Manage a class of students engaged in hands-on/project-based work	6			
[1.8]	Use the textbook as a resource rather than the primary instructional tool.				6
[3.1]	Recognize and respond to student cultural diversity	6			
[2.3]	Use calculators/computers for mathematics learning games	6			
[7.2]	Involve parents in the mathematics education of their children	5	1		
[2.1]	Lead a class of students using investigative strategies		4	2	
[2.3]	Use calculators/computers for drill and practice.	2	4		
[2.3]	Use calculators/computers to demonstrate mathematics principles	6			
[2.3]	Use calculators/computers to collect and analyze data	6			
[2.3]	Use calculators/computers for simulations and applications	6			
[2.3]	Use the Internet in your mathematics teaching for general reference	4	2		
[2.3]	Use the Internet in your mathematics teaching for data acquisition	6			
[2.3]	Use the Internet in your mathematics teaching for collaborative projects with classes/individuals in other schools	6			

[6.4] In the past three years, how many hours of professional development have you had in mathematics or mathematics education?

5	None
	6 hours or less
1	7–15 hours
	16–35 hours
	More than 35 hours

FIGURE A.2	SUMMARY DATA FROM TEACHER SELF-PERCEPTION QUESTIONNAIRES *(continued)*

Compiler's Use

[6.4] If you have had professional development related to your mathematics teaching in the past three years, what was the format? (Check all that apply.)

- [5] N/A
- [1] Attendance at a workshop on mathematics teaching
- [ ] Observation of other teachers teaching mathematics as part of your own professional development (formal or informal)
- [ ] Study group of teachers on mathematics teaching issues
- [ ] A formal college/university course in the teaching of mathematics (math ed)
- [ ] A formal college/university mathematics course
- [ ] Service as a mentor and/or peer coach in mathematics teaching as part of a formal arrangement that is recognized or supported by the school or district
- [ ] Attendance at a national or state mathematics teacher association meeting
- [ ] Collaboration on mathematics teaching issues with a group of teachers at a distance using telecommunications (distance learning)

Instruction

How much emphasis does your instruction place on each of the following elements?

		Not Much	Some	Moderate	Extensive
[2.1]	Mathematical concepts				6
[2.2a]	Problem solving				6
[2.1]	Mathematical reasoning			5	1
[1.7a]	Computational skills				6
[1.6]	How mathematics ideas connect with one another		3	3	
[5.1]	Increasing interest in mathematics	4	2		
[5.1]	Preparing for further study in mathematics				6
[1.7a]	Mathematical algorithms/procedures				6
[1.7a]	Ability to perform computations with speed and accuracy				6
[9.1b]	Standardized test preparation				6
[1.4]	Expression of mathematical ideas (orally and in writing)	5	1		
[1.6]	The logical structure of mathematics	6			
[5.4]	Applications of mathematics in business and industry	6			
[5.4]	The history and nature of mathematics	6			

[2.4] How much homework do you assign in an average school <u>week</u>?

- [ ] 0–10 minutes
- [ ] 11–20 minutes
- [ ] 21–40 minutes
- [ ] 41–90 minutes
- [4] 91–120 minutes
- [2] More than 120 minutes

FIGURE A.2	SUMMARY DATA FROM TEACHER SELF-PERCEPTION QUESTIONNAIRES *(continued)*

Compiler's Use

[2.3]

Technology Use

In which of the following ways do students use calculators or computers in your math class? (Check all that apply.)

- [6] Do drill and practice
- [ ] Demonstrate mathematics principles
- [ ] Play mathematics learning games
- [ ] Do probability simulations
- [ ] Collect data using sensors or probes
- [ ] Retrieve or exchange data
- [ ] Solve problems using simulations
- [ ] Take a test or quiz

[1.8]

Resources/Equipment

Indicate the degree of use of each of the following in your math instruction.

	Do Not Use (Not Needed)	Do Not Use (Not Available)	Use
Overhead projector	[ ]	[ ]	[6]
Videotape player	[6]	[ ]	[ ]
Videodisc player	[6]	[ ]	[ ]
DVD player	[6]	[ ]	[ ]
Four-function calculator (class set)	[ ]	[ ]	[6]
Fraction calculators (class set)	[6]	[ ]	[ ]
Graphing calculators (class set)	[6]	[ ]	[ ]
Scientific calculators (class set)	[6]	[ ]	[ ]
Computers	[6]	[ ]	[ ]
Calculator/computer lab interfacing devices	[6]	[ ]	[ ]
Computers with Internet connection	[2]	[4]	[ ]

[1.8]

Use of Textbooks/Commercial Programs

Which of the following best describes your use of textbooks or alternative commercial programs in your math classes?

- [6] Use one textbook or program all or most of the time
- [ ] Use multiple textbooks or programs
- [ ] Do not use a textbook or commercial program

FIGURE A.3	PRINCIPAL'S SELF-PERCEPTION QUESTIONNAIRE

SCHOOL Harder-Not-Smarter Middle School

Compiler's Use	**Professional Development**
[3.4]	1. To what extent are professional development policies and practices focused on student needs (heterogeneous classes, learning styles, multiple intelligences, brain-based research, abilities, etc.)? We provide four days of professional development annually. One of these days is provided by the district office and always involves a state requirement (such as blood pathogens or sexual harassment). The school provides one day on integration of reading into the different content areas. The final two days are flexible days in which teachers can be approved for training that meets their specific needs.
[6.8] [6.5]	2. What local, state, and federal funds are made available to the school for professional development to support innovative delivery systems, such as teacher academies; school-university partnerships; teacher networks; internships; courses for college credit; and active involvement in local, regional, state, or national professional mathematics associations? The district office and I encourage teachers to become members of their professional organizations and attend the relevant conferences that are provided.
[6.4]	3. What professional development needs related to mathematics have teachers identified? Our mathematics scores are below the scores of other schools in the district and state. Mathematics will be a focus this next school year.
[6.2] [8.5c]	4. To what extent are there opportunities for continuous, sustained professional development with ongoing study of a topic and in-school coaching? Until now we have focused on reading, but we will begin providing professional development training in mathematics next year.
[6.4]	5. Have teachers been trained on the program/materials/textbooks adopted for teaching mathematics? All of our math teachers have been trained on the adopted materials except for Ms. Newbie, who was hired this year.

FIGURE A.3	**PRINCIPAL'S SELF-PERCEPTION QUESTIONNAIRE** *(continued)*

Compiler's Use

[6.8]

6. What kinds of opportunities are there for you and your teachers to broaden and deepen your knowledge of mathematics subject matter; content-specific pedagogy; child pedagogy and adolescent development; new assessment strategies; how to address learning differences and disabilities; how to expand the range of teaching strategies; how to use technologies as part of the curriculum; and, how to work well with parents?

Teachers can study any of these topics during their flexible inservice training days.

[9.7]

7. Does your school use mathematics achievement standards and professional teaching standards as a basis for professional development design?

All professional development programs must be approved by me and by the district instructional supervisor.

Resources

[10.1]
[10.5]

1. How are resources (money, teachers, other staff, materials, equipment, and facilities) allocated to the teaching of mathematics? Is there sufficient technology available to meet the needs of the mathematics program?

All teachers are provided a budget of $300 annually. In addition, our budget is set to cover as many photocopies as the teachers would like to use.

[10.1]

2. What share of the total budget goes to support mathematics instruction in regular classrooms?

All teachers receive the same allocation regardless of what they teach. We believe in an equitable distribution of our available funds.

[6.6]

3. How much time do teachers have to plan and work together in teams and schoolwide?

Each teacher has two periods of planning daily. The teams are required to meet once a week. Rarely does this meeting take more than one of these periods.

[6.6]

4. How much individual planning time do teachers have each week?

See above—at least eight periods each week are set aside for individual planning.

[9.8]
[10.4]

5. Are funds available to support extracurricular and cocurricular activities, such as remediation and enrichment programs, clubs, competitions, and field trips?

The state provides funding for an after-school tutorial program. We also have some funds for field trips—up to one per year.

FIGURE A.4	PRINCIPAL'S CHECKLIST FOR THE MATHEMATICS PROGRAM

SCHOOL _Harder-Not-Smarter Middle School_

The Mathematics Program Improvement Review includes self-reported data that is cross-referenced with observational and interview data. As the instructional leader of your school, your perceptions and understanding of the mathematics program are critical to the analysis of the program. Consequently, we need you to complete this checklist, the results of which will be included in the program analysis. Thank you.

Please mark under the heading "Y" for Yes, "N" for No, and "?" for "No Data."

Compiler's Use	**A. School Organization**	Y	N	?
[6.1a]	1. Does your school have written instructional goals and objectives describing what students should be learning in math?	✔		
[1.1]	2. Is there a written plan describing coordinated and sequential math experiences for all grade levels or courses?	✔		
[1.5]	3. Is the school's math curriculum aligned to the state objectives?	✔		
[1.3] [7.2]	4. Did development of the math curriculum involve teachers, administrators, parents, and anyone else responsible for implementing and maintaining that curriculum?	✔		
[9.6]	5. Does the curriculum provide for vertical articulation in math instruction/learning (i.e., coordination with feeder schools)?		✔	
[1.9] [6.1a]	6. Do all classroom math teachers understand the goals, curriculum, and time allocations for math instruction?			✔
[8.6]	7. Is adequate time for teaching math scheduled on a daily basis?	✔		
[10.1]	8. Does the annual budget specify funds to adequately finance the math program?	✔		
[9.1]	9. Do you regularly re-examine the math goals, teaching/learning strategies, and materials?		✔	
[10.5]	10. Are there budgeted funds to cover costs for math materials, supplies, software, equipment (e.g., calculators), and books?	✔		
[10.1]	11. Are teachers permitted to use petty cash funds to buy consumables for math?		✔	
[6.5]	12. Does the budget include funds for professional development for math (e.g., consultants for local programs, travel to conferences, and teacher attendance at conventions)?	✔		
[10.4]	13. Does the budget provide for transportation and other costs for activities, such as field trips?	✔		
Compiler's Use	**B. Principal Leadership**	Y	N	?
[7.4]	1. Do you conduct public awareness sessions about math with parents?		✔	
[8.2]	2. Do classroom math teachers have an opportunity to provide input into the professional development plan?		✔	
[9.7]	3. Do you feel the math section of the state assessment is a valid measure of your school's math program's goals, curriculum, and experiences?		✔	
[9.1]	4. Over the past two years, have you assessed the effectiveness of your math program using curricular reviews, teacher surveys, student interviews, review of state test data, and other means?		✔	

FIGURE A.4	PRINCIPAL'S CHECKLIST FOR THE MATHEMATICS PROGRAM *(continued)*			
Compiler's Use	**B. Principal Leadership** (continued)	Y	N	?
[9.7]	5. Have your school's state assessment math scores shown a positive trend over the past several years?		✔	
[9.9]	6. Do you evaluate the quality of teachers' math instruction?	✔		
[9.7]	7. Do your students perform as well as or better than the state average on the math portion of the state assessment?		✔	
[8.5b]	8. Are you an active participant in math professional development programs with your teachers?		✔	
[7.3]	9. Are parents and the general community made aware of the school math program through parent–teacher meetings, math contests, or local media publicity?		✔	
[8.4]	10. If a committee is formed to select a new math program/textbook, will you be an active participant?			✔
[9.4a]	11. Is the school's policy for grading and evaluating students consistent with the math program's objectives and instruction?			✔
Compiler's Use	**C. Support for Teachers**	Y	N	?
[8.5e]	1. Do you let the teachers know that *you* are interested in good math education by discussing best practices in math?	✔		
[8.5a]	2. Do your teachers understand that they are expected to teach math as stated in the curriculum?	✔		
[1.2] [2.6]	3. Does the school's math curriculum offer teachers specific skills, techniques, and materials they can use in their classrooms?		✔	
[6.8]	4. Is there a means for teachers to try out new experiences before they use them in their classrooms?		✔	
[6.5]	5. Have most of your teachers had recent exposure to professional workshops and meetings about math sponsored by the school or school system, regional education agencies, colleges, or professional organizations?	✔		
[6.5]	6. Does the school provide funding for released time for teachers to attend programs on improving math education?		✔	
[1.9]	7. Does the school maintain a professional library of math journals and other resources, and do the math teachers use it regularly?			✔
[8.5c]	8. Are the teachers given a written copy of what you are looking for in your walk-throughs?		✔	
Compiler's Use	**D. Program Materials**	Y	N	?
[2.1]	1. Do the math texts and materials encourage students to explore, discover, and find answers for themselves?			✔
[1.4]	2. Are the processes of math—including reasoning, communications, representations, connections and problem solving—an integral part of the materials used in math?			✔
[1.6]	3. Is your math program aligned with both NCTM standards and state objectives?			✔

FIGURE A.4	PRINCIPAL'S CHECKLIST FOR THE MATHEMATICS PROGRAM *(continued)*			
Compiler's Use	**D. Program Materials** (continued)	Y	N	?
[2.6]	4. Are all written materials consistent with the math goals and objectives set by your school?	✔		
[3.1]	5. Do program materials go from the simple to the complex and appear to fit the students' appropriate developmental levels?	✔		
[5.1]	6. Do the materials draw upon the students' own interests and experiences?			✔
[5.4]	7. Do the program materials introduce students to math-related careers?	✔		
[6.4]	8. Is the teacher's guide useful as a planning tool (rather than as a crutch)?	✔		
	E. Walk-Through Observations and Informal Discussions	Y	N	?
[8.5d]	1. Are the attitudes of the math teachers positive when you discuss math with them/ when they teach?	✔		
[2.2]	2. Do the teachers make full use of two-way discussion, reading, writing, small-group projects, lecturing, cooperative group work, and individualized instruction?	✔		
[2.2a]	3. Are the teachers teaching skills, concepts, applications, and problem solving?		✔	
[2.1]	4. Do teachers give students opportunities to investigate and do mathematics independently?			✔
[2.1]	5. Are students given opportunities to explore math materials before a concept is introduced?			✔
[2.1]	6. Do teachers ask open-ended, divergent questions and give all students time to respond?			✔
[2.2f]	7. Do teachers listen to what the students have to say?	✔		
[3.3]	8. Are students with special needs given opportunities to become involved in math activities?	✔		
[5.3]	9. Are teachers regularly connecting mathematics to other subjects like writing, science, or art?			✔
[3.3]	10. Are students with limited reading skills achieving in the math program?		✔	
[4.1]	11. Do your school's students seem to like mathematics?	✔		
[4.1]	12. When you talk with students about math, are their attitudes positive?	✔		
[2.4]	13. Is a substantial part of class time in mathematics spent on activities beyond reading, listening, and pencil-and-paper work?		✔	
[2.2f]	14. Do teachers use alternative assessments to continually monitor how well their students are acquiring math skills and concepts and how their students feel about mathematics?	✔		
[2.2e]	15. Do students join freely in discussions about math activities, often initiating their own observations and ideas?	✔		
[2.2b]	16. Are there lots of opportunities for individualized math projects, independent work, and peer-group tutoring?			✔

FIGURE A.4	PRINCIPAL'S CHECKLIST FOR THE MATHEMATICS PROGRAM *(continued)*			
Compiler's Use	**F. Resources and Facilities**	Y	N	?
[8.7]	1. Does each teacher have adequate storage space for math supplies, equipment, and materials?		✔	
[1.6]	2. Are math materials (e.g., calculators) sufficiently available so that all students can work with them?		✔	
[1.9]	3. Does the school library have a good collection of up-to-date books about math?			✔
[5.2]	4. Are there displays of student work in math classrooms as well as in the building?		✔	
[5.2]	5. Do math classes show evidence of activities—bulletin boards, student projects, learning centers?	✔		
[1.9], [10.5]	6. Are math supplies and materials regularly replaced?	✔		
[10.5]	7. Do teachers have easy access to computers that their students can use in math learning?			✔
[10.3]	8. Do teachers collectively determine the need for mathematics resources, and is the ordering process reasonable, simple, and efficient?	✔		
[10.1]	9. Are all those who teach math involved in selecting what will be used for instruction and reference?	✔		

G. Summary

I. Checklist Response Totals

Yes: 29   No: 21   No Data: 15

2. On a scale of 1–5, with 5 being the highest, what overall rating would you give to your school's math program?
4

3. List the major strengths of your school's math program.

– Teachers
– Parental support
– Resources

4. List the areas of the program most in need of improvement.

– Professional development
– More use of technology
– Focus on every child's learning

5. List five priority actions for next year.

1. Professional development.
2. Purchase computers for math instruction.
3. Increase true collaboration between regular ed and special ed teachers.
4. Analyze state test data more quickly as a faculty.
5. Replace the retiring teacher with a real "go getter."

FIGURE A.5	CLASS DESCRIPTION QUESTIONNAIRE

SCHOOL *Harder-Not-Smarter Middle School*

Teacher *Rather B. Wright*   Room # *204*

Grade Level and Subject *7th grade math*   # of Students *29*

IEP Students *2*   # IDEA/Section 504 Students *0*   # G/T Students *0*

Grouping approaches used: (homogenous/heterogeneous/other _____)

1. Name of the mathematics text or other materials used:

   Traditional Mathematics and worksheets

2. A brief description of the lesson planned during MPIR observation:

   Check homework, explain how to do the next lesson by demonstrating examples on the board, assign homework, and provide individual assistance to those who need it.

3. Professional organizations you belong to, journals you read or subscribe to on a regular basis, and professional development you have attended in the past three years:

   No professional organizations. I read Teacher and Instructor. I've never attended any math inservice training.

4. Technology or software used in your class:

   The students use calculators to check their work, but not until they have shown me that they have worked everything out for themselves.

5. Other information the review team should know about you or your students:

FIGURE A.6	PARENT DESCRIPTIONS

Parent 1: Mrs. Gon

Mrs. Gon's daughter, Polly, is an 8th grader who is bright and likes math and school. Mrs. Gon believes that the math teachers in the school are very good. Her daughter's teacher this year is using the textbook as the basis for his math instruction. Polly has described several geometry activities that have been done at school—string art, geometric constructions, holiday ornaments from student-made geometric solids, and others. On parent conference day, the teacher indicated that Polly definitely shows some interest in math and willingly participates in math activities and class discussion. That is the only time that Mrs. Gon has been in the school this year. She is *very* interested in Polly's education and is willing to work with the school in any way that will improve her daughter's educational opportunities. She has never been asked to do any volunteer work, even though she offered to help at the parent conference day.

Parent 2: Mr. Fox

Mr. Fox has two sons in the middle school: Wiley, who is repeating the 7th grade, and Sly, a 7th grader receiving mathematics instruction through a self-contained special education program.

Wiley told his dad that the reason that he failed math last year is that the teacher just talked to the whole class all the time and never came around much to give him help. He said that sometimes the teacher put the students in groups to do homework, but the other students didn't really show him how to do the work; they just let him copy what they were doing (when they weren't making fun of him). Wiley said that he doesn't like math because he is always told to do the same kinds of problems over and over again. Wiley's teacher this year said that she assigns homework at least three nights a week, but Wiley has time to do the assignments in class. Wiley doesn't like to do the work in class ("It's not any fun"), and he hardly ever does it when he gets home ("Playing with friends, playing video games, and watching TV is more fun than homework").

Mr. Fox's younger son, Sly, is passing all of his courses. Sly doesn't do any homework either, but his teacher said that is because she has a small class and she works with each student during class to help them get their work done. Mr. Fox wonders whether Wiley would be better off in a special education class for his math (an arrangement like Sly's), but no one has ever talked to him about that possibility.

Parent 3: Mrs. Root

Mrs. Root's daughter, Ima, is an 8th grader this year. Ima is in the advanced math class and loves her teacher. She says that her teacher believes students learn best by doing things and encourages students to use a wide variety of math manipulatives. The manipulatives are always available to students who want to use them for practice or for problem solving. The teacher often asks the students to explain their math work—sometimes in writing, but usually in oral discussions. Mrs. Root feels confident that Ima is getting the background she'll need to succeed in high school algebra next year. Ima is also on the school academic team and won recognition last year in the mathematics competition. She has been doing well this year and hopes that she will get her name on the plaque in the school display case again for her achievement in the mathematics competition.

FIGURE A.6	PARENT DESCRIPTIONS *(continued)*

Parent 4: Mrs. Lution

Mrs. Lution's son, Saul, is a 6th grader taking advanced math. Although Saul was identified as "gifted" when he was in elementary school, he frequently got into trouble in math class all the way through elementary school. So far, he hasn't been in as much trouble in middle school, but Mrs. Lution doesn't feel like Saul has achieved to his potential. Saul says that he is frustrated because he can often work the problems in his head or with just a few steps, but the teacher requires him to write every step because this is the process she has taught. Saul sometimes has to help others when they get stuck. Although there seem to be adequate math manipulatives and calculators in the classroom, Saul says that much of the math instruction involves the teacher using overhead manipulatives to "demonstrate" the math, followed by the students completing problems assigned from the textbook. Mrs. Lution has not been asked to contribute anything for math class and does not really feel comfortable visiting the school. She is of the opinion that "gifted" children are not challenged by the school, particularly in math, and is contemplating sending Saul to a private school next year.

Parent 5: Mr. Rhythm

Mr. Rhythm's son, Algo, is in the 7th grade and seems to be a class leader—not only of his math class, but of the entire grade level. Algo loves to participate in school activities—both clubs and sports (he is on both the football and basketball teams)—and is still able to maintain good grades. Math has always been his favorite subject. His teacher oftentimes divides the class into groups, where students read the lesson overview and begin the assignments together. The teacher doesn't provide whole-class instruction unless several groups get hung up, and usually only works with small groups when they ask questions or express concerns. The students are each responsible for completing the assignments in their notebooks, and each is graded individually on tests and quizzes. Algo says that the teacher sometimes demonstrates concepts with materials on the overhead when several groups don't understand the lesson, and groups have the option to use the materials whenever they want (but rarely do). Mr. Rhythm has heard some parents complain that they can see why so many students fail math—the teacher doesn't teach—but Algo seems to be doing well with this arrangement.

FIGURE A.7	TEACHER DESCRIPTIONS

Teacher 1: Mrs. Flo Meter (6th grade)

Mrs. Meter has taught 6th grade mathematics at the school for 18 years after graduating with a teaching certificate for grades 1–8. She enjoys working with students at the 6th grade level. Even though she does use the textbook for many of her daily assignments, she has also developed some favorite units over the years. She loves to teach these units, especially the unit on measurement. The state test includes measurement among the tested concepts, and her students always do well. The curriculum for most of the year, however, deals with computation of whole numbers with some work on decimals and a little on fractions. She doesn't do much with geometry other than teach the formulas. The only statistics that she teaches is reading and making bar graphs. Among the activities in the statistics unit are student-conducted surveys done of other 6th, 7th, and 8th graders in the school.

Mrs. Meter is very popular with the parents because the students in her math classes always earn good grades (very few receive a grade below a *B;* most make *A*s). She is popular with students because she doesn't give very much homework. Students usually don't have more than one worksheet to be completed every three or four weeks. Homework is usually completed in class.

Teacher 2: Mrs. Gracie Kindness (6th grade)

Mrs. Kindness taught for 11 years at a feeder elementary school before coming to the middle school to teach 6th grade mathematics 12 years ago. She is certified to teach grades 1–6. She has been to a couple of state mathematics teacher conferences since coming to the middle school. She lacks confidence in her ability to teach mathematics and wants to do what is right. Mrs. Kindness gets along well with all of the other teachers (except she is not sure yet about Ms. Newbie because "she does things differently than the rest of us").

All of the students love Mrs. Kindness. She is known to her students and the community as "Mrs. Gracie." She is always complimenting her students and telling them how well they are doing. Students are always happy to do the worksheets that she assigns because she places stickers on them before returning them. She does have a class set of calculators, but students can only use them to check their work. They have to show her the completed worksheet before they can get a calculator out of the caddy. She allows students to use base-10 blocks or counters for some selected activities.

Teacher 3: Mr. Rather B. Wright (7th grade)

Mr. Wright has been teaching 7th grade mathematics at the school for his entire teaching career: 23 years. He grew up in the community and went to the junior high school that was the predecessor for HNS Middle School. He graduated from the district high school, attended the local community college, and then transferred to a university known for its teacher education program, where he earned a degree in mathematics.

Mr. Wright is a strong proponent of students mastering basic skills. Students in his class are not permitted to use calculators. He assigns homework regularly: usually a worksheet he has created, but occasionally problems from the textbook. Students are permitted to work on homework assignments in groups.

Mr. Wright seldom uses whole-class instruction to teach a lesson. He generally has students read the lesson openers in the textbook and then work on the examples in their group. Once they begin the assignment, they can ask him for help if no one in the group understands what to do. He sometimes uses manipulatives in his demonstrations. He has enough of some types of manipulatives (geoboards, fraction circles, counters) for all of his students to use if they like.

Mr. Wright has not taken any additional mathematics classes since he received his degree. He rarely attends professional development related to mathematics (none within the past five years). He has never attended a state, regional, or national mathematics teacher conference.

FIGURE A.7	TEACHER DESCRIPTIONS *(continued)*

Teacher 4: Mr. Trey Ditional (8th grade)

Mr. Ditional grew up in the community in which he now teaches. Everyone in the community seems to know him. His reputation is so strong that even those parents who didn't have him for a teacher said that they did, and they all have their favorite "Ditional stories" to tell. He has taught 8th grade mathematics for 30 years. He likes to weave stories into his lessons that relate to mathematics. Some are related to careers of his former students, some are related to basketball (which he used to coach), but most are whimsical, lighthearted stories that are meant to both interest the students and make the class entertaining.

Mr. Ditional has never allowed his students to use calculators, and he is not about to start now. He does sometimes use a computer and an LCD projector to teach mathematics using favorite Web sites, but his students never use a computer. Nor are students allowed to use manipulatives. He says they are "toys" and have no place in an 8th grade classroom.

For assignments, he uses the textbook or workbook pages from the adopted program, but often uses copies of favorite worksheets that he has had for years. His tests are variations of ones he has always given. Students must show the processes they use to solve the problems. Student solutions are not counted as correct unless they also show all of the work. No partial credit is given if they miss a sign or if they fail to reduce a fraction. If the problem says to work out the solution to the nearest 10th and the student gives the answer to the nearest 100th, it is incorrect. "Part of my math class is learning how to follow directions. It is a life skill that they will need as much as they will need the math."

Mr. Ditional is the school's mathematics department chair.

Teacher 5: Ms. Ima Newbie (8th grade)

Ms. Newbie joined the math faculty this year after teaching in another school for five years. Although she grew up in the state, she is new to the community. She graduated from the state university, where her mathematics education class emphasized the national mathematics standards. Her husband is also a mathematics educator (an instructor at the local community college).

Ms. Newbie believes that mathematics is more than skills. She agrees with the NCTM that a strong mathematics program should also include the development of reasoning, problem solving, communications, connections, and representations. She tries to include these in her classroom through frequent use of cooperative learning, manipulatives, and student projects and presentations. She has tried to develop integrated lessons with teachers within other departments, but has not had any success so far.

She used money from the budget allocated to her to purchase some calculators and encouraged her students to purchase their own calculators. She believes that students in her 8th grade mathematics classes should be able to use calculators at any time. Although she does teach the computational processes (integer rules, etc.), she emphasizes problem solving. She has some manipulatives that she has accumulated on her own over the years that she has been teaching, but she doesn't have all that she would like to have. She frequently borrows manipulatives from her husband's mathematics department for specific lessons.

Although the other mathematics teachers are polite to her, she feels like they haven't really accepted her into the department yet. She believes that it is just because the rest of them have been together so long that it will take some time for them to get used to somebody new in the department.

FIGURE A.8	STUDENT INTERVIEW RESPONSES

SCHOOL Harder-Not-Smarter Middle School

INTERVIEW GROUP INFORMATION 12 students, 4 from each grade level: 6th, 7th, and 8th

Compiler's Use	Question	Response

[1.3]	1. Which of the following do you think is most important?
	  a. Basic skills (math facts, computation)
	  b. Concepts (e.g., place value)
	  c. Real-life applications
	  d. Problem solving
	Which do you think your teacher feels is most important?
		6th graders—all said basic skills
		
		7th graders—2 said basic skills and 1 said applications; 1 no opinion
		
		8th grader—2 said concepts and 1 said applications; 1 no opinion
		
		All said that their teachers seemed to think basic skills were most important, except for Ms. Newbie, who emphasizes problem solving.

[1.4]
[1.4]
[1.7e]
[1.7h]
[2.5]
[2.5]
[2.5]
[2.5c]
	2. Which of the following have you done this year?
	  a. Described answers to problems in writing
	  b. Wrote a math report
	  c. Created your own math models or design
	  d. Collected data through a survey
	  e. Did a probability experiment
	  f. Went on a math field trip
	  g. Did a math project
	  h. Discussed different ways to solve math problems
		a. All said they had done some of this.
		b. None has written a math report.
		c. Only in Ms. Newbie's class . . .
		d. Only in Ms. Newbie's class . . .
		e. All said yes, but only Ms. Newbie's students have done an experiment using manipulatives.
		f. None
		g. None
		h. All said they have discussed different procedures for doing problems.

[1.6]
[2.4]
	3. Which of these best describes how your teacher begins a new lesson?
	  a. Teacher reviews what you have learned previously and talks about how it will relate to the new lesson.
	  b. Teacher goes straight into the new lesson without discussing previous lessons.
		a. Ms. Newbie usually does this.
		
		b. The other teachers do this.

FIGURE A.8	STUDENT INTERVIEW RESPONSES *(continued)*

Compiler's Use	Question	Response

[1.4]	4. Does it help you to learn math by . . .
	  a. Listening to how other students solved problems?
	  b. Writing so that your teacher understands your thoughts?
		a. Students agreed. "I usually learn more from another student than I do from the teacher."
		b. "All of our tests are multiple choice, so we don't ever have to write anything."

[2.2b]	5. Do you work with other students in groups? What kind of groups (e.g., small groups, large groups, pairs)? Do you feel that group work helps you to learn better or not?	7th graders: "We do some group work—usually working on homework with a partner." All 8th graders said yes. "It does help me to talk it out with someone else."
[2.2d]	6. Do you use manipulatives? Which do you use most often?	7th: "We never use manipulatives." 8th: "Ms. Newbie has us use manipulatives at least once every week or so. In her class, we can use whatever we want to help us understand the problem."

[2.4]	7. Do you have math homework? Does it take you more than 20 minutes on average to complete your homework?
	
	What type of homework do you usually do? Is it usually
	  a. Textbook problems to practice a new concept?
	  b. A real-life application, such as collecting data?
	  c. Writing in a math journal?
		7th: "We usually get most of our homework done in class."
		"It usually takes less than 20 minutes."
		
		7th: Homework always comes from the math textbook or worksheets.
		
		Students in other grades agreed or were noncommittal.

[2.2a]	8. What are some of the problem-solving strategies you have used in math this year?	Most said addition, subtraction, multiplication, and division. Only Ms. Newbie's students gave appropriate responses (working backward, guess-and-check, make a table).
[4.2]	9. Do you sometimes wish that the math was more difficult or more challenging?	All but two replied yes. "Math class is boring."

FIGURE A.8	STUDENT INTERVIEW RESPONSES *(continued)*

Compiler's Use	Question	Response

[2.2f]	10. Which of these best describes your teacher's method of getting answers to questions?
	  a. Calls only on students whose hands are raised
	  b. Calls on no one; students call out the answers each time
	  c. Calls on students in a predictable pattern, like going down the row
	  d. Calls on students randomly
		Most replied that their teacher usually had a combination of calling on those whose hands are raised and calling on students randomly (although they said that people selected randomly were usually ones who were talking or not paying attention).

[9.3]	11. Which of the following types of tests have you taken this year?
	  a. Multiple choice
	  b. Short answer
	  c. Matching
	  d. Problems in which you have to show all your work
	  e. Problems where you have to explain or justify your solution (open response)
	
	Do you get partial credit on test questions in which you have to show your work?
		All said that all tests have been multiple choice.
		
		Students don't have to show their work and don't get any partial credit for it if they do.

[5.1]	12. Does your teacher ever ask you what you are interested in and then find math problems related to those interests?	Only Ms. Newbie does this.
[5.4]	13. Who in the school talks about how math is important later—in high school, in college, or in the working world? Your math teacher? Principal? Counselor? Who tells you what kind of math is needed in particular careers?	Teacher and counselor Teacher
[1.8] [2.3]	14. How often do you use computers in math? How do you use them?	"We don't use computers in math." "Sometimes the teacher will show us something using her computer."
	15. What would you change about the math program to improve it or make it more interesting?	"Do stuff like the students do in Ms. Newbie's class." Use computer games. Play math games. Make it fun. Don't give so much homework.
	16. What do you like about the math program that you think the school should keep and not change?	Ms. Newbie

FIGURE A.9	ADDITIONAL INFORMATION FROM PARENT INTERVIEWS

- All the parents felt that the school has very good mathematics teachers who are willing to stay after school to help students who have questions.

- The school Web site has each teacher's e-mail address for students or parents to send questions, but none of the parents have ever sent an e-mail to any teacher. Two of the parents don't have Internet access at home or work.

- The parents remember getting the state report card mailed home in the fall, and they think the math scores went up, but no one knows for sure.

- Teachers gave each student a copy of a course syllabus on the first day of school. Two parents were not aware of this. Those who had seen a syllabus said that it included a grading policy to show how much of the grade came from tests, quizzes, participation, homework, notebooks, and so on, but none could remember the exact percentages.

- One of the parents was a member of the curriculum committee and two were PTA officers, but none could remember ever attending a general school meeting to discuss the math program (or any other academic area).

- The school doesn't have a regular mailing such as a school newsletter. The school has a newsletter club sponsored by a language arts teacher. The group of students in this club put out a newsletter once or twice a semester. It mostly contains stories about students, sports, dances, etc.

- The parents think the principal is a very strong instructional leader who runs a tight ship. They don't know what his teaching background is, but a couple of parents remember that he used to be a coach.

- The only field trips the parents know about are those made by the academic teams.

- All but one of the parents feel that the mathematics program is generally pencil-and-paper and not much hands-on (except for Ms. Newbie's classes).

- The school has a career day each spring, but the parents weren't aware of any career discussion in math classes.

- The parents felt that the emphasis in math seemed to be on skills—getting the students able to do the problems in the text—although one parent said that her child's teacher seemed to really emphasize problem solving.

- Except for one parent who had a special education student, none of the parents were aware of students having any experiences in measurement of any type (linear, area, capacity, etc.) in math classes.

- The parents thought the teachers were fair to everyone. They didn't think there were any biases or discrimination based on gender, race, ability, or special education status. However, when teaching to learning styles was explained, all but one of the parents thought that the teachers may be weak in that area. They did think they were doing the best they could considering the number of students the teachers had to work with each day.

- None of the parents had been asked for suggestions, to serve on a committee related to the mathematics program, or to be a guest speaker in a math class.

- All the parents thought that the school goal was to improve the math scores on the state test.

FIGURE A.10	ADDITIONAL SCHOOL INFORMATION COLLECTED

- The school's math curriculum is not available for review. Teachers comment that they think someone worked on the curriculum last summer. One teacher remarked that she thinks that Mrs. _____ has a copy. The principal states that a consultant assisted the district with writing a math curriculum last summer for two days.

- Classroom observations in some classrooms included the following:

  - Students taking a test during three periods of one teacher's class.

  - Students doing seatwork/homework for at least 30 minutes of each 48-minute class in one teacher's classes.

  - One teacher demonstrating multiplication of fractions using overhead fraction pieces and transparencies.

  - One teacher letting students use calculators to check their answers after they had completed all the problems by hand first.

  - One teacher demonstrating dropping a ball from different heights and measuring the height of each bounce. One student then recorded the data on the board for other students to record on their papers. Students then graphed their results.

- Teachers report that they are evaluated regularly. The principal states that he "doesn't have a math background, but he has strong teachers and trusts them to know what to teach and how to teach it." The principal, teachers, and students report that whenever the principal is in classrooms conducting observation, he sits in the back and is not involved in the lesson. The principal states that he attends all professional development sessions with his teachers. However, both he and the teachers say there haven't been any math professional development offerings for quite some time.

- Teachers say that each receives $250 to $300 per year for instructional materials and supplies, but that "we are luckier than some because we can have as much paper as we need for copies." The principal says that teachers can get anything else they need or can attend professional conferences (with substitutes paid, but not registration or other expenses) as long as they "make a good case for it."

- Each math class has one networked computer that appears to be used for administrative purposes (recording grades and attendance, e-mails to staff, etc.). Students do not report any use of technology in their math classes.

- The principal states that he often requires teachers to submit assessment items along with their lesson plans when he collects them each week. He states that he does not "go over every detail" of the items or the lesson plans, but checks to see that the teachers are completing them.

| FIGURE A.11 | SCHOOL IMPROVEMENT PLAN FOR MATHEMATICS |

SCHOOL: Harder-Not-Smarter Middle School

Priority Need

According to the math subdomain score on the state assessment, 8th grade students scored significantly below the state mean on geometry and measurement. The student questionnaire that accompanied the state test indicated that students are not using manipulatives to verify reasoning, nor are they using a variety of tools to develop their mathematical knowledge.

Causes or Contributing Factors

Based on professional development records

- Math teachers have not received training on the use of manipulatives to teach geometry.
- Teachers have not received training on measurement concepts for middle school students.

Based on test data

- Students are unaware or unable to apply problem-solving strategies or higher-order thinking skills to the solution of geometry problems.

Based on examination of the curriculum

- The geometry chapter is late in the textbook—after the 8th grade testing—and students may have forgotten what they have learned in previous years.

Goal

A. To improve students' understanding of geometry and measurement concepts so that they are able to apply their understanding in multiple settings and problem situations.

Measurable Objectives

A1. Introduce at least 80 percent of all geometry concepts through the use of manipulatives or math tools.

A2. One hundred percent of math teachers will attend a minimum of six hours of professional development on the use of manipulatives to introduce geometry concepts, to practice skills, and to do problem solving.

A3. One hundred percent of math teachers will attend six hours of professional development on problem solving.

A4. One hundred percent of 8th grade math teachers will teach at least one geometry unit and one measurement unit prior to state testing.

A5. The percentage of students who score Novice will be no more than 50 percent.

APPENDIX B

TOOLS

THIS APPENDIX PROVIDES THE TOOLS NECESSARY TO CONDUCT MATHEMATICS Program Improvement Reviews. The reproducible forms are also available for download in a password-protected PDF format from the ASCD Web site: www.ascd.org. Follow the Publications link to the Books page, click on "Browse by Title," and then select this book's title. You may also search for the book's title from the home page. To access the PDFs, enter the password *ASCD105126* when prompted.

FIGURE B.1	RATING FORM FOR THE MATHEMATICS PROGRAM IMPROVEMENT REVIEW STANDARDS

Standards and Indicators for a Quality Mathematics Program

5 = Completely consistent with best practices   N/O = Not observed

3 = Moderately consistent with best practices   N/A = Not applicable

1 = Inconsistent with best practices

Standard 1: Curriculum

The curriculum uses problem-centered content that develops students' conceptual understanding of mathematics, ability to apply mathematics, ability to communicate mathematically, and knowledge and skills in using mathematics algorithms.

	Indicators	Rating
1.1	The math curriculum is written and is used in planning the instructional program.	
1.2	The curriculum is research-based and redesigned periodically to respond to our changing society.	
1.3	Problem solving is an integral part of all mathematical activity.	
1.4	Students understand that communicating mathematically requires a variety of processes—observing, representing, discussing, analyzing, thinking creatively, reading, writing, and listening.	
1.5	The math curriculum is aligned with the state standards and state assessments.	
1.6	Students understand that mathematical ideas are connected and that all of mathematics is an integrated whole.	
1.7 **(K–8)**	The curriculum develops students'	
	a. Number sense, operation sense, and computational skills.	
	b. Mastery of estimation and mental computation.	
	c. Understanding of patterns, sequences, and series.	
	d. Knowledge of measurement and geometry.	
	e. Spatial sense and reasoning.	
	f. Ability to collect, organize, represent, and interpret data.	
	g. Facility using statistical methods and exploring chance and probability models.	
	h. Facility using algebraic skills and concepts.	
1.7 **(9–12)**	The curriculum develops students'	
	a. Operations on real numbers (absolute value, factorial, etc.).	
	b. Mastery of estimating strategies, including real number properties.	
	c. Ability to use matrices to solve problems.	
	d. Understanding of sequences and series.	
	e. Knowledge of algebraic and geometric transformations.	
	f. Use of indirect measurement and the Pythagorean theorem.	
	g. Ability to collect, organize, and display two-variable data.	

FIGURE B.1	RATING FORM FOR THE MATHEMATICS PROGRAM IMPROVEMENT REVIEW STANDARDS *(continued)*	

	Indicators	Rating
1.7	h. Ability to understand statistical models, probability, and combinatorics.	
	i. Ability to solve and graph a variety of equations and inequalities.	
	j. Ability to identify the characteristics of the graphs of functions.	
	k. Understanding of linear, quadratic, and exponential equations and functions.	
	l. Ability to apply right triangle trigonometry.	
1.8	Appropriate instructional materials are provided and used to reinforce the objectives of the math curriculum.	
1.9	Teachers demonstrate thorough understanding of the written mathematics curriculum.	

Standard 2: Instruction

Instruction engages students in a variety of learning experiences designed to develop mathematical discovery and reasoning.

	Indicators	Rating
2.1	Instructional strategies reflect a constructivist orientation, including student exploration, development of concepts from direct experience, and questioning to elicit higher-order thinking.	
2.2	Teachers use appropriate instructional strategies relevant to the objectives of the mathematics curriculum, including	
	a. Multiple problem-solving strategies and application of these strategies in routine and nonroutine problems.	
	b. A variety of instructional grouping patterns.	
	c. Reading, writing about, and discussing mathematical ideas.	
	d. The use of manipulatives to introduce concepts, practice skills, practice problem solving, and verify mathematical reasoning.	
	e. Provisions for students to pose problems, analyze their own mistakes, and discover new solutions.	
	f. Monitoring of student performance, giving immediate response, and adjusting instruction accordingly.	
2.3	Students use a variety of technological tools—including computers, calculators, and other scientific equipment—to develop and extend their mathematical understanding.	
2.4	Instruction includes a developmentally appropriate balance of preteach/teach/reteach, review, guided practice, monitored classwork, and independent homework.	
2.5	Field trips, math fairs, speakers, and other supplementary programs and enrichment activities extend instruction beyond the classroom into the school and the community.	
2.6	Course objectives are linked to materials and activities and guide the teachers' instruction.	

FIGURE B.1	RATING FORM FOR THE MATHEMATICS PROGRAM IMPROVEMENT REVIEW STANDARDS *(continued)*

Standard 3: Equity and Diversity

The school provides learning environments that meet students' diverse learning needs.

	Indicators	Rating
3.1	Students of all ethnic groups, cultural groups, ability groups, economic levels, learning styles (multiple intelligences), and genders have equal access to information, assistance, classroom interaction, and technology.	
3.2	Teachers use fair and flexible grouping practices.	
3.3	Teachers accommodate students' special needs, abilities, and disabilities.	
3.4	Teachers use specific strategies to motivate underachievers and address students' particular learning needs.	
3.5	The classroom environment reflects the diversity of students' cultures and values, thereby inviting participation by every student.	
3.6	Professional development relating to equity and diversity is provided to the staff.	
3.7	The teaching staff selects mathematics curriculum materials that avoid bias and stereotyping and encourage cultural and gender appreciation.	

Standard 4: School Climate

The school climate creates positive attitudes toward and about mathematics and encourages and recognizes students' accomplishments in mathematics.

	Indicators	Rating
4.1	Students, parents, and teachers believe all students are capable of achievement in mathematics.	
4.2	Students help develop high expectations and standards for themselves and for others.	
4.3	Teachers exhibit high expectations for all students.	
4.4	The school recognizes and rewards the mathematics achievements of all students, especially girls, minority students, developing English speakers, and those with special education needs.	
4.5	Students are rewarded for originality, accuracy, personal initiative, and creativity in mathematics.	
4.6	Students feel free to make mistakes and are encouraged to take risks.	
4.7	School support personnel (teachers, counselors, administrators, instructional aides, etc.) actively promote the mathematics program.	
4.8	The mathematical accomplishments of students and school personnel are appropriately recognized.	

FIGURE B.1	RATING FORM FOR THE MATHEMATICS PROGRAM IMPROVEMENT REVIEW STANDARDS *(continued)*

Standard 5: Usefulness

The mathematics program relates instruction and learning to students' interests, experiences, and future goals.

	Indicators	Rating
5.1	Teachers relate mathematics to individual student interests and to subsequent mathematical studies.	
5.2	The school environment—across classrooms and in the halls, the media center, the cafeteria, and other public places—stimulates interest and demonstrates the usefulness and value of mathematics.	
5.3	Teachers integrate mathematics with other content areas when appropriate.	
5.4	Teachers highlight applications of mathematics in the everyday life and culture of students and the community and its importance in students' future career choices.	

Standard 6: Professional Environment

The professional environment inspires collegiality and understanding among the faculty and the administrative staff to work together to implement an effective mathematics program.

	Indicators	Rating
6.1	Staff members can	
	a. Articulate the instructional goal(s) for mathematics.	
	b. State specific instructional and noninstructional activities directed toward meeting those goals.	
	c. Explain what the school's improvement plan contains and use it in planning their activities during the school year.	
6.2	The school staff and district support teachers' continuing education in mathematics.	
6.3	Professional development programs in mathematics are evaluated for effectiveness.	
6.4	Teachers have been trained in the use of the program/materials that they have adopted for the teaching of mathematics.	
6.5	School and district administrators encourage and fund active involvement in local, state, and national professional mathematics associations, societies, and research activities.	
6.6	Cross-grade collaboration and/or interdisciplinary planning strengthen mathematics teaching.	
6.7	Interruptions during academic learning time are kept to a minimum.	
6.8	Principals and teachers are informed of and participate in opportunities to expand their mathematical knowledge.	

FIGURE B.1	RATING FORM FOR THE MATHEMATICS PROGRAM IMPROVEMENT REVIEW STANDARDS *(continued)*

Standard 7: Community

The school involves the parents and the community in a collaborative effort to develop mathematical knowledge among students.

	Indicators	Rating
7.1	The school encourages families to expect and support mathematics achievement by all students.	
7.2	Parents are provided opportunities to make suggestions that they think may improve the curriculum.	
7.3	Communication to the community regarding the instructional program and state/national test results occurs on a regular basis.	
7.4	Parents are informed of	
	a. Available academic support and instructional assistance in mathematics.	
	b. The purpose and structure of the instructional program in mathematics.	
	c. Their child's curriculum options and their child's future career possibilities.	
7.5	Joint school/community activities related to the mathematics instructional program take place regularly.	

Standard 8: Organization and Leadership
The school facility and school leadership enhance opportunities for effective and consistent mathematics instruction.

	Indicators	Rating
8.1	Nonteaching responsibilities and extra duties are equitable and kept to a minimum.	
8.2	The design of the professional development program for mathematics is based on needs identified from analyses of student and teacher data.	
8.3	Classroom teachers are assigned classes at or under recommended capacity size.	
8.4	The main focus of the principal is instructional leadership that promotes and supports teaching excellence.	
8.5	The principal	
	a. Conveys high expectations for students, staff, and self.	
	b. Actively pursues a program of professional development focusing on improving mathematics instruction.	
	c. Confers with teachers immediately following observations, reinforcing effective practices and providing guidance to improve ineffective ones.	
	d. Demonstrates effective interpersonal skills that enable facilitation of change in the school.	
	e. Articulates his or her beliefs about effective instruction in mathematics.	
8.6	An appropriate amount of time is scheduled for instruction in mathematics.	
8.7	Classrooms have adequate space and furnishings to facilitate a standards-based investigative program.	

FIGURE B.1	RATING FORM FOR THE MATHEMATICS PROGRAM IMPROVEMENT REVIEW STANDARDS *(continued)*

Standard 9: Assessment and Evaluation

The school continually assesses student achievement, evaluates program effectiveness, and uses the results to determine if there is a need for improvement.

	Indicators	Rating
9.1	Mathematics program evaluation includes	
	a. Self-examination as well as evaluation by external sources.	
	b. Examination of a variety of qualitative and quantitative data, including state assessment results, survey results, and student work.	
9.2	Evaluations directly relate to both instructional and assessment goals established for the program.	
9.3	Students have adequate opportunities to demonstrate their achievements through multiple methods of assessment.	
9.4	To report results:	
	a. Teachers use various forms of documentation to report student progress, achievement, and participation.	
	b. The results of evaluations are made available to parents and interested parties and discussed in relation to state standards and school goals.	
9.5	All mathematics teachers participate in mathematics program planning and evaluation.	
9.6	The school coordinates needs identification and improvement activities with the programs in other schools in the district, particularly schools in the feeder pattern.	
9.7	Teachers and administrators use state assessment results, student feedback, and other data to identify strengths and weaknesses in the curriculum.	
9.8	Academic support activities (remediation/enrichment) provide additional opportunities for student learning.	
9.9	Evaluation criteria distinguish between effective and ineffective teaching practices.	

Standard 10: Financial and Material Resources

The mathematics curriculum is supported by adequate financial and material resources.

	Indicators	Rating
10.1	Funds allocated are sufficient to meet the needs generated by the program.	
10.2	The school makes use of appropriate resources from other educational institutions, parents, businesses, industries, and service clubs.	
10.3	Expenditures are determined collectively by the affected staff.	
10.4	Funding is provided to enable students to experience extracurricular and cocurricular activities, such as field trips, regional competitions, and math fairs.	
10.5	Appropriate technology is available in sufficient quantities to meet the needs of the instructional program.	

FIGURE B.2	GUIDE FOR RATING MPIR INDICATORS AND STANDARDS

This guide is designed to provide direction in completing the ratings for the program standards and indicators in the Mathematics Program Improvement Review process conducted for schools. Each indicator under a standard is assigned a rating reflective of the mathematics program at the school. A capsule rating is then assigned to the standard, based holistically on the indicator ratings.

Each indicator is rated on a five-point scale. This guide contains descriptors to help assign the appropriate ratings. Having a consistent and reliable method of assigning and interpreting the ratings will aid school staff members in using the MPIR report in their improvement planning.

Using This Guide

1. Persons assigning the ratings should examine all the evidence collected that relates to the indicator and then select the rating whose descriptor most closely matches the evidence.

2. The descriptors given for a particular indicator are intended to represent the typical range of conditions that could exist in the school's mathematics program. The descriptors do not reflect the entire set of possibilities, nor are the brief statements sufficient to completely characterize the rating levels. The descriptors are a guide, not a prescription. Persons assigning the ratings will need to use their informed judgment, based on the evidence collected, when deciding the most appropriate rating to assign.

3. Indicators do not have descriptors for all five rating levels. The "in-between" rating should be assigned if the evidence gathered indicates that such a situation exists.

   Example: For the indicator below, suppose the evidence indicates that the teachers use a curriculum consisting of the list of state standards, but nothing else. Thus, the situation is better than the descriptor for "1" but does not satisfy the descriptor for "3." Therefore, the appropriate rating would be "2."

Indicator	1	3	5
1.1 The math curriculum is written and is used in planning the instructional program.	No written curriculum exists.	Curriculum consists of state standards, together with a topic list.	Curriculum contains standards, scope and sequence, learning objectives, and suggested activities.

4. In some cases, circumstances may be such that no evidence addressing a particular indicator was collected, or the evidence collected was insufficient for the team to make a confident rating. In these cases, the indicator should be marked "N/O" for "not observed." Because the MPIR is a data-based process, it is important that ratings be based on evidence gathered, not on hunches or opinions.

5. In some cases, the situation at a school may make some indicators inappropriate or irrelevant. The appropriate rating in this case is "N/A" for "not applicable." For example, Standard 6.1 addresses the goals that the school has set for its mathematics programs. If the school has not set any goals for mathematics, then Indicator 6.1a and 6.1b would be rated "N/A."

FIGURE B.2   GUIDE FOR RATING MPIR INDICATORS AND STANDARDS *(continued)*

Standard 1: Curriculum	1	3	5
1.1 The math curriculum is written and is used in planning the instructional program.	No written curriculum exists.	Curriculum consists of state standards, together with a topic list.	Curriculum contains standards, scope and sequence, learning objectives, and suggested activities.
1.2 The curriculum is research-based and redesigned periodically to respond to our changing society.	Curriculum is not reviewed except during districtwide revisions (if at all).	Curriculum consists of state standards and a basal textbook scope and sequence; individual teachers make adjustments, but changes are not incorporated into the curriculum document.	Curriculum is based on NCTM standards and is reviewed/revised prior to text adoption or change in state assessment; all affected teachers actively participate in curricular changes, based on analysis of data.
1.3 Problem solving is an integral part of all mathematical activity.	The emphasis is on basic skills with minimal daily use of problem solving.	Problem solving consists of a problem of the day that is not integrated into the day's lesson.	Problem solving is a major part of lesson—labs, written work, cooperative activities, and so on.
1.4 Students understand that communicating mathematically requires a variety of processes—observing, representing, discussing, analyzing, thinking creatively, reading, writing, and listening.	Most students associate learning with memorizing and repeating facts and formulas.	Students receive different learning experiences—some are in classes with active engagement, while others are in classes that stress rote learning.	Most students associate learning with intellectual engagement that addresses interesting ideas and problems.
1.5 The math curriculum is aligned with the state standards and state assessments.	Curriculum bears no relation to state or district content standards or to assessment goals for student learning.	Curriculum's connections to state content standards and assessments are uneven; some items are clearly connected, whereas others do not appear linked at all.	Curriculum is clearly connected to state and district content standards and to state assessment goals for student learning.
1.6 Students understand that mathematical ideas are connected and that all of mathematics is an integrated whole.	Most/all teachers work through lessons and units as separate activities; students often do not see how facts are related and build into concepts.	Most/all teachers make reference to how facts and/or ideas in a topic are related together, but do not spend specific time on illustrating the connections.	Most/all teachers use concept mapping and other strategies to help students tie facts to concepts and to show connections among concepts.

Criterion				
1.7 The curriculum develops students' a. Number sense, operation sense, and computational skills (including real numbers for high school). b. Mastery of estimation and mental computation. c. Understanding of patterns, sequences, and series. d. Knowledge of measurement and geometry (including indirect measurement). e. Spatial sense and reasoning (including algebraic and geometric transformations in high school). f. Ability to collect, organize, represent, and interpret data (including two-variable data in high school). g. Facility using statistical methods and exploring chance and probability models. h. Facility using algebraic skills and concepts (including matrices, graphing equations and inequalities, line of best fit, characteristics of the graph of a function, and linear/quadratic/exponential/functions in high school).	Evidence from state test data, teacher interviews, and classroom observations suggests that this content received minimal effective instruction, e.g., students scored well below the national mean on a related objective.	Evidence from state test data, teacher interviews, and/or classroom observations suggests that students are receiving instruction on this content, but it is ineffective.		Evidence from state test data, teacher interviews, and classroom observations suggests that this content is taught effectively with students demonstrating mastery.
1.8 Appropriate instructional materials are provided and used to reinforce the objectives of the math curriculum.	Instructional materials are not present, old or outdated, or are not used appropriately.	Instructional materials are present in ample supply but are more traditional, less appropriate for teaching to the standards; not all teachers use relevant materials.		Innovative instructional materials are present in ample supply and are used to support teaching to the standards.
1.9 Teachers demonstrate thorough understanding of the written mathematics curriculum.	Most teachers have little knowledge of the curriculum for their grade level/subject.	Most teachers can discuss details of the curriculum at their grade level or in their subject.		Each teacher can discuss details of their grade level/subject curriculum, plus its relation to other grade levels/math subjects.

FIGURE B.2	GUIDE FOR RATING MPIR INDICATORS AND STANDARDS *(continued)*		
Standard 2: Instruction	1	3	5
2.1 Instructional strategies reflect a constructivist orientation, including student exploration, development of concepts from direct experience, and questioning to elicit higher-order thinking.	Students are uninvolved or only partially engaged in learning as a result of poor communication, low-level questions, little student participation in discussion, little or no feedback on learning, and the teachers' rigid adherence to an instructional plan despite evidence that it should be modified.	Students are engaged in learning as a result of clear communication, appropriate instructional strategies, and productive use of feedback. The majority of the teachers demonstrate flexibility when contributing to the success of lessons and of each student.	All students are highly engaged in learning and make material contributions to the success of the class by asking questions and participating in discussions, getting actively involved in learning activities, and using feedback in their learning. Teachers ensure the success of every student by creating a high-level learning environment; providing timely, high-quality feedback; and continuously searching for approaches that meet student needs.
2.2 Teachers use appropriate instructional strategies relevant to the objectives of the mathematics curriculum, including			
a. Multiple problem-solving strategies and application of these strategies in routine and nonroutine problems.	Teachers typically act as the providers of knowledge who know all the answers; mistakes and alternate methods are discouraged.	Most teachers provide instruction on problem-solving strategies included in texts; most teachers encourage students to find alternate approaches but still emphasize correctness above all.	All teachers provide opportunities for students to use multiple problem solving strategies developed by students or a variety of resources; teachers value students finding other methods.
b. A variety of instructional grouping patterns.	Teachers use mostly whole-class strategies, with students working individually on tasks.	Most teachers use small-group as well as whole-group strategies at least some of the time.	All teachers vary grouping patterns as appropriate for the variety of tasks; when learning needs change, tasks are differentiated.
c. Reading, writing about, and discussing mathematical ideas.	Teachers use traditional lecture methods with little student-initiated interaction.	Some teachers—but not all—provide opportunities for student reflection (writing, discussing).	All teachers provide daily opportunities for students to initiate learning through reading, writing, and discussing.

Criterion			
d. The use of manipulatives to introduce concepts, practice skills, practice problem solving, and verify mathematical reasoning.	Manipulatives are used rarely, if ever, in most classrooms.	Most teachers use manipulatives to introduce concepts and/or to practice skills—none use them for problem solving or verification of reasoning.	All teachers regularly use manipulative materials as an integral part of lessons, including problem solving and verification of reasoning.
e. Provisions for students to pose problems, analyze their own mistakes, and discover new solutions.	Teachers—either through lecture or text examples—provide one method of solution.	Students are given opportunities to discover different methods to solve problems but do not create their own; there is some effort to have students analyze their own mistakes.	Each lesson provides time for students to analyze mistakes and discover methods of solution; students are periodically given opportunities to pose problems to each other.
f. Monitoring of student performance, giving immediate response, and adjusting instruction accordingly.	Teachers only use student assessment data for assigning grades to students and provide little or no feedback to students on their learning.	Teachers attempt to use student assessment data for more than student grading, with uneven results. They offer limited feedback to students and use the data only intermittently to improve their performance.	Teachers use student assessment data to provide specific and timely feedback to students, reflect on their own practice, monitor progress toward content standards, and contribute to student grades.
2.3 Students use a variety of technological tools—including computers, calculators, and other scientific equipment—to develop and extend their mathematical understanding.	Technology is used rarely, if ever, in most classrooms.	Most teachers use calculators to some degree; a few make use of other technology.	All teachers regularly use technology as an integral part of lessons.
2.4 Instruction includes a developmentally appropriate balance of preteach/reteach, review, guided practice, monitored classwork, and independent homework.	An inordinate amount of class time is spent on reviewing and doing seatwork.	Some teachers overemphasize drill and seatwork, but a few provide better balance in using instructional time.	Class time focuses on developing understanding; seatwork and homework are instructional tools, not just drill.
2.5 Field trips, math fairs, speakers, and other supplementary programs and enrichment activities extend instruction beyond the classroom into the school and the community.	No evidence of cocurricular or extracurricular activities in mathematics.	Various cocurricular and extracurricular activities take place using community resources, but often are only loosely connected to instructional objectives at the time.	Various cocurricular and extracurricular activities occur regularly, utilize community resources, and are specifically linked to the instructional focus at the time.
2.6 Course objectives are linked to materials and activities and guide the teachers' instruction.	No objectives exist outside of those listed in the textbook.	Course objectives have been developed, but instructional resources (software, manipulatives, activity pages, etc.) have not been linked.	Course objectives have been developed and guide instruction; instructional materials have been linked to most, if not all, objectives.

FIGURE B.2   GUIDE FOR RATING MPIR INDICATORS AND STANDARDS *(continued)*

Standard 3: Equity and Diversity	1	3	5
3.1 Students of all ethnic groups, cultural groups, ability groups, economic levels, learning styles (multiple intelligences) and genders have equal access to information, assistance, classroom interaction, and technology.	Teachers direct most of their instruction to selected members of the class.	Most teachers—but not all—provide all students with equal access to instruction.	All students have equal access to instruction and materials, including technology.
3.2 Teachers use fair and flexible grouping practices.	Most/all teachers rarely, if ever, utilize student groups during instruction.	Most teachers use student groups to meet diverse learning styles.	All teachers use a variety of strategies for grouping and organizing students to accommodate learning styles.
3.3 Teachers accommodate students' special needs, abilities, and disabilities.	Teachers provide instruction to the middle with no variation for special needs students or high-achieving students.	Most teachers provide instruction to all students, including differentiated assignments, learning centers, or other accommodations.	All teachers provide varied instructional strategies to meet varied needs and provide alternative methods for students to demonstrate understanding.
3.4 Teachers use specific strategies to motivate underachievers and address students' particular learning needs.	Most/all teachers believe it is not necessary to use special strategies to meet individual needs.	Some teachers show evidence of using a variety of specific strategies, but others do not.	Most/all teachers both discuss and are observed using strategies intended to meet the needs of particular students.
3.5 The classroom environment reflects the diversity of students' cultures and values, thereby inviting participation by every student.	Most/all classrooms have no pictures, posters, or other resources that illustrate diversity in math or how mathematics is approached in other locations and cultures.	Most/all classrooms display multicultural materials at certain times of the year (e.g., Black History Month, Women's History Month).	Most/all classrooms prominently display pictures, posters, or other resources that illustrate diversity in mathematics and how the subject is approached in other locations and cultures.
3.6 Professional development relating to equity and diversity is provided to the staff.	No professional development has been provided on equity or diversity.	Professional development has been provided on either gender or racial equity.	Equity/diversity training is periodically provided to all staff members.
3.7 The teaching staff selects mathematics curriculum materials that avoid bias and stereotyping and encourage cultural and gender appreciation.	Materials are in evidence that include bias or stereotyping.	Materials do not have bias or stereotyping, but these were not criteria of the review process.	Rubrics or other evaluation materials are used by staff in reviewing and selecting software, texts, and other math materials to ensure that there is no bias or stereotyping.

Standard 4: School Climate	1	3	5
4.1 Students, parents, and teachers believe all students are capable of achievement in mathematics.	Most students, parents, and teachers accept that some students cannot learn mathematics well.	Most students, parents, and teachers believe that some students will excel to a greater degree, but all students can achieve in mathematics to a certain minimum level.	Most/all students, parents, and teachers voice a strong belief that all students can succeed in mathematics.
4.2 Students help develop high expectations and standards for themselves and for others.	Students have no role in setting expectations for performance.	Students regularly assess their own work, using standards developed by the teacher.	Students regularly are involved in assessing their own work and that of others according to standards they have helped to create.
4.3 Teachers exhibit high expectations for all students.	Most/all teachers express different levels of expectations for different groups of students.	Most/all teachers verbally express high expectations for all; specific actions to support and encourage all students are less evident.	Through words and actions, most/all teachers regularly communicate encouragement and expectations to individual students as well as the whole class.
4.4 The school recognizes and rewards the mathematics achievements of all students, especially girls, minority students, developing English speakers, and those with special education needs.	School provides no academic recognition program beyond honor rolls.	School staff recognizes academic achievements by those who participate in extracurricular activities and competitions.	School staff recognizes and rewards academic achievements within all classes and all students have equal opportunities for such recognition.
4.5 Students are rewarded for originality, accuracy, personal initiative, and creativity in mathematics.	Students are expected to "do it the way they are shown."	Students are encouraged to find alternate methods, but grading is based on "doing it the teacher's way."	Students are encouraged and rewarded for finding different methods and for explaining their reasoning clearly.
4.6 Students feel free to make mistakes and are encouraged to take risks.	Mistakes result in a lower grade, with little or no opportunity to learn from them.	Most teachers verbally encourage risk taking but do not model it.	Most teachers model risk taking and use student mistakes as an opportunity to further refine.
4.7 School support personnel (teachers, counselors, administrators, instructional aides, etc.) actively promote the mathematics program.	No evidence that school staff discuss options with students.	Counselors and administrators present class options to students but do not give priority to mathematics.	Support and administrative staff actively promote mathematics.
4.8 The mathematical accomplishments of students and school personnel are appropriately recognized.	School has no mechanisms to formally recognize achievements of students or teachers in mathematics (awards received, performance in competitions, etc.).	Accomplishments of teachers and students in mathematics are publicly recognized through spoken announcements, hallway displays, and so on.	Public recognition of accomplishments in mathematics extends beyond awards and contests to include achievements within the work of the instructional program.

FIGURE B.2	GUIDE FOR RATING MPIR INDICATORS AND STANDARDS *(continued)*		
Standard 5: Usefulness	1	3	5
5.1 Teachers relate mathematics to individual student interests and subsequent mathematical studies.	Most/all teachers use topics and activities as given in the text (or other source); little adaptation for interests in a particular class.	Most/all teachers use special projects or other specific instructional activities to address student interests; little or no adaptation of general instruction.	Most/all teachers regularly adapt activities, examples, and assessments to place them in contexts related to student interests.
5.2 The school environment—across classrooms, in the halls, the media center, the cafeteria, and other public places—stimulates interest and demonstrates the usefulness and value of mathematics.	Neither classrooms nor public areas of the school have items that call attention to or engage students in thinking about mathematics.	Mathematics classrooms have a variety of engaging visual items; mathematics is not apparent in public areas of the school.	Students are exposed to a variety of images of mathematics throughout the school (e.g., "mathematical art" display, math books featured in the library, pictures or posters in the hallways).
5.3 Teachers integrate mathematics with other content areas when appropriate.	Most/all teachers show little or no evidence of connecting mathematics with other areas.	Most/all teachers have specific units that are integrated with other subject areas, but integration is not an ongoing focus.	Most/all teachers regularly work together to coordinate units across subject areas and to reinforce knowledge/skills in other subject areas throughout the year.
5.4 Teachers highlight applications of mathematics in the everyday life and culture of students and the community and its importance in students' future career choices.	Most/all teachers rarely, if ever, tie concepts in mathematics to the local community or careers.	Most/all teachers discuss applications of concepts during certain times of the year (e.g., National Engineering Week, Earth Day, career fairs).	Most/all teachers frequently highlight applications of concepts to everyday life and how they are used in careers of interest to students.

Standard 6: Professional Environment	1	3	5
6.1 Staff members can			
a. Articulate the instructional goal(s) for mathematics.	Most/all teachers are unaware of instructional goals.	Most teachers can discuss goals—but the focus is on the assessment goals.	All affected teachers can discuss the instructional goals and why they were identified.
b. State specific instructional and noninstructional activities directed toward meeting those goals.	Most/all teachers are unaware of the instructional goals.	Most teachers give general strategies (e.g., "more hands-on").	All teachers can discuss specific strategies to meet the instructional goals.

c. Explain what the school's improvement plan contains and use it in planning their activities during the school year.	Most/all school staff are unaware of the contents of the current improvement plan; no evidence of impact on activities in the school.	Most/all school staff can discuss the contents of the improvement plan, but little evidence exists that the plan is guiding mathematical activities at the school.	Most/all school staff can articulate the goals and objectives of the plan, as well as what they are doing to support achieving the goals of the mathematics program.
6.2 The school staff and district support teachers' continuing education in mathematics.	Principal and teaching staff are unaware of the availability of local, state, or federal funds to support continuing education.	Staff are aware of the availability of funds, but few if any—teachers make use of these funds.	Administrative staff actively encourage teachers to make use of continuing education funding and a number periodically do so.
6.3 Professional development programs in mathematics are evaluated for effectiveness (impact on instruction, school culture, etc.).	Attendance/participation in professional development has had *no* impact on instructional practices, school culture, and so on.	Professional development has had *some* impact on one or more components (school culture, instructional practices, etc.).	Professional development has had a *significant* impact on most/all of the components (school culture, instructional practices, etc.).
6.4 Teachers have been trained in the use of the program/materials that they have adopted for the teaching of mathematics.	Teachers are provided—at best—an overview of the program components by the textbook representative.	Teachers receive at least one day of training on the program resources and how they can be adapted to meet various needs.	All teachers participate in periodic training beyond the adoption year on effective ways to utilize the program resources and how to adapt them to meet changing instructional needs.
6.5 School and district administrators encourage and fund active involvement in local, state, and national professional mathematics associations, societies, and research activities.	No evidence of support for professional memberships; teachers typically are not released to attend state or national meetings.	Teachers are encouraged to join professional associations; limited funding is available to attend conferences.	School/district support professional involvement (e.g., institutional memberships to provide journals, encouraging presentations) and expect teachers to be professionally active.
6.6 Cross-grade collaboration and/or interdisciplinary planning strengthen mathematics teaching.	Teachers work entirely independently, without coordinating or integrating instruction between them.	Teachers find opportunities to coordinate their efforts; however, no integration is attempted.	Teachers create extensive opportunities for students to integrate their learning across disparate curricular areas.
6.7 Interruptions during academic learning time are kept to a minimum.	Interruptions are frequent throughout the day and disrupt instruction.	Interruptions are not frequent but are disruptive when they occur.	Classes proceed with no (or only minor) interruptions.
6.8 Principals and teachers are informed of and participate in opportunities to expand their mathematical knowledge.	No opportunities for increasing knowledge about mathematics content or pedagogy are provided.	Study groups, video lessons, Internet lessons, and so on are used by some teachers but not by all and not by the principal.	Principal and most mathematics teachers participate in school-centered opportunities (study groups, etc.) to expand their mathematical knowledge.

FIGURE B.2	GUIDE FOR RATING MPIR INDICATORS AND STANDARDS *(continued)*		
Standard 7: Community	**1**	**3**	**5**
7.1 The school encourages families to expect and support mathematics achievement by all students.	Parents receive little or no information about how to help their children succeed.	School/teachers regularly send information home about how parents can help their children in mathematics.	School/teachers regularly send information home about how parents can help their children in mathematics; periodic workshops for parents are also conducted.
7.2 Parents are provided opportunities to make suggestions that they think may improve the curriculum.	Parents have no awareness of the curriculum and no opportunities for input.	Parents are invited to review curriculum, but mechanisms to enable it are not well defined.	A formal mechanism exists to gather and incorporate feedback about the curriculum from a broad group of parents.
7.3 Communication to the community regarding the instructional program and state/national test results occurs on a regular basis.	Communication with families, other educators, and the community is nonexistent or minimal, or the information communicated is inaccurate.	School's attempts to communicate with families, other educators, and the community are partially successful, but misinformation or gaps in understanding persist.	School's attempts to communicate with families, other educators, and the community are fully successful. All members of the faculty are engaged in the communication effort, using all available means.
7.4 Parents are informed of			
a. Available academic support and instructional assistance in mathematics.	Parents receive little or no information about academic support.	School sends parents information about academic support available for mathematics.	School/teachers regularly send information to all parents but also contact specific parents whose children could benefit from support available.
b. The purpose and structure of the instructional program in mathematics.	Parents report little or no knowledge of the instructional program in mathematics.	Teachers send parents information about the program in mathematics, typically at the beginning of the school year, explaining what the students are going to learn and the methods to be used.	Teachers send parents periodic updates about what the class is doing in mathematics, reinforcing the importance of the concepts addressed and the methods used; information is also discussed at parent meetings.
c. Their child's curriculum options and their child's future career possibilities.	Parents receive little or no information about curriculum options.	School sends parents information to help parents assist their child in making course selections that support possible career interests.	Curriculum options are discussed at parent meetings and specific events for that purpose (e.g., career fairs).

	1	3	5
7.5 Joint school/community activities related to the mathematics instructional program take place regularly.	No evidence of joint activities related to mathematics.	School regularly hosts jointly planned learning-related activities for the community (family nights, workshops, speakers, etc.).	School and community regularly plan and provide joint activities; in addition, community members are included on school committees working on the math instructional program.

Standard 8: Organization and Leadership	1	3	5
8.1 Nonteaching responsibilities and extra duties are equitable and kept to a minimum.	Teachers are burdened with numerous extra duties (hall supervision, bus dismissal, etc.).	Nonteaching responsibilities and extra duties are reasonable and fairly assigned to all certified staff.	Nonteaching responsibilities are reasonable; most extra duties are assigned to staff without classroom responsibilities.
8.2 The design of the professional development program for mathematics is based on needs identified from analyses of student and teacher data.	Professional development decisions are made at the top, and teachers are afforded little opportunity to determine what avenues to pursue. The professional atmosphere in the school is closed and isolated.	Teachers have some input into professional development offerings, although the offerings are primarily assigned by others. Teachers have limited opportunities to work with colleagues. The culture of professional inquiry is fairly positive.	Teachers design the professional development offerings in the school in order to improve student learning and meet the school's goals. The culture of professional inquiry is open and provides teachers with multiple opportunities to collaborate on their work.
8.3 Teachers are assigned classes at or under recommended capacity size.	Most classes regularly exceed recommended size.	Only one or two classes exceed recommended size.	No classes exceed recommended size.
8.4 The main focus of the principal is instructional leadership that promotes and supports teaching excellence.	Principal is management-focused; little indication of attention to instruction issues.	Principal's words and actions both demonstrate commitment to instruction, but time and attention are concentrated on other subject areas.	Principal's words and actions both demonstrate commitment of time, attention, and energy to instruction in mathematics.

FIGURE B.2 | GUIDE FOR RATING MPIR INDICATORS AND STANDARDS *(continued)*

Standard 8: Organization and Leadership *(continued)*	1	3	5
8.5 The principal			
a. Conveys high expectations for students, staff, and self.	Principal conveys different levels of expectation for different teacher and student groups.	Principal verbally expresses high expectations, but actions are infrequent.	Principal's words and actions regularly and consistently urge all teachers and students to do their best.
b. Actively pursues a program of professional development focusing on improving mathematics instruction.	Principal has attended no professional development related to mathematics improvement.	Principal has attended workshops or other professional development activities related to math improvement strategies in the past two years.	Principal is currently engaged in ongoing mathematics professional development activities and is applying the strategies to daily work.
c. Confers with teachers immediately following observations, reinforcing effective practices and providing guidance to improve ineffective ones.	Classroom observations are typically isolated events, with no follow-up or feedback to the teacher.	Teachers receive written feedback after an observation, usually with strengths and weaknesses noted.	Principal holds a follow-up meeting to provide specific feedback about an observation, focusing on effective and ineffective methods.
d. Demonstrates effective interpersonal skills that enable facilitation of change in the school.	Principal is perceived by the staff as one who cannot communicate his/her personal feelings effectively.	Principal is respected and teachers follow his/her lead, but more because of the position than through personal charisma.	Teachers' perception of the principal is that he/she cares about the well-being of each person (staff, student) in the school.
e. Articulates his or her beliefs about effective instruction in mathematics.	Principal has difficulty articulating a vision for what constitutes effective mathematics instruction.	Principal discusses a standards-based vision, but it is a general description, lacking detail about specific strategies for mathematics.	Principal articulates a comprehensive vision of standards-based instruction in mathematics, including role of content, teaching strategies, and assessment.
8.6 An appropriate amount of time is scheduled for instruction in mathematics.	No specific amount of time per day or per week is scheduled; left to teacher discretion.	Time is scheduled, but is not sufficient at some levels.	Adequate time is regularly scheduled each week.
8.7 Classrooms have adequate space and furnishings to facilitate a standards-based investigative program.	All classrooms are crowded; minimal storage; furniture inhibits use of hands-on student work.	Space, storage, and/or furniture provide some barriers to hands-on work in some classrooms.	All classrooms have ample space, storage, and furniture to maximize student learning.

Standard 9: Assessment and Evaluation	1	3	5
9.1 Mathematics program evaluation includes			
a. Self-examination as well as evaluation by external sources.	Little or no evidence of existing program evaluation mechanisms in mathematics.	Teachers in mathematics have previously engaged in a general self-assessment of the program.	School has previously engaged in a detailed self-assessment, as well as gathering input from sources outside the school.
b. Examination of a variety of qualitative and quantitative data, including state assessment results, survey results, and student work.	Program evaluation is not at all data-based; judgments are based on perceptions of a few key persons.	The only real data examined in the program evaluation are state assessment results.	The evaluation process examines multiple sources of data beyond state assessments, including other measures of student performance and measures of program status.
9.2 Evaluations directly relate to both instructional and assessment goals established for the program.	No goals have been established for the program in mathematics.	Program evaluation is tailored to mathematics but is organized around assessment goals; no specific focus on instructional goals.	Program evaluation is tailored to mathematics and to the specific instructional and assessment goals set for the program.
9.3 Students have adequate opportunities to demonstrate their achievements through multiple methods of assessment.	Grading is based on only a few major assignments and pencil-and-paper tests; daily work is typically not checked by the teacher.	Grading is based on tests in which students have to show all of their work, classroom discussion, and homework/classwork.	Assessments throughout the year include multiple formats (e.g., open response, cooperative group projects, individual investigations, and daily assignments).
9.4 To report results			
a. Teachers use various forms of documentation to report student progress, achievement, and participation.	Reports of student performance are limited to letter grades on a report card.	Students receive periodic reports of their current standing, typically points earned or percent completion.	Students receive regular formal feedback about their overall performance, their understanding of key concepts, and their degree of progress.
b. The results of evaluations are made available to parents and interested parties and discussed in relation to state standards and school goals.	Results of evaluations are kept within the school; no evidence of subsequent use or discussions.	General results of evaluations are publicly disseminated without discussion, through school newsletters, announcements at PTA meetings, and so on.	General results of evaluations are publicly disseminated; specific meetings are scheduled to discuss findings and enable teachers, parents, and others to work together on what should be done.

FIGURE B.2	GUIDE FOR RATING MPIR INDICATORS AND STANDARDS *(continued)*		
Standard 9: Assessment and Evaluation *(continued)*	1	3	5
9.5 All mathematics teachers participate in program planning and evaluation.	Improvement plan is developed by the principal or counselor.	A small group of teachers volunteer or are assigned to develop the improvement plan; upon completion of a draft, other teachers react to the plan and contribute to revisions.	All teachers in mathematics are regularly involved in analysis and discussions leading to development of the improvement plan.
9.6 The school coordinates needs identification and improvement activities with the programs in other schools in the district, particularly schools in the feeder pattern.	Little or no evidence of communication with other schools in the district regarding data, needs, or improvement activities.	Schools in the district share data, particularly about students coming up through the feeder pattern; little or no collaboration on improvement activities.	Schools in the district regularly share data; improvement plans target individual school needs but also include activities that address needs common among schools in the district.
9.7 Teachers and administrators use state assessment results, student feedback, and other data to identify strengths and weaknesses in the curriculum.	School staff does not examine state assessment results beyond overall scores.	An individual or a small group analyzes state assessments and provides results to rest of faculty.	School staff as a group uses data in addition to item analyses to target curricular weaknesses.
9.8 Academic support activities (remediation/enrichment) provide additional opportunities for student learning.	No evidence of academic support activities in mathematics.	Academic support in mathematics is available through the school, typically in an after-school program; activities may or may not be tied directly to classroom studies.	Academic support programs are available in a variety of settings (in-school, after-school, evening) to accommodate students with different access; activities are directly linked to classroom studies.
9.9 Evaluation criteria distinguish between effective and ineffective teaching practices.	Evaluation criteria focus more on contextual features (e.g., orderliness) than on effective practices.	Evaluation criteria examine specific effective practices for general instruction; no reference to strategies associated with effective teaching in mathematics.	Evaluation criteria examine both strategies for general instruction and strategies of particular importance to mathematics; criteria emphasize current goals of the school.

Standard 10: Financial and Material Resources	1	3	5
10.1 Funds allocated are sufficient to meet the needs generated by the program.	Funds are not made available specifically for mathematics.	Funds are limited, but program operates at a subsistence level.	Funds are available for new materials as well as for established needs.
10.2 The school makes use of appropriate resources from other educational institutions, parents, businesses, industries, and service clubs.	School makes no effort to collaborate or forge partnerships with public/private agencies or the business community.	Some opportunities are provided for both students and teachers to collaborate with public/private agencies or businesses, but efforts are spotty and poorly organized and involve only a small percentage of students or teachers.	School has developed an extensive program of collaboration with public/private agencies and businesses, resulting in valuable opportunities for both students and teachers.
10.3 Expenditures are determined collectively by the affected staff.	Decision-making and budgeting systems are secretive and involve only a few teachers and/or the principal in the processes. There is no screening process to ensure that the decisions made will support student learning.	Decision-making and budgeting systems are moderately clear to everyone, and permit some teachers to be involved in the processes. The processes yield decisions that may support student learning.	Decision-making and budgeting systems are transparent to everyone and permit all teachers to be involved in the processes. The processes yield decisions that unambiguously support student learning.
10.4 Funding is provided to enable students to experience extracurricular and cocurricular activities, such as field trips, regional competitions, and math fairs.	No funding is available for field trips or other extracurricular/cocurricular activities.	Funding is available for one field trip per year and funding is provided for small groups of students (e.g., academic teams).	If need can be supported, then funding is available for extracurricular/cocurricular activities, including field trips.
10.5 Appropriate technology is available in sufficient quantities to meet the needs of the instructional program.	Technology is unavailable or outdated.	Technology is available, but access is limited by placement or policies.	Sufficient technology is regularly available to classes as needed.

FIGURE B.3	TEACHER SELF-PERCEPTION QUESTIONNAIRE

SCHOOL _____

Your school leadership has requested that a team visit your school to conduct a Mathematics Program Improvement Review. This review will use self-reported data from this questionnaire as well as interviews and observations on the day of the visit. None of the collected data will be used to identify or single out any teacher. The report issued as a result of the visit will be an analysis of the overall mathematics program. After completing this form, return it to your school secretary to be placed anonymously in an envelope.

Compiler's Use

Professional Background and Affiliation

a. I have _____ total years of classroom teaching experience.

b. I have a certification to teach mathematics in the following grade-span (circle one):

     K–4   K–6   K–8   5–8   7–12   9–12

[6.5]   c. I am a member of a state mathematics organization and/or NCTM.

     ☐ Yes   ☐ No

[6.5]   d. I have attended a state, regional, or national mathematics conference in the past three years.

     ☐ Yes   ☐ No

Instructional Approaches

How often do you use each of the following techniques to teach math in your classes?

		Daily	Weekly	Monthly	Rarely	Never
[5.4]	a. Students solving real-life problems	☐	☐	☐	☐	☐
[2.2c]	b. Library research	☐	☐	☐	☐	☐
[2.2c]	c. Mathematical writing (reflections)	☐	☐	☐	☐	☐
[2.1]	d. Demonstrating/modeling	☐	☐	☐	☐	☐
[2.2d]	e. Students using manipulatives*	☐	☐	☐	☐	☐
[2.2b]	f. Students in groups or teams	☐	☐	☐	☐	☐
[2.2b]	g. Group projects	☐	☐	☐	☐	☐
[1.4]	h. Workbooks	☐	☐	☐	☐	☐
[2.3]	i. Calculator problem solving	☐	☐	☐	☐	☐
[2.3]	j. Computer drill and practice	☐	☐	☐	☐	☐
[2.4]	k. Review of skills and procedures	☐	☐	☐	☐	☐
[2.4]	l. Individual projects	☐	☐	☐	☐	☐
[2.5]	m. Math-related field trips	☐	☐	☐	☐	☐
[1.3]	n. Computer problem solving	☐	☐	☐	☐	☐
[2.4]	o. Lecture with student note taking	☐	☐	☐	☐	☐

*Note: *Manipulatives* are items like geoboards, counters, algebra tiles, base-10 blocks, and so on. *Math tools* are single-purpose items like calculators, graph paper, rulers, compasses, and protractors.

FIGURE B.3	TEACHER SELF-PERCEPTION QUESTIONNAIRE *(continued)*

Compiler's Use

		Daily	Weekly	Monthly	Rarely	Never
[2.4]	p. Whole-class discussion	☐	☐	☐	☐	☐
[1.4]	q. Student-led discussion	☐	☐	☐	☐	☐
[2.4]	r. Individualized assignments	☐	☐	☐	☐	☐
[2.5]	s. Guest speakers	☐	☐	☐	☐	☐
[5.3]	t. Interdisciplinary lessons	☐	☐	☐	☐	☐

Concerns

To what extent is each of the following a problem that limits students' mathematics learning in your school?

		Not a Problem	Slight Problem	Moderate Problem	Major Problem
[10.1]	Availability of funds for mathematics materials and supplies	☐	☐	☐	☐
[1.8]	Availability of appropriate curriculum materials (texts, calculators, software, etc.)	☐	☐	☐	☐
[10.5]	Availability of and access to computers and other technology	☐	☐	☐	☐
[9.1b]	Pressure to prepare students for state assessment	☐	☐	☐	☐
[8.2]	Availability of inservice opportunities for math teachers	☐	☐	☐	☐

Training

Reflect on the inservice training you have received and evaluate how prepared you feel to perform the following activities.

		Not Well Prepared	Somewhat Prepared	Well Prepared	Very Well Prepared
[1.3]	Develop lessons with a problem-solving focus	☐	☐	☐	☐
[1.6]	Use an approach that provides mathematical connections	☐	☐	☐	☐
[2.1]	Develop lessons that provide opportunities for students to actively construct their own mathematical knowledge	☐	☐	☐	☐
[2.2d]	Provide opportunities for students to use manipulatives to verify mathematical reasoning	☐	☐	☐	☐
[2.2b]	Use cooperative learning groups	☐	☐	☐	☐
[2.2a]	Model multiple problem-solving strategies and have students apply what they have learned	☐	☐	☐	☐
[2.2e]	Have students pose their own problems	☐	☐	☐	☐
[3.1]	Teach classes containing students of heterogeneous abilities	☐	☐	☐	☐
[3.3]	Use appropriate techniques for students with special needs	☐	☐	☐	☐
[3.1]	Teach classes containing students with different learning styles	☐	☐	☐	☐
[5.4]	Connect math to real-life contexts and careers	☐	☐	☐	☐
[9.3]	Use a variety of assessment strategies to measure students' success	☐	☐	☐	☐

FIGURE B.3	TEACHER SELF-PERCEPTION QUESTIONNAIRE *(continued)*

Compiler's Use

Preparation

Do you feel well prepared—either through professional development or coursework—to do the following?

	Not Well Prepared	Somewhat Prepared	Well Prepared	Very Well Prepared
[3.1] Encourage participation of males in mathematics	☐	☐	☐	☐
[2.2c] Listen/ask questions as students work in order to gauge their understanding	☐	☐	☐	☐
[5.1] Encourage students' interest in mathematics	☐	☐	☐	☐
[2.1] Develop students' conceptual understanding of mathematics	☐	☐	☐	☐
[3.1] Encourage participation of minorities in mathematics	☐	☐	☐	☐
[2.2f] Take students' prior understanding into account when planning curriculum and instruction	☐	☐	☐	☐
[2.2d] Manage a class of students engaged in hands-on/project-based work	☐	☐	☐	☐
[1.8] Use the textbook as a resource rather than the primary instructional tool . . .	☐	☐	☐	☐
[3.1] Recognize and respond to student cultural diversity	☐	☐	☐	☐
[2.3] Use calculators/computers for mathematics learning games	☐	☐	☐	☐
[7.2] Involve parents in the mathematics education of their children	☐	☐	☐	☐
[2.1] Lead a class of students using investigative strategies	☐	☐	☐	☐
[2.3] Use calculators/computers for drill and practice	☐	☐	☐	☐
[2.3] Use calculators/computers to demonstrate mathematics principles	☐	☐	☐	☐
[2.3] Use calculators/computers to collect and analyze data	☐	☐	☐	☐
[2.3] Use calculators/computers for simulations and applications	☐	☐	☐	☐
[2.3] Use the Internet in your mathematics teaching for general reference	☐	☐	☐	☐
[2.3] Use the Internet in your mathematics teaching for data acquisition	☐	☐	☐	☐
[2.3] Use the Internet in your mathematics teaching for collaborative projects with classes/individuals in other schools	☐	☐	☐	☐

[6.4] In the past three years, how many hours of professional development have you had in mathematics or mathematics education?

☐ None

☐ 6 hours or less

☐ 7–15 hours

☐ 16–35 hours

☐ More than 35 hours

FIGURE B.3	TEACHER SELF-PERCEPTION QUESTIONNAIRE *(continued)*

Compiler's Use

[6.4] If you have had professional development related to your mathematics teaching in the past three years, what was the format? (Check all that apply.)

- ☐ N/A
- ☐ Attendance at a workshop on mathematics teaching
- ☐ Observation of other teachers teaching mathematics as part of your own professional development (formal or informal)
- ☐ Study group of teachers on mathematics teaching issues
- ☐ A formal college/university course in the teaching of mathematics (math ed)
- ☐ A formal college/university mathematics course
- ☐ Service as a mentor and/or peer coach in mathematics teaching as part of a formal arrangement that is recognized or supported by the school or district
- ☐ Attendance at a national or state mathematics teacher association meeting
- ☐ Collaboration on mathematics teaching issues with a group of teachers at a distance using telecommunications (distance learning)

Instruction

How much emphasis does your instruction place on each of the following elements?

	Not Much	Some	Moderate	Extensive
[2.1] Mathematical concepts	☐	☐	☐	☐
[2.2a] Problem solving	☐	☐	☐	☐
[2.1] Mathematical reasoning	☐	☐	☐	☐
[1.7a] Computational skills	☐	☐	☐	☐
[1.6] How mathematics ideas connect with one another	☐	☐	☐	☐
[5.1] Increasing interest in mathematics	☐	☐	☐	☐
[5.1] Preparing for further study in mathematics	☐	☐	☐	☐
[1.7a] Mathematical algorithms/procedures	☐	☐	☐	☐
[1.7a] Ability to perform computations with speed and accuracy	☐	☐	☐	☐
[9.1b] Standardized test preparation	☐	☐	☐	☐
[1.4] Expression of mathematical ideas (orally and in writing)	☐	☐	☐	☐
[1.6] The logical structure of mathematics	☐	☐	☐	☐
[5.4] Applications of mathematics in business and industry	☐	☐	☐	☐
[5.4] The history and nature of mathematics	☐	☐	☐	☐

[2.4] How much homework do you assign in an average school <u>week</u>?

- ☐ 0–10 minutes
- ☐ 11–20 minutes
- ☐ 21–40 minutes
- ☐ 41–90 minutes
- ☐ 91–120 minutes
- ☐ More than 120 minutes

FIGURE B.3	TEACHER SELF-PERCEPTION QUESTIONNAIRE *(continued)*

Compiler's Use

[2.3]

Technology Use

In which of the following ways do students use calculators or computers in your math class? (Check all that apply.)

- ☐ Do drill and practice
- ☐ Demonstrate mathematics principles
- ☐ Play mathematics learning games
- ☐ Do probability simulations
- ☐ Collect data using sensors or probes
- ☐ Retrieve or exchange data
- ☐ Solve problems using simulations
- ☐ Take a test or quiz

Resources/Equipment

[1.8]

Indicate the degree of use of each of the following in your math instruction.

	Do Not Use (Not Needed)	Do Not Use (Not Available)	Use
Overhead projector	☐	☐	☐
Videotape player	☐	☐	☐
Videodisc player	☐	☐	☐
DVD player	☐	☐	☐
Four-function calculator (class set)	☐	☐	☐
Fraction calculators (class set)	☐	☐	☐
Graphing calculators (class set)	☐	☐	☐
Scientific calculators (class set)	☐	☐	☐
Computers	☐	☐	☐
Calculator/computer lab interfacing devices	☐	☐	☐
Computers with Internet connection	☐	☐	☐

Use of Textbooks/Commercial Programs

[1.8]

Which of the following best describes your use of textbooks or alternative commercial programs in your math classes?

- ☐ Use one textbook or program all or most of the time
- ☐ Use multiple textbooks or programs
- ☐ Do not use a textbook or commercial program

FIGURE B.4	**CLASS DESCRIPTION QUESTIONNAIRE**

SCHOOL _____

Teacher _____ Room # _____

Grade Level and Subject _____ # of Students _____

IEP Students _____ # IDEA/Section 504 Students _____ # G/T Students _____

Grouping approaches used: (homogenous/heterogeneous/other _____)

1. Name of the mathematics text or other materials used:

2. A brief description of the lesson planned during MPIR observation:

3. Professional organizations you belong to, journals you read or subscribe to on a regular basis, and professional development you have attended in the past three years:

4. Technology or software used in your class:

5. Other information the review team should know about you or your students:

FIGURE B.5	PRINCIPAL'S SELF-PERCEPTION QUESTIONNAIRE

SCHOOL _____

Compiler's Use	
	Professional Development
[3.4]	1. To what extent are professional development policies and practices focused on student needs (heterogeneous classes, learning styles, multiple intelligences, brain-based research, abilities, etc.)?
[6.8] [6.5]	2. What local, state, and federal funds are made available to the school for professional development to support innovative delivery systems, such as teacher academies; school-university partnerships; teacher networks; internships; courses for college credit; and active involvement in local, regional, state, or national professional mathematics associations?
[6.4]	3. What professional development needs related to mathematics have teachers identified?
[6.2] [8.5c]	4. To what extent are there opportunities for continuous, sustained professional development with ongoing study of a topic and in-school coaching?
[6.4]	5. Have teachers been trained on the program/materials/textbooks adopted for teaching mathematics?

FIGURE B.5	PRINCIPAL'S SELF-PERCEPTION QUESTIONNAIRE *(continued)*

Compiler's Use

[6.8]   6. What kinds of opportunities are there for you and your teachers to broaden and deepen your knowledge of mathematics subject matter; content-specific pedagogy; child pedagogy and adolescent development; new assessment strategies; how to address learning differences and disabilities; how to expand the range of teaching strategies; how to use technologies as part of the curriculum; and, how to work well with parents?

[9.7]   7. Does your school use mathematics achievement standards and professional teaching standards as a basis for professional development design?

Resources

[10.1]
[10.5]   1. How are resources (money, teachers, other staff, materials, equipment, and facilities) allocated to the teaching of mathematics? Is there sufficient technology available to meet the needs of the mathematics program?

[10.1]   2. What share of the total budget goes to support mathematics instruction in regular classrooms?

[6.6]   3. How much time do teachers have to plan and work together in teams and schoolwide?

[6.6]   4. How much individual planning time do teachers have each week?

[9.8]
[10.4]   5. Are funds available to support extracurricular and cocurricular activities, such as remediation and enrichment programs, clubs, competitions, and field trips?

FIGURE B.6	PRINCIPAL'S CHECKLIST FOR THE MATHEMATICS PROGRAM

SCHOOL _____

The Mathematics Program Improvement Review includes self-reported data that is cross-referenced with observational and interview data. As the instructional leader of your school, your perceptions and understanding of the mathematics program are critical to the analysis of the program. Consequently, we need you to complete this checklist, the results of which will be included in the program analysis. Thank you.

Please mark under the heading "Y" for Yes, "N" for No, and "?" for "No Data."

Compiler's Use	A. School Organization	Y	N	?
[6.1a]	1. Does your school have written instructional goals and objectives describing what students should be learning in math?			
[1.1]	2. Is there a written plan describing coordinated and sequential math experiences for all grade levels or courses?			
[1.5]	3. Is the school's math curriculum aligned to the state objectives?			
[1.3] [7.2]	4. Did development of the math curriculum involve teachers, administrators, parents, and anyone else responsible for implementing and maintaining that curriculum?			
[9.6]	5. Does the curriculum provide for vertical articulation in math instruction/learning (i.e., coordination with feeder schools)?			
[1.9] [6.1a]	6. Do all classroom math teachers understand the goals, curriculum, and time allocations for math instruction?			
[8.6]	7. Is adequate time for teaching math scheduled on a daily basis?			
[10.1]	8. Does the annual budget specify funds to adequately finance the math program?			
[9.1]	9. Do you regularly re-examine the math goals, teaching/learning strategies, and materials?			
[10.5]	10. Are there budgeted funds to cover costs for math materials, supplies, software, equipment (e.g., calculators), and books?			
[10.1]	11. Are teachers permitted to use petty cash funds to buy consumables for math?			
[6.5]	12. Does the budget include funds for professional development for math (e.g., consultants for local programs, travel to conferences, and teacher attendance at conventions)?			
[10.4]	13. Does the budget provide for transportation and other costs for activities, such as field trips?			
Compiler's Use	B. Principal Leadership	Y	N	?
[7.4]	1. Do you conduct public awareness sessions about math with parents?			
[8.2]	2. Do classroom math teachers have an opportunity to provide input into the professional development plan?			
[9.7]	3. Do you feel the math section of the state assessment is a valid measure of your school's math program's goals, curriculum, and experiences?			
[9.1]	4. Over the past two years, have you assessed the effectiveness of your math program using curricular reviews, teacher surveys, student interviews, review of state test data, and other means?			

FIGURE B.6	PRINCIPAL'S CHECKLIST FOR THE MATHEMATICS PROGRAM *(continued)*			

Compiler's Use	**B. Principal Leadership** (continued)	Y	N	?
[9.7]	5. Have your school's state assessment math scores shown a positive trend over the past several years?			
[9.9]	6. Do you evaluate the quality of teachers' math instruction?			
[9.7]	7. Do your students perform as well as or better than the state average on the math portion of the state assessment?			
[8.5b]	8. Are you an active participant in math professional development programs with your teachers?			
[7.3]	9. Are parents and the general community made aware of the school math program through parent–teacher meetings, math contests, or local media publicity?			
[8.4]	10. If a committee is formed to select a new math program/textbook, will you be an active participant?			
[9.4a]	11. Is the school's policy for grading and evaluating students consistent with the math program's objectives and instruction?			

Compiler's Use	**C. Support for Teachers**	Y	N	?
[8.5e]	1. Do you let the teachers know that *you* are interested in good math education by discussing best practices in math?			
[8.5a]	2. Do your teachers understand that they are expected to teach math as stated in the curriculum?			
[1.2] [2.6]	3. Does the school's math curriculum offer teachers specific skills, techniques, and materials they can use in their classrooms?			
[6.8]	4. Is there a means for teachers to try out new experiences before they use them in their classrooms?			
[6.5]	5. Have most of your teachers had recent exposure to professional workshops and meetings about math sponsored by the school or school system, regional education agencies, colleges, or professional organizations?			
[6.5]	6. Does the school provide funding for released time for teachers to attend programs on improving math education?			
[1.9]	7. Does the school maintain a professional library of math journals and other resources, and do the math teachers use it regularly?			
[8.5c]	8. Are the teachers given a written copy of what you are looking for in your walk-throughs?			

Compiler's Use	**D. Program Materials**	Y	N	?
[2.1]	1. Do the math texts and materials encourage students to explore, discover, and find answers for themselves?			
[1.4]	2. Are the processes of math—including reasoning, communications, representations, connections and problem solving—an integral part of the materials used in math?			
[1.6]	3. Is your math program aligned with both NCTM standards and state objectives?			

FIGURE B.6	PRINCIPAL'S CHECKLIST FOR THE MATHEMATICS PROGRAM *(continued)*			
Compiler's Use	**D. Program Materials** (continued)	Y	N	?
[2.6]	4. Are all written materials consistent with the math goals and objectives set by your school?			
[3.1]	5. Do program materials go from the simple to the complex and appear to fit the students' appropriate developmental levels?			
[5.1]	6. Do the materials draw upon the students' own interests and experiences?			
[5.4]	7. Do the program materials introduce students to math-related careers?			
[6.4]	8. Is the teacher's guide useful as a planning tool (rather than as a crutch)?			
	E. Walk-Through Observations and Informal Discussions	Y	N	?
[8.5d]	1. Are the attitudes of the math teachers positive when you discuss math with them/ when they teach?			
[2.2]	2. Do the teachers make full use of two-way discussion, reading, writing, small-group projects, lecturing, cooperative group work, and individualized instruction?			
[2.2a]	3. Are the teachers teaching skills, concepts, applications, and problem solving?			
[2.1]	4. Do teachers give students opportunities to investigate and do mathematics independently?			
[2.1]	5. Are students given opportunities to explore math materials before a concept is introduced?			
[2.1]	6. Do teachers ask open-ended, divergent questions and give all students time to respond?			
[2.2f]	7. Do teachers listen to what the students have to say?			
[3.3]	8. Are students with special needs given opportunities to become involved in math activities?			
[5.3]	9. Are teachers regularly connecting mathematics to other subjects like writing, science, or art?			
[3.3]	10. Are students with limited reading skills achieving in the math program?			
[4.1]	11. Do your school's students seem to like mathematics?			
[4.1]	12. When you talk with students about math, are their attitudes positive?			
[2.4]	13. Is a substantial part of class time in mathematics spent on activities beyond reading, listening, and pencil-and-paper work?			
[2.2f]	14. Do teachers use alternative assessments to continually monitor how well their students are acquiring math skills and concepts and how their students feel about mathematics?			
[2.2e]	15. Do students join freely in discussions about math activities, often initiating their own observations and ideas?			
[2.2b]	16. Are there lots of opportunities for individualized math projects, independent work, and peer-group tutoring?			

FIGURE B.6	PRINCIPAL'S CHECKLIST FOR THE MATHEMATICS PROGRAM *(continued)*			

Compiler's Use	F. Resources and Facilities	Y	N	?
[8.7]	1. Does each teacher have adequate storage space for math supplies, equipment, and materials?			
[1.6]	2. Are math materials (e.g., calculators) sufficiently available so that all students can work with them?			
[1.9]	3. Does the school library have a good collection of up-to-date books about math?			
[5.2]	4. Are there displays of student work in math classrooms as well as in the building?			
[5.2]	5. Do math classes show evidence of activities—bulletin boards, student projects, learning centers?			
[1.9], [10.5]	6. Are math supplies and materials regularly replaced?			
[10.5]	7. Do teachers have easy access to computers that their students can use in math learning?			
[10.3]	8. Do teachers collectively determine the need for mathematics resources, and is the ordering process reasonable, simple, and efficient?			
[10.1]	9. Are all those who teach math involved in selecting what will be used for instruction and reference?			

G. Summary

I. Checklist Response Totals

   Yes: No: No Data:

2. On a scale of 1–5, with 5 being the highest, what overall rating would you give to your school's math program?

3. List the major strengths of your school's math program.

4. List the areas of the program most in need of improvement.

5. List five priority actions for next year.

FIGURE B.7	TEACHER INTERVIEW QUESTIONS—ELEMENTARY AND MIDDLE SCHOOL

SCHOOL _____

INTERVIEW GROUP INFORMATION _____

Compiler's Use	Question	Response
[1.3]	1. In your opinion, which comes first, understanding or skills?	
[1.3]	*2. Which is more important over the course of the school year? a. Computational skills b. Conceptual understanding c. Real-life applications d. Problem solving?	

[1.7a]
 	
[1.7b]
 	
[1.7c]
 	
[1.7d]
	*3. This year, have you taught (or will you teach) the following topics?
	a. Number sense and operation sense
	  – Number theory (primes, factors, multiples, etc.)
	  – Mental computation
	  – Equivalent forms of numbers (percents, fractions, decimals)
	  – Ratios, percents, proportions
	  – Concept of fractions
	  – Operations with fractions
	b. Estimation techniques
	  – Strategies other than rounding (front-end, compatible numbers, etc.)
	  – Using estimation to solve problems
	  – Using estimation to check reasonableness of an answer
	c. Patterns and functions
	  – How to describe, extend, and create patterns
	  – How to use patterns/functions to solve problems, including algebra problems
	d. Measurement and geometry
	  – How to describe, compare, and sketch geometric figures (2–D, 3–D)
	  – Properties of figures (2–D, 3–D)
	  – Time and money (elapsed time, time schedules, making change, denominate measurements)
	  – Perimeter, area, volume, angle measure (formula and measure)
	  – Use of appropriate measurement tools (spring balances, trundle wheel, platform scales, etc.)	

*Questions marked with an asterisk are foundational to the MPIR and must be asked in all teacher interviews.

FIGURE B.7	TEACHER INTERVIEW QUESTIONS—ELEMENTARY AND MIDDLE SCHOOL *(continued)*

Compiler's Use	Question	Response
[1.7e]	e. Spatial sense and reasoning – Tessellations – Transformations (reflections, rotations, translations, dilations) – Line of symmetry – Scale drawing	

[1.7f]	f. Data collection and interpretation
	– Reading/interpreting graphs, tables, and charts brought in from newspaper
	– Collecting, organizing, and interpreting data
	– How to create the following:
	    pictographs
	    bar graphs
	    line plots
	    line graphs
	    circle graphs (pie charts)
	    double bar/double line graphs
	    histograms
	    glyphs
	    stacked bar graphs
	    stem-and-leaf plots
	    Venn diagrams
	    scatter plots
	    box-and-whiskers plots
	    line of best fit
	– Finding mean, median, mode, range, outliers
	– Making predictions based on data analysis (random vs. population sample vs. biased sample)	

[1.7g]	g. Probability and statistics – Conducting probability simulations – Using theoretical probability to predict (organized list, tree diagram, area model, Fundamental Counting Principle)	
[1.7h]	h. Algebra – Plotting coordinates – Operations with integers – Solving equations – Graphing equations – Finding slope/intercept – The Pythagorean theorem	
[1.8]	4. How much and how often do your students use a textbook?	

FIGURE B.7	TEACHER INTERVIEW QUESTIONS—ELEMENTARY AND MIDDLE SCHOOL *(continued)*

Compiler's Use	Question	Response
[1.8]	5. Do you make use of school library resources (trade books, videos) to teach math? If so, how?	
[1.8]	6. Do you have access to a professional library of math materials (e.g., professional math journals, appropriate blackline master publications)?	
[9.3]	*7. Which of the following approaches do you use to assess students' progress? – Reflective writing (journal, log, exit slip, etc.) – Group project with a group product (oral report, model, poster, etc.) – Anecdotal records – Self/peer assessment – Individual hands-on investigations – Group performance events – Open-response questions on tests – Open-response questions in class	
[2.2d]	*8. How often do you use manipulatives? Do you use them to introduce concepts or to practice skills? Do you use them for problem solving, i.e., students choose manipulatives to solve a problem? Do students use manipulatives to verify solutions?	
[2.2b]	9. How often do your students work in cooperative groups? How do you place students in groups?	
[2.3]	10. When do students use calculators in class? Are there any restrictions on their use?	
[2.3]	11. Do students use computers? How?	

FIGURE B.7	TEACHER INTERVIEW QUESTIONS—ELEMENTARY AND MIDDLE SCHOOL *(continued)*

Compiler's Use	Question	Response

[10.1]
 	
[10.3]
 	
[10.4]
	*12. Do you have an adequate number of resources to teach math? What do you feel that you could use to improve your instruction?
	   a. Who makes decisions on budget allocations for math?
	   b. Is there funding for extracurricular experiences, such as field trips or after-school enrichment?	

[2.4]	13. How much, how often, and what type of homework do you assign? How much time do you expect students to spend on doing math homework at home?	
[5.4] [2.6]	14. How do you demonstrate the connections between math and the real world other than through class discussion and the problems in the text?	
[5.1]	15. What process do you have to relate lessons to student interests or subsequent mathematics topics?	
[2.2e]	16. How do you help students develop their ability to pose problems and to discover solutions for themselves?	
[3.1] [3.3]	*17. What efforts do you make to assure girls, minority students, students from poor families, and students with different learning styles, needs, abilities and disabilities have an opportunity to participate equally in your class?	
[3.4]	18. What do you do to challenge students who excel in math?	
[3.4]	19. What adaptations do you make to meet the needs of lower-achieving or special needs students?	

FIGURE B.7	TEACHER INTERVIEW QUESTIONS—ELEMENTARY AND MIDDLE SCHOOL *(continued)*

Compiler's Use	Question	Response
[6.4]	20. Do you think that you have had enough training on technology to be able to use it adequately in your classes? What training have you had?	
[4.4] [4.8]	21. What does the school do to recognize students' and teachers' achievements in mathematics learning or teaching?	
[5.3]	22. What are some examples of how you show the usefulness of math in other subject areas?	
[6.6]	*23. What opportunities during the school day do the teachers in your team/department and the total group of teachers in your school have to plan together (common planning, early dismissal, professional development days), to observe one another (peer observation), and to exchange feedback?	
[6.5]	24. Does the school or district administration encourage participation in local, state, and national associations or meetings? How?	
[8.5c]	*25. Does the principal coach you on effective instructional practices that help you to teach mathematics?	
[7.1]	26. What do you or other school staff do to encourage families to support mathematics achievement among all students?	
[7.4b]	27. How do you inform parents about the purpose and structure of the math program (syllabus, course outline, written expectations)?	
[7.4a] [7.4c]	28. How are parents informed of specialized programs (for example, after-school tutoring)? How are they informed of curriculum options as well as future educational and career options?	

FIGURE B.7	TEACHER INTERVIEW QUESTIONS—ELEMENTARY AND MIDDLE SCHOOL *(continued)*

Compiler's Use	Question	Response
[9.4]	29. How do you communicate student successes or problems to parents (midterm progress reports, written notes, letters, e-mails, etc.)?	
[9.5]	30. Do all teachers participate in mathematics planning and evaluation (for example, development of the school improvement plan, curriculum development, test disaggregation)?	
[9.6]	31. How often do you meet with teachers from other schools, especially feeder schools, to plan and coordinate the math program?	
[6.1]	32. Does the school have written instructional goals apart from assessment goals? What are they? Is math included in the school's improvement plan? How?	
[6.4]	*33. What specialized training and experiences have helped you to teach math (e.g., Box It or Bag It or T³)? Is there any "teacher-to-teacher" training?	
[3.6]	34. Have teachers in your school had professional development relating to equity and diversity?	
[6.4]	35. Have you been trained in the use of the programs/ materials that you use to teach mathematics? How long?	
[8.5c]	36. Does the principal provide you with written feedback after observations? How quickly?	
[8.5d]	37. Does the principal have the interpersonal skills that encourage you to want to make changes he or she has suggested?	

FIGURE B.7	TEACHER INTERVIEW QUESTIONS—ELEMENTARY AND MIDDLE SCHOOL *(continued)*

Compiler's Use	Question	Response
[1.1]	*38. What documents do you use to plan what and how you will teach? Are these documents aligned to the state assessment? To texts and other resources? Is there a timeline or pacing guide? Do you know which skills/concepts that you are accountable for teaching?	
	*39. What do you see as the major strength(s) of the overall math program?	
	*40. What are the areas most in need of improvement?	

FIGURE B.8	TEACHER INTERVIEW QUESTIONS—HIGH SCHOOL

SCHOOL _____

INTERVIEW GROUP INFORMATION _____

Compiler's Use	Question	Response
[1.3]	*1. In your opinion, which is most important: skills, concepts, applications, or problem solving?	
	*2. This year, have you taught (or will you teach) the following topics?	
[1.7a]	a. Operations on real numbers (absolute value, factorial)	
[1.7b]	b. Estimation strategies (including use of real number properties)	
[1.7c]	c. Using matrices to solve problems	
[1.7d]	d. Sequences and series	
[1.7e]	e. Algebraic and geometric transformations	
[1.7f]	f. Indirect measurement and the Pythagorean theorem	
[1.7g]	g. Collecting, organizing, and displaying two-variable data	
[1.7h]	h. Statistical models (standard deviation, chi square)	
[1.7i]	i. Solving and graphing a variety of equations (including systems) and inequalities	
[1.7j]	j. Identifying the characteristics of the graphs of a function	
[1.7k]	k. Linear, quadratic, and exponential equations and functions	
[1.7l]	l. Right triangle trigonometry (sine, cosine, tangent)	
[1.8]	3. How much and how often do your students use a textbook?	
[1.8]	4. Do you make use of school library resources (trade books, videos) to teach math? If so, how?	

*Questions marked with an asterisk are foundational to the MPIR and must be asked in all teacher interviews.

FIGURE B.8	TEACHER INTERVIEW QUESTIONS—HIGH SCHOOL *(continued)*

Compiler's Use	Question	Response
[1.8]	5. Do you have access to a professional library of math materials (e.g., professional math journals, appropriate blackline master publications)?	
[9.3]	*6. Which of the following approaches do you use to assess students' progress? – Reflective writing (journal, log, exit slip, etc.) – Group project with a group product (oral report, model, poster, etc.) – Anecdotal records – Self-/peer assessment – Individual hands-on investigations – Group performance events – Student-teacher-parent conferences – Open-response questions on tests – Open-response questions for homework	
[2.2d]	*7. How often do you use manipulatives? Do you use them to introduce concepts or to practice skills? Do you permit students to determine which manipulative, if any, they need when doing problem solving? Do students use manipulatives to verify solutions?	
[2.2b]	8. How often do your students work in cooperative groups? How do you place students in groups?	
[2.3]	9. When do students use calculators in class? Are there any restrictions on their use?	
[2.3]	10. Do students use computers? How?	
[10.1] [10.3] [10.4]	*11. Do you have an adequate number of manipulatives, calculators, and so on? a. Who makes decisions on budget allocations for math? b. Is there funding for extracurricular experiences, such as field trips or after-school enrichment?	

FIGURE B.8	TEACHER INTERVIEW QUESTIONS—HIGH SCHOOL *(continued)*

Compiler's Use	Question	Response
[2.4]	12. How much, how often, and what type of homework do you assign? How much time do you expect students to spend on doing math homework at home?	
[5.4] [2.6]	13. How do you demonstrate the connections between math and the real world other than through class discussion and the problems in the text?	
[2.2e]	14. How do you help students develop their ability to pose problems and to discover solutions for themselves?	
[5.1]	15. What process do you have to relate lessons to student interests or subsequent mathematics topics?	
[3.1] [3.3]	*16. What efforts do you make to assure girls, minority students, students from poor families, and students with different learning styles, needs, abilities and disabilities have an opportunity to participate equally in your class?	
[3.4]	17. What do you do to challenge and motive students who excel in mathematics?	
[3.4]	18. What adaptations do you make to meet the needs of lower-achieving or special needs students?	
[6.4]	19. Do you think that you have had enough training on technology to be able to use it adequately in your classes? What training have you had?	

FIGURE B.8	TEACHER INTERVIEW QUESTIONS—HIGH SCHOOL *(continued)*

Compiler's Use	Question	Response
[4.4] [4.8]	20. What does the school do to recognize students' and teachers' achievements in mathematics learning or teaching?	
[5.3]	21. What are some examples of how you show the usefulness of math in other subject areas?	
[6.6]	*22. What opportunities during the school do the teachers in your department and throughout the faculty have to plan together (common planning, early dismissal, professional development days), to observe one another (peer observation), and to exchange feedback?	
[6.5]	23. Does the school or district administration encourage participation in local, state, and national associations or meetings? How?	
[8.5c] [8.5d]	*24. Does the principal coach teachers on effective instructional strategies? Does the principal have the interpersonal skills that encourage you to make changes he or she may have suggested for your instructional approach?	
[7.1]	25. What do you or other school staff do to encourage families to support mathematics achievement among all students?	
[7.4b]	26. How do you inform parents about the purpose and structure of the math program (syllabus, course outline, written expectations) and how the grading system works (percentage of grade based on homework, on tests, etc.)?	

FIGURE B.8	TEACHER INTERVIEW QUESTIONS—HIGH SCHOOL *(continued)*

Compiler's Use	Question	Response
[7.4a] [7.4c]	27. How are parents informed of specialized programs (e.g., after-school tutoring)? How are they informed of curriculum options as well as future educational and career options?	
[9.4]	28. How do you communicate student successes or problems to parents (midterm progress reports, written notes, letters, e-mails, etc.)?	
[9.5]	29. Do all teachers in the mathematics department participate in program planning and evaluation (for example, development of a program improvement plan, curriculum development, test disaggregation)?	
[9.6]	30. How often do you meet with teachers from other schools, especially feeder schools, to plan and coordinate the math program?	
[6.1]	31. What are the school's goals with regard to mathematics instruction? Is math included in the school's improvement plan? How?	
[6.4]	*32. What specialized training and experiences have helped you to teach math (e.g., Lattice Algebra or T^3)? Is there any "teacher-to-teacher" training?	
[1.1]	*33. What documents do you use to plan what and how you will teach? Are these documents aligned to the state assessment? To texts and other resources? Is there a timeline or pacing guide? Do you know which skills/concepts you are accountable for teaching?	
[8.5c]	34. Does the principal provide you with written feedback after observations? How quickly?	

FIGURE B.8	TEACHER INTERVIEW QUESTIONS—HIGH SCHOOL *(continued)*

Compiler's Use	Question	Response
[3.6]	35. Have teachers in your school had professional development relating to equity and diversity?	
[3.4]	36. Have you been trained in the use of the programs/ materials that you use to teach mathematics?	
	*37. What do you see as the major strength(s) of the overall math program?	
	*38. What are the areas most in need of improvement?	

FIGURE B.9	STUDENT INTERVIEW QUESTIONS

SCHOOL _____

INTERVIEW GROUP INFORMATION _____

Compiler's Use	Question	Response

[1.3]	1. Which of the following do you think is most important?
	  a. Basic skills (math facts, computation)
	  b. Concepts (e.g., place value)
	  c. Real-life applications
	  d. Problem solving
	
	Which do you think your teacher feels
	is most important?	

[1.4]
[1.4]
[1.7e]
[1.7h]
[2.5]
[2.5]
[2.5]
[2.5c]
	2. Which of the following have you done this year?
	  a. Described answers to problems in writing
	  b. Wrote a math report
	  c. Created your own math models or design
	  d. Collected data through a survey
	  e. Did a probability experiment
	  f. Went on a math field trip
	  g. Did a math project
	  h. Discussed different ways to solve math problems	

[1.6]
[2.4]
	3. Which of these best describes how your teacher begins a new lesson?
	  a. Teacher reviews what you have learned previously and talks about how it will relate to the new lesson.
	  b. Teacher goes straight into the new lesson without discussing previous lessons.	

FIGURE B.9	STUDENT INTERVIEW QUESTIONS *(continued)*

Compiler's Use	Question	Response

[1.4]	4. Does it help you to learn math by . . .
	   a. Listening to how other students solved problems?
	   b. Writing so that your teacher understands your thoughts?	

[2.2b]	5. Do you work with other students in groups? What kind of groups (e.g., small groups, large groups, pairs)? Do you feel that group work helps you to learn better or not?	
[2.2d]	6. Do you use manipulatives? Which do you use most often?	

[2.4]	7. Do you have math homework? Does it take you more than 20 minutes on average to complete your homework?
	
	What type of homework do you usually do? Is it usually
	   a. Textbook problems to practice a new concept?
	   b. A real-life application, such as collecting data?
	   c. Writing in a math journal?	

[2.2a]	8. What are some of the problem-solving strategies you have used in math this year?	
[4.2]	9. Do you sometimes wish that the math was more difficult or more challenging?	

FIGURE B.9	STUDENT INTERVIEW QUESTIONS *(continued)*

Compiler's Use	Question	Response

[2.2f]	10. Which of these best describes your teacher's method of getting answers to questions?
	  a. Calls only on students whose hands are raised
	  b. Calls on no one; students call out the answers each time
	  c. Calls on students in a predictable pattern, like going down the row
	  d. Calls on students randomly	

[9.3]	11. Which of the following types of tests have you taken this year?
	  a. Multiple choice
	  b. Short answer
	  c. Matching
	  d. Problems in which you have to show all your work
	  e. Problems where you have to explain or justify your solution (open response)
	
	Do you get partial credit on test questions in which you have to show your work?	

[5.1]	12. Does your teacher ever ask you what you are interested in and then find math problems related to those interests?	
[5.4]	13. Who in the school talks about how math is important later—in high school, in college, or in the working world? Your math teacher? Principal? Counselor? Who tells you what kind of math is needed in particular careers?	
[1.8] [2.3]	14. How often do you use computers in math? How do you use them?	
	15. What would you change about the math program to improve it or make it more interesting?	
	16. What do you like about the math program that you think the school should keep and not change?	

FIGURE B.10	PARENT INTERVIEW QUESTIONS

SCHOOL _____

INTERVIEW GROUP INFORMATION _____

Compiler's Use	Question	Response
[1.3]	1. **Curriculum.** Historically, math instruction has tended to emphasize four things in varying degrees: a. Basic skills (math facts, computation) b. Concepts (e.g., place value) c. Real-life applications d. Problem solving Where do you think this school is currently placing its emphasis?	
[1.6]	2. **Curriculum.** Based on your child's experience, would you say students in this school are taught a variety of math topics over the years, or do they do much of the same each year? Do you feel the math program is balanced among computation, geometry, measurement, probability, algebra, and statistics?	
[2.2d]	3. **Instruction.** Would you say the school tends to use a more hands-on approach to math learning or more of a textbook and paper-and-pencil approach?	
[1.7e] [1.7d] [2.3] [2.3] [2.5] [2.5] [5.4]	4. **Instruction.** Which of these activities did your child do this year? a. Made math models or design b. Measured shapes or objects c. Used a calculator d. Worked math on a computer e. Did a special project f. Went on a math-related field trip g. Practically applied math as related to everyday life	

FIGURE B.10	PARENT INTERVIEW QUESTIONS *(continued)*

Compiler's Use	Question	Response
[4.1] [3.1]	**5. Classroom/School Environment.** Are there high expectations for all learners? Would you say that all students are treated equally and fairly within the classroom, regardless of gender, race, ethnicity, achievement level, learning styles, or socioeconomic status?	
[3.3]	**6. Accommodating Student Needs.** Based on your child's experience, would you say that math homework assignments are reasonable in terms of how often they are given and how long it takes to complete them?	
[7.3] [9.4]	**7. Student Success.** Are students in this school achieving in mathematics at a high level? Is the school going in the right direction with regard to math? What information on math achievement have you received?	
[7.2]	**8. Monitoring.** Have you had an opportunity to offer suggestions or support for improving the math curriculum? For example, has anyone ever asked you to be a guest speaker, suggest a field trip site, participate in a discussion of the math program, or serve in the math classroom as an instructional volunteer?	
[7.3] [8.4]	**9. Leadership.** Do you think the principal shows interest in the math program? Does the principal make any written reports to parents or the community about the math program?	
[6.1] [9.4b]	**10. School Goals.** Does the school have goals for math instruction? If so, how were they developed and how were they communicated to you?	
[7.4]	**11. Communication.** Have you ever attended a program or received a newsletter to show you how math is taught or tested? Have you ever received information about support or assistance that was available to students for math? Has there been any discussion about future consequences (high school course offerings, university admission requirements, careers) based on students' results in math?	

FIGURE B.10	PARENT INTERVIEW QUESTIONS *(continued)*

Compiler's Use	Question	Response
[9.4]	**12. Evaluation/Assessment.** What is the grading scale within your child's math class? How much of the grade is based on homework, tests, participation, and so on? How do you know?	
[9.4]	**13. Assessment Goals.** How are your child's math test results and progress reported to you? How often does this happen? Has this reporting been adequate?	
[8.6]	**14. Time Allotment.** (Grades K–8): How much time does your child spend in math class each day? Is this adequate? (Grades 9–12): Do you feel that students are required to take enough math?	
	15. Program Strengths. What would you say are the strongest features of the math program in this school?	
	16. Program Weaknesses. What areas of the math program would you say need to be changed or improved?	

FIGURE B.11	PRINCIPAL INTERVIEW QUESTIONS

SCHOOL _____

INTERVIEW GROUP INFORMATION _____

Compiler's Use	Question	Response
[1.1]	**1. Curriculum.** Does the school have a written curriculum?	
[1.3]	Do you feel that computation, concepts, applications, or problem solving is the major focus of the math program?	
[10.3]	Who makes the recommendations and budget decisions on math expenditures?	
[10.1]	Is the budget for math based on the needs shown within the curriculum?	
[8.4]	**2. Instruction.** How do you monitor instruction? Do you observe each teacher during a math lesson? Do you review math lesson plans to determine if they are aligned to the curriculum? Are pacing guides or other scheduling expectations set?	
[2.6]	Do you review the objectives for math, particularly to see if they are aligned?	
[8.5e]	What is your vision of effective mathematics instruction?	
[3.1]	**3. Equity and Diversity.** What do you do to ensure that all students, regardless of gender, race, ethnicity, socioeconomic background, or learning style have equal access to good math instruction?	
[3.4]	What do you do to ensure that both high-achieving and low-achieving students get access to math instruction that meets their needs? Do you ability group for math? How are students placed in classes?	
[4.3]	**4. School Climate.** What have the math teachers done to ensure that there are high expectations for all students?	
[4.4] [4.8]	What is done within the school to recognize and reward math achievement by students and school personnel? Do classes or programs for struggling students receive additional support? Are there enrichment programs for math?	

FIGURE B.11	PRINCIPAL INTERVIEW QUESTIONS *(continued)*

Compiler's Use	Question	Response
[6.3]	5. **Training and Development.** Are professional development programs evaluated for effectiveness? Does the school provide opportunities for "teacher-to-teacher" training?	
[8.5c]	Do you coach teachers on effective instructional practices?	
[8.5b]	Do you regularly attend and participate in mathematics professional development?	
[7.1]	6. **Community.** What does the school do to encourage families to support the math program?	
[7.3] [7.4]	How do you inform parents and the community about the purpose of the math program, special assistance, and test results in math?	
[10.2]	What do you do to involve the business and professional community in the math program?	
[9.1]	7. **Continuing Assessment.** What efforts have been made by the school staff to evaluate the math program?	
[9.2]	What use has been made of data from state and national tests in planning and implementing program improvements? How have you used parent and/or student surveys?	
[9.6]	What efforts have been made to coordinate the math program here with the math program in the feeder schools as well as other schools in the district?	
[6.1] [9.4b]	8. **Organization.** Does the school have goals for math instruction?	
[10.1]	Are the goals used in the planning of professional development and the budget?	
[8.3]	Are all teachers assigned classes with fewer than 28 students?	
[9.9]	Are there specific criteria for evaluating math instruction? Does the teacher evaluation system distinguish between competent and incompetent math teachers?	
[8.1	Are math teachers required to have their students complete entries for their writing portfolios? How are extra duties (bus, bathroom, etc.) assigned?	

FIGURE B.12	CLASSROOM OBSERVATION INSTRUMENT

TEACHER _____ **LEVEL/CLASS** _____

LESSON TITLE _____

1. Physical Setting/Classroom Environment   Section Rating _____
(Mark all that apply.)

A. Classroom Facility
☐ Classroom adequate size for student number
☐ Adequate storage for resources/materials/equipment
☐ Furnishings allow for activity-based instruction
☐ Student seating is flexible to allow for differing needs (projects, investigations, cooperative groups, etc.)
☐ Room size will accommodate activities (CBL, etc.)
☐ Flat top surfaces are sufficient for investigations, projects, displays, etc.

B. Classroom Environment
☐ Math manipulatives/tools evident
☐ Math displays/posters promote learning
☐ Student textbooks evident
☐ Class set of calculators available
☐ Computers available, # _____
☐ Math student work displayed
☐ Adequate resources available for hands-on lesson (as appropriate)

2. Lesson Effectiveness   Section Rating _____
(Mark all that apply.)

A. Major Instructional Resources Used

☐ Textbook
☐ Other print materials
☐ Overhead
☐ Videotape, audiotape
☐ DVD
☐ Math tools

☐ Hands-on/manipulative materials
☐ Calculators
☐ Overhead calculator
☐ Computer to access Internet
☐ Computer to collect or analyze data

☐ Computer to learn or practice a skill or concept (software program)
☐ Instructional resources were used appropriately
☐ Resources contributed to the quality of lesson

B. Content Focus
☐ Number/computation
☐ Geometry
☐ Measurement
☐ Probability/statistics
☐ Algebra/precalculus/calculus

FIGURE B.12	CLASSROOM OBSERVATION INSTRUMENT *(continued)*

C. Place in Instructional Sequence

☐ Introduce new concept
☐ Develop conceptual understanding
☐ Apply concept to new situation
☐ Review concept or procedure
☐ Assess student understanding

D. Grouping Arrangement Used

☐ Whole group
☐ Small groups working on same task
☐ Small groups working on different tasks
☐ Individuals working on same task
☐ Individuals working on different tasks
The grouping arrangement was appropriate for the apparent instructional goal and activity   ☐ Yes ☐ No

E. Teacher and Student Behaviors Observed

Teacher Behaviors

☐ Setting up and guiding students through meaningful problems
☐ Moving around the room monitoring/questioning
☐ Encouraging students to consider multiple ways to solve problems/test solutions
☐ Guiding students in the use of manipulatives/technology
☐ Promoting student use of inquiry/creativity through questioning/group work
☐ Facilitating discussions about problem-solving processes' efficiency/effectiveness
☐ Leading students through discussion/journaling of their understanding

Student Behaviors

☐ Interacting with others and working alone
☐ Applying math to real-life problems with adopted program
☐ Working in groups to test solutions
☐ Sharing solution processes and listening to others share their thinking
☐ Defending solution processes' efficiency and usefulness
☐ Communicating math ideas: demonstrations, models, drawings, and arguments
☐ Working in teams to challenge and defend solutions
☐ Helping to clarify each other's learning through discussion/modeling
☐ Activity in progress was appropriate for the apparent instructional goal

Activity was   ☐ ineffective/poor   ☐ mediocre/minimum impact   ☐ somewhat effective
                ☐ effective/good   ☐ exceptionally effective/high quality

FIGURE B.12	CLASSROOM OBSERVATION INSTRUMENT *(continued)*

F. Inclusion of Open-Response Questions

Students solved one or more nonroutine, or open-response, questions   ☐ Yes   ☐ No

G. Instructional Design

☐ Established academic focus (e.g., essential question)
☐ Reviewed/connected to previous learning
☐ Included closure

3. Questioning Strategies   Section Rating _____

(Mark all that apply.)

☐ Wait Time I   ☐ Wait Time II   ☐ No/limited wait time
☐ Questions were higher-order and stimulated broad student responses
☐ Questions were lower-cognitive and stimulated narrow student responses
☐ No questions were asked by teacher or posed through the activity being conducted
☐ Teacher used strategy to ensure all students had opportunity to respond
☐ Teacher asked probing follow-up questions
☐ Student(s) asked follow-up questions
☐ Teacher provided specific praise
☐ Teacher provided general praise
☐ Teacher provided no praise
The questioning strategies were checked for student understanding of apparent instructional goal   ☐ Yes   ☐ No

4. Classroom Climate   Section Rating _____

A. Student Involvement

☐ Majority of students demonstrated interest
☐ Majority of students were engaged and on task
☐ Majority of students uninterested or apathetic
☐ Majority of students were frequently off task

B. Classroom Management

☐ Classroom orderly, no student disruptions that impaired learning environment
☐ Classroom generally orderly, but some student disruptions required disciplinary action
☐ Classroom disorderly, frequent student disruptions seriously impaired the learning environment
☐ The climate was generally positive
☐ The climate enhanced learning opportunities for students

FIGURE B.12	CLASSROOM OBSERVATION INSTRUMENT *(continued)*

5. Development of Higher-Order Thinking Skills
(Check all skills that were introduced and/or developed in the observed lesson.)

Section Rating _____

A. Basic Process Skills
☐ Observing actions of others
☐ Reciting/recalling facts
☐ Classifying
☐ Measuring/estimating
☐ Collecting/recording data
☐ Constructing charts/graphs

B. Higher-Level Skills
☐ Interpreting/analyzing data
☐ Computing/calculating
☐ Investigating
☐ Applying theorems/principles
☐ Evaluating relevancy of data
☐ Selecting problem-solving strategy
☐ Creating/formulating patterns/equations
☐ Evaluating logical consistency
☐ Justifying/verifying solutions/strategies

C. Learner Attitudes Demonstrated
☐ Curiosity
☐ Cooperation
☐ Persistence
☐ Responsibility
☐ Confidence
☐ Enthusiasm
☐ Objectivity
☐ Accuracy
☐ Critical thinking

6. Overall Classroom Observation Rating
(Consult criteria in Section 6 of the Classroom Observation Instrument Scoring Rubric.)

_____

FIGURE B.13	CLASSROOM OBSERVATION INSTRUMENT SCORING RUBRIC	
1. Physical Setting/Classroom Environment		
1	**3**	**5**
Student furnishings are not flexible and in many cases will not allow for appropriate student-student or student-teacher interaction.	Student furnishings are not flexible enough to allow for quality student-student and student-teacher interaction in all types of mathematics instruction.	Student furnishings are flexible and can be arranged to accommodate any type of mathematics activity and to provide for maximum student-student and student-teacher interaction.
Classroom is inadequate in size, with little or no storage space for mathematics materials (e.g., manipulatives and other resources).	Classroom is adequate in size, with some storage space for mathematics materials (e.g., manipulatives and other resources).	The classroom is large with sufficient storage for mathematics materials (e.g., manipulatives and other resources).
Classroom furnishings are not conducive to hands-on instruction (e.g., there are slant-top desks).	Classroom has a variety of furnishings, some of which are appropriate for hands-on activities.	Classroom furnishings are varied and appropriate for hands-on activities.
Mathematics manipulatives and/or calculators are absent or extremely limited.	Manipulatives and calculators are available (either out for student access or in cabinets), but not in sufficient quantities for all students to be involved.	Manipulatives and calculators are evident and easily obtained by the students.
There is no student work in mathematics displayed.	Limited amount of student work is displayed.	Student work in mathematics is displayed.
There are no computer stations available for student use.	Some computers and printers are available, but not enough for all student teams to access simultaneously.	Sufficient computers and printers are available for all student teams to have access.

FIGURE B.13	CLASSROOM OBSERVATION INSTRUMENT SCORING RUBRIC *(continued)*

2. Lesson Effectiveness		
1	**3**	**5**
Instructional resources utilized are not appropriate for the activity.	Instructional resources utilized are appropriate for the activity; however, other better-designed or more up-to-date resources are available.	Instructional resources utilized are appropriate for the activity and are well designed and up to date.
Technology is not used by students when needed or is unavailable.	Appropriate technology is available but not used by all students or not fully integrated into the instructional activity.	Appropriate technology is incorporated as an integral part of instruction and increases student learning opportunities.
Lesson objectives are not apparent and the lesson is not well designed (no review or connection to previous learning and no closure).	Lesson objectives are not readily apparent and/or the lesson design is not suited to achieve them (ambiguous connection made to previous learning and no closure).	Lesson objectives are apparent and the lesson is well designed to achieve them (including review or connection to previous learning and lesson closure).
Students are not seated in a configuration that is conducive to accomplishing instructional goals.	Students are seated in a configuration appropriate for the current lesson, but grouping is not flexible enough for all types of instruction.	Students are seated in a configuration that is flexible and appropriate for the lesson being taught.
Instruction is inconsistent with research-based best practice.	Instruction has some elements of research-based best practice, but it is not likely that all students will achieve the instructional objectives.	Instruction is consistent with research-based practice and all students have an excellent chance of achieving the instructional objectives.
There is little or no evidence that students are learning.	There is some evidence that all students are learning or, at least, evidence that *some* students are learning.	There is much evidence that all students are learning (quality of student–student and student–teacher interaction, completion of assigned tasks, ability to plan and carry out a discovery lesson, etc.).

FIGURE B.13	CLASSROOM OBSERVATION INSTRUMENT SCORING RUBRIC *(continued)*

3. Questioning Strategies

1	3	5
Few or no significant questions are posed by either the teacher or students.	Some significant questions are posed by the teacher and students.	Many significant questions are posed by both the teacher and students.
Activity does not utilize questions to clarify the concept or extend learning.	Activity utilizes the teacher's and students' questions to clarify the concept or extend learning.	Activity is based on questions asked by the teacher or students.
All questions asked are narrow (lower-cognitive) in nature.	Some broad questions asked; however, narrow (lower-cognitive) questions are more abundant.	Broad, higher-cognitive, questions elicit a variety of student responses.
Many students in the class are not engaged or are not participating in the activity.	Most students in the class are engaged and participate in the activity.	All students in the class are engaged and participate in the activity.
Questions do not extend student learning.	Questions have limited value in extending student learning.	Questions extend student learning and lead students into further discussion or inquiry.
Student gender, race, or socioeconomic status appears to influence the quantity or quality of questions asked.	Student gender, race, or socioeconomic status does not appear to influence the *quality* of questions asked, but few questions are asked of minority students in proportion to their numbers; or does not appear to influence the *number* of questions asked, but the questions asked of minority students are of a lesser quality (i.e., lower cognitive).	Student gender, race, or socioeconomic status does not appear to influence the quantity or quality of questions asked.
Wait time is not used.	Wait time is used after questions are asked but not after students respond.	Wait time of 3 seconds or longer is used after questions are asked and after students respond.
General praise is given to student responses.	A mixture of general praise and specific praise is provided.	Specific praise is given to student responses.

FIGURE B.13	CLASSROOM OBSERVATION INSTRUMENT SCORING RUBRIC *(continued)*

4. Classroom Climate

1	3	5
Few or no students demonstrate interest in the topic being taught.	Many or most students demonstrate interest in the topic being taught.	All students demonstrate interest in the topic being taught.
Few students are engaged in the instructional activity.	Most students are engaged in the instructional activity.	All students are engaged in the instructional activity.
Few students appear to know classroom routines and procedures.	Many or most students appear to know classroom routines and procedures.	All students appear to know classroom routines and procedures.
Few or no students take initiative in discussion and activity sessions.	Many students take initiative in discussion and activity sessions.	Most students take initiative in discussion and activity sessions.
Classroom lacks structure and/or is not well managed.	Classroom is generally orderly and well managed with occasional disruptions.	Classroom is orderly and well managed.
Class time is lost "starting up" and/or at the end of the period.	Class time is well utilized, with minimal loss of time "starting up" or at the end of the period.	Class time is well utilized, with no loss of time "starting up" or at the end of the period.
Overall instructional time is lost because teacher must stop frequently to discipline students who misbehave.	Some students occasionally require disciplinary action, resulting in a loss of instructional time.	No instructional time is lost to disciplinary action.
There are two or more instances of classroom interruptions (intercom, knock at door, students entering/leaving, etc.).	There is one classroom interruption (intercom, knock at door, students entering/leaving, etc.).	There are no classroom interruptions.

FIGURE B.13	CLASSROOM OBSERVATION INSTRUMENT SCORING RUBRIC *(continued)*

5. Development of Higher-Order Thinking Skills

1	3	5
Students are involved only in basic process skills without hands-on instruction.	Students *discover* or *investigate* a mathematics concept/relationship using a preplanned activity that provides a definitive procedure or requires the collection and analysis of data (may or may not be recorded on spreadsheets/graphs).	In addition to requirements of a 4, the students independently determine to justify or verify their solutions and strategies.

6. Overall Classroom Observation Rating

1	3	5
Instruction observed was of poor quality and was not effective for any students.	Instruction observed was somewhat effective for most students.	Instruction observed was effective for all students.
No objectives were stated for the lesson and it was not clear if the teacher's perceived objectives were aligned to state standards.	Instruction was based on student objectives aligned with state standards but these were not clearly defined in the lesson.	Instruction was based on clearly defined and presented objectives aligned with state and local standards.
No students were engaged in activities that required higher-level thinking skills.	Some students were engaged in activities that required higher-level thinking skills.	All students were engaged in activities that required higher-level thinking skills.

FIGURE B.14	CLASSROOM OBSERVATION SUMMARY

SCHOOL _____ **DATE OF VISIT** _____

SCHOOL ADDRESS _____

1. Classroom Observation Rating Summary

NUMBER OF CLASSES OBSERVED:

Category	# Classes Rating 1	# Classes Rating 2	# Classes Rating 3	# Classes Rating 4	# Classes Rating 5	Average Rating
1. Physical Setting/Classroom Environment						
2. Lesson Effectiveness						
3. Questioning Strategies						
4. Classroom Climate						
5. Development of Higher-Order Skills						
# Observations/Average Rating						
						Overall Average

2. Overall Classroom Observation Rating Summary

NUMBER OF CLASSES OBSERVED:

# Classes Rating 1	# Classes Rating 2	# Classes Rating 3	# Classes Rating 4	# Classes Rating 5	Average Rating of All Observations

For information on the overall rating, see the Classroom Observation Instrument Scoring Rubric, Section 6.

3. Summary of Observations of Specific Strategies/Activities

NUMBER OF CLASSES OBSERVED:

Observations	# Classes Where Observed	% of All Classes Observed
1. Classroom was of adequate size, with appropriate furniture to conduct mathematical investigations.		
2. Classroom displayed student work.		
3. Classroom mathematics resources were adequate, were used appropriately, and contributed to the quality of the mathematics instruction.		

FIGURE B.14	CLASSROOM OBSERVATION SUMMARY *(continued)*		
Observations		**# Classes Where Observed**	**% of All Classes Observed**
4. Students were using a computer to collect, interpret, or communicate data.			
5. Students were using technology (computer or calculator) to learn or reinforce a mathematics fact or concept.			
6. Grouping arrangement was appropriate for the apparent instructional goal and activity.			
7. Students were engaged in an investigation.			
8. Students were engaged in a data-based activity that required data collection, inputting data, analyzing data, or graphing.			
9. Students were engaged in a print-based activity, such as doing mathematics problems from a text or worksheet.			
10. Questioning strategies were effective for the activity and apparent instructional goal.			
11. Classroom atmosphere was generally positive and enhanced learning opportunities for students.			
12. Students were solving one or more nonroutine or open-response problem.			
13. Students were engaged in a higher-level process skill.			

Comments:

Resources

American Council on Education. (1999). *To touch the future: Transforming the way teachers are taught: An action agenda for college and university presidents*. Washington, DC: Author.

Black, P. J., & William, D. (1998). Inside the black box: Raising standards through classroom assessment. *Phi Delta Kappan, 80*(2), 39–46.

Blank, R. K. (1997). Mathematics and science content standards and curriculum frameworks: States' progress on development and implementation. In *Interstate school leaders licensure consortium: Standards for school leaders* (pp. 1–159). Washington, DC: Council of Chief State School Officers.

Blank, R. K., Porter, A., & Smithson, J. (2001). *New tools for analyzing teaching, curriculum, and standards in mathematics and science: Results from survey of enacted curriculum project* (final report). Washington, DC: Council of Chief State School Officers.

Boonin, T., & Neuwirth, P. (1983, April). Pro: Boards need independent, impartial experts to audit administrative performance. *American School Board Journal, 170*(4), 31–34.

Brewster, C., & Fager, J. (2000, October). *Increasing student engagement and motivation: From time-on-task to homework*. Portland, OR: Northwest Regional Educational Laboratory.

Brooks, J. G., & Brooks, M. G. (1993). *In search of understanding: The case for constructivist classrooms*. Alexandria, VA: Association for Supervision and Curriculum Development.

Burrill, G. (2001, May–June). It's not all or nothing! *Mathematics Education Dialogues*. Available: http://www.nctm.org/dialogues/2001-05/20010504.htm.

Buttram, J., Corcoran, T. B., & Hansen, B. J. (1986). *Sizing up your school system: The district effectiveness audit*. Trenton, NJ: New Jersey School Boards Association.

Campbell, P. F., & Silver, E. A. (2000). *Teaching and learning mathematics in poor communities: Report of a task force*. Reston, VA: National Council of Teachers of Mathematics.

Ceperley, P. E., & Squires, D. A. (2001). *Standards implementation indicators: Charting your course to high achievement*. Charleston, WV: Appalachia Educational Laboratory.

Cooley, W. W. (1983, June–July). Improving the performance of an educational system. *Educational Researcher, 12*(6), 4–12.

Council of Chief State School Officers/State Education Assessment Center. (1996). *Interstate school leaders licensure consortium: Standards for school leaders*. Washington, DC: Author.

DuFour, R., & Eaker, R. (1998). *Professional learning communities at work: Best practices for enhancing student achievement*. Alexandria, VA: Association for Supervision and Curriculum Development.

English, F. (1979, November–December). Effective ways to improve public education. *Management Focus, 2–9.*

English, F. (1984, September). Curriculum mapping and management. In B. D. States (Ed.), *Promoting school excellence through the application of effective schools research: Summary and proceedings of a 1984 regional exchange workshop.* Charleston, WV: Appalachia Educational Laboratory. (ERIC Document Reproduction Service No. 251972)

English, F. W. (1988). *Curriculum auditing.* Lancaster, PA: Technomic Publishing.

English, F. W. (1999). *Deciding what to teach and test: Developing, aligning, and auditing the curriculum.* Newbury Park, CA: Corwin Press.

Ferrini-Mundy, J., & Johnson, L. (1994). Recognizing and recording reform in mathematics: New questions, many answers. *Mathematics Teacher, 87*(3), 190–193.

Fitzpatrick, K. (1997). *Indicators of schools of quality: Volume 1. Schoolwide indicators of quality.* Schaumburg, IL: National Study of School Evaluation.

Frase, L. E., English, F., & Posten, W. K., Jr. (Eds.). (2000). *The curriculum management audit: Improving school quality.* Lanham, MD: The Scarecrow Press.

Genck, F. H. (1987, August). How to improve performance results in your district. *The School Administrator, 44*(8), 17–19.

Grouws, D. A., & Cebulla, K. J. (2000). Improving student achievement in mathematics: Recommendations for the classroom (Educational Practice Series–4). Brussels, Belgium: International Academy of Education. (ERIC Document Reproduction Service No. ED463953)

Haberman, M. (1991, December). The pedagogy of poverty versus good teaching. *Phi Delta Kappan, 73*(4), 290–294.

Hansen, B. J., & Corcoran, T. B. (1986, March–April). Sizing up your school system. *School Leader, 17.*

Hunter, M. C. (1982). *Mastery Teaching: Increasing instructional effectiveness in elementary and secondary schools, colleges, and universities (Madeline Hunter Collection Series).* Thousand Oaks, CA: Corwin Press.

Hunter, R. (2004). *Madeline Hunter's mastery teaching: Increasing instructional effectiveness in elementary and secondary schools* (Updated ed.). Thousand Oaks, CA: Corwin Press.

Johnson, D. W., & Johnson, R. T. (1990). Using cooperative learning in math. In N. Davidson (Ed.), *Cooperative learning in mathematics: A handbook for teachers* (pp. 103–125). New York: Addison-Wesley.

Kagan, S. (1989 December–1990 January). The structural approach to cooperative learning. *Educational Leadership, 47*(4), 12–16.

Kauffman, D., Johnson, S. M., Kardos, S., Liu, E., & Penske, H. G. (2002, Summer). Lost at sea: Without a curriculum, navigating can be tough. *American Educator, 104*(2), 273–300.

Kirkpatrick, J., Martin, W. G., & Schifter, D. (2003). *A research companion to principles and standards for school mathematics.* Reston, VA: National Council of Teachers of Mathematics.

Lindly, C. A. (1987, Winter). Districtwide K–12 evaluation: An effective format for school improvement. *North Central Association Quarterly, 61*(3), 387–390. (ERIC Document Reproduction Service No. EJ354500)

Louis, K. S., Marks, H. M., & Kruse, S. (1996). Teacher's professional community in restructuring schools. *American Educational Research Journal, 33*(4), 757–798.

Love, N. (2002). *Using data/getting results: A practical guide for school improvement in mathematics and science.* Norwood, MA: Christopher-Gordon Publishers.

The Madeline Hunter direct instruction model. (n.d.). Included in *Some basic lesson presentation elements* [Online]. Humboldt State University. Available: http://www.humboldt.edu/~tha1/hunter-eei.html.

Marzano, R. J. (2003). *What works in schools: Translating research into action.* Alexandria, VA: Association for Supervision and Curriculum Development.

Marzano, R. J., Pickering, D. J., & Pollock, J. E. (2001). *Classroom instruction that works: Research-based strategies for increasing student achievement.* Alexandria, VA: Association for Supervision and Curriculum Development.

National Council of Teachers of Mathematics. (2000, March). *Teacher time* [Position paper]. Reston, VA: Author.

National Council of Teachers of Mathematics. (2001). Principals and standards for school mathematics. Reston, VA: Author. Available: http://standards.nctm.org/.

National Partnership for Excellence and Accountability in Teaching. (1999). *Revisioning professional development: What learner-centered professional development looks like* (Report No. B97 CLRNC). Available: http://www.nsdc.org/library/policy/npeat213.pdf.

National Research Council Board on Mathematical Sciences & Mathematical Sciences Education Board. (1989). *Everybody counts: A report to the nation on the future of mathematics education.* Washington, DC: National Research Council.

Phi Delta Kappa. (2004, September). The curriculum management audit [Online]. Available: http://www.pdkintl.org/icmc/features.htm.

Reavis, H. K., Jenson, W. R., Morgan, D. P., Andrews, D. J., Fister, S. L., & Taylor, M. (Eds.). (1996). *Best practices: Behavioral and educational strategies for teachers.* Longmont, CO: Sopris West.

Slavin, R. (1990). Student team learning in mathematics. In N. Davidson (Ed.), *Cooperative learning in mathematics: A handbook for teachers* (pp. 69–102). New York: Addison-Wesley.

Sowell, E. J. (1989). Effects of manipulative materials in mathematics instruction. *Journal for Research in Mathematics Education, 20*(5), 498–505.

Steffy, B. E., & English, F. W. (1997). *Curriculum and assessment for world-class schools.* Lancaster, PA: Technomic Publishing.

Sutton, J., & Krueger, A. (Eds.). (2002). *EDThoughts: What we know about mathematics teaching and learning.* Aurora, CO: Mid-continent Research for Education and Learning.

U.S. Department of Education. (2000). *Blue Ribbon Schools Program: National review panel elementary scoring guidelines 2000–2001.* Available: http://www.ed.gov/programs/nclbbrs/2000-2001scoringguidelines.pdf.

U.S. Department of Education. (2001). *Blue Ribbon Schools Program: National review panel middle and high school scoring guidelines 2001–2002.* Available: http://www.ed.gov/programs/nclbbrs/2001-2002scoringguidelines.pdf.

Weissglass, J. (1990). Cooperative learning using a small-group laboratory approach. In N. Davidson (Ed.), *Cooperative learning in mathematics: A handbook for teachers* (pp. 295–334). New York: Addison-Wesley.

Wellman, B., & Lipton, L. (2004). *Data-driven dialogue: A facilitator's guide to collaborative inquiry.* Sherman, CT: MiraVia.

Wiggins, G., & McTighe, J. (1998). *Understanding by design.* Alexandria, VA: Association for Supervision and Curriculum Development.

Wilhoit, G. (2004, September). Commissioner's comments: Increasing mathematics skills must be a priority. *Kentucky Teacher,* 3.

Williams, B. (Ed.). (2003). *Closing the achievement gap: A vision for changing beliefs and practices* (2nd ed.). Alexandria, VA: Association for Supervision and Curriculum Development.

Zemelman, S., Daniels, H., & Hyde, A. (1998). *Best practices: New standards for teaching and learning in America's schools.* Portsmouth, NH: Heinemann.

Index

Page references for figures are indicated by an *f*.

About the Author

RON PELFREY HAS LED THE EVALUATION OF MORE THAN 300 elementary, middle, and high school mathematics programs and has trained several hundred teachers and administrators in the process of conducting these reviews. Before returning to the classroom in 2004, Dr. Pelfrey was a mathematics supervisor for 20 years. A recipient of the Outstanding Mathematics Educator Award in Kentucky, he has served as an adjunct professor of mathematics education at the University of Kentucky and as the chair of the Department of Education and associate professor of mathematics at Midway College in Midway, Kentucky. He is the co-author of *Mathematics: Applications and Connections (Book 1, Book 2,* and *Book 3)*, the leading middle school mathematics series in the United States.

You may contact Dr. Pelfrey at 2137 Rollingdale Road, Lexington, KY 40513.

Related ASCD Resources: Mathematics

At the time of publication, the following ASCD resources were available; for the most up-to-date information about ASCD resources, go to www.ascd.org. ASCD stock numbers are noted in parentheses.

Audio

Improving Mathematics Instruction Through Coaching by Glenda Copeland (CD: #505298)

Linking Classroom Practice to Student Learning in Mathematics by Kathleen Morris and Jo Ellen Roseman (audio cassette: #204095; CD: #504129)

Online Courses

Early Childhood Mathematics Professional Development Course by Penni Ross

Middle School Mathematics Professional Development Course by Diane L. Jackson and Patrick Bathras

(Available: http://pdonline.ascd.org/pd_online/new/)

Print Products

Administrator's Guide: How to Support and Improve Mathematics Education in Your School by Amy Mirra (#303398)

Literacy Strategies for Improving Mathematics Instruction by Joan M. Kenney, Euthecia Hancewicz, Loretta Heuer, Diana Metsisto, and Cynthia L. Tuttle (#105137)

Math Wonders to Inspire Teachers and Students by Alfred S. Posamentier (#103010)

Teaching Children Who Struggle with Mathematics: A Systematic Approach to Analysis and Correction by Helene J. Sherman, Lloyd I. Richardson, and George J. Yard (#305135)

Teaching Reading in Mathematics, 2nd Edition by Mary Lee Barton and Clare Heidema (#302053)

Videotapes

The Brain and Mathematics Series (Two 30- to 40-minute videotapes with facilitator's guide) (#400237)

The Lesson Collection: Math Strategies, Tapes 17–24 (Eight 10- to 20 minute videotapes) (#401044)

For more information, visit us on the World Wide Web (http://www.ascd.org), send an e-mail message to member@ascd.org, call the ASCD Service Center (1-800-933-ASCD or 703-578-9600, then press 2), send a fax to 703-575-5400, or write to Information Services, ASCD, 1703 N. Beauregard St., Alexandria, VA 22311-1714 USA.